INTOLERANT RELIGION IN A TOLERANT-LIBERAL DEMOCRACY

This book aims to examine and critically analyse the role that religion has and should have in the public and legal sphere. The main purpose of the book is to explain why religion, on the whole, should not be tolerated in a tolerant-liberal democracy and to describe exactly how it should not be tolerated—mainly by addressing legal issues.

The main arguments of the book are, first, that as a general rule illiberal intolerance should not be tolerated; secondly, that there are meaningful, unique links between religion and intolerance, and between holding religious beliefs and holding intolerant views (and ultimately acting upon these views); and thirdly, that the religiosity of a legal claim is normally a reason, although not necessarily a prevailing one, not to accept that claim.

Intolerant Religion in a Tolerant-Liberal Democracy

Yossi Nehushtan

·HART·
PUBLISHING
OXFORD AND PORTLAND, OREGON
2015

Published in the United Kingdom by Hart Publishing Ltd
16C Worcester Place, Oxford, OX1 2JW
Telephone: +44 (0)1865 517530
Fax: +44 (0)1865 510710
E-mail: mail@hartpub.co.uk
Website: http://www.hartpub.co.uk

Published in North America (US and Canada) by
Hart Publishing
c/o International Specialized Book Services
920 NE 58th Avenue, Suite 300
Portland, OR 97213-3786
USA
Tel: +1 503 287 3093 or toll-free: (1) 800 944 6190
Fax: +1 503 280 8832
E-mail: orders@isbs.com
Website: http://www.isbs.com

Hart Publishing is an imprint of Bloomsbury Publishing plc.

British Library Cataloguing in Publication Data
Data Available

ISBN: 978-1-84946-605-9

Typeset by Compuscript Ltd, Shannon
Printed and bound in Great Britain by
CPI Group (UK) Ltd, Croydon CR0 4YY

Acknowledgements

Some parts of this book are the latest though not necessarily the final version of ideas and arguments I started to develop as an undergraduate law student in the mid-1990s. Other parts reflect ideas and arguments I have developed more recently. I have been writing about topics pertaining to law and religion as a student and lecturer, presenting my ideas in numerous workshops and conferences, and teaching about them in various courses and seminars. During this long period I have received excellent comments from fellow students, participants in academic events, colleagues, and from my own students in various law schools in Israel and the UK. Their names will not be mentioned here but if you are one of them and happen to read this—thank you for reading, listening, disagreeing and criticising.

My deep thanks are also due to (in alphabetical order) Nick Barber, Eyal Benvenisti, Peter Cane, David Enoch, Carolyn Evans, Marie Failinger, Leslie Green, Alon Harel, Kate Hofmeyr, Douglas Husak, Tsachi Keren-Paz, Matthew Kramer, Mordechai Kremnitzer, Maleiha Malik, Barak Medina, Frances Raday and Eli Shimelevich. They have all read previous versions of one or more chapters of this book either because they had to (as supervisors, editors or examiners) or because they chose to. They all improved my arguments and it is a pleasure and privilege to be indebted to them.

Special thanks are due to Joseph Raz and Nicholas Bamforth who read earlier versions of many parts of the book and challenged me with helpful comments and questions. Their ongoing advice and support cannot be overstated.

The publication of this book has been made possible thanks to the generosity of the Oxford Centre for Ethics and Philosophy of Law (CEPL), University College, Oxford University—which had me as HLA Hart Visiting Fellow and enabled me to start working on the book; the School of Law at Keele University, which allowed me time off teaching so I could finish writing the book; and the Emile Zola Chair for Human Rights, which supported the research by a generous research grant. Lastly, I thank Deborah Renshaw for excellent editing assistance and Marieanne Oludhe and Or Sadan who provided accurate and helpful research assistance.

Earlier versions of (parts of) some chapters were published in the *Oxford Journal of Law and Religion* (2012), *Religion and Human Rights* (2012), *Tel-Aviv University Law Review* (2011), *Philosophy and Theology* (2011), *Law and Philosophy* (2010), and *Ratio Juris* (2007). I thank the publishers for permission to include revised versions of these articles.

This book is dedicated to my beloved Sarit, Itay and Yuval who are the reason for almost everything I do and almost everything I feel.

Contents

1

Introduction

THE BROAD AND sometimes implied purpose of this book is to explain why religion should not be tolerated in a tolerant-liberal democracy. The more focused and explicit purpose of the book is to explain why a tolerant-liberal democracy should be reluctant to tolerate religious claims for accommodation. Special consideration is given to the argument that religious demands to be granted conscientious exemptions from legal norms should be treated differently and less favourably than non-religious demands.

During the last decades there has been extensive writing about issues concerning law and religion. Most publications in this subject share two characteristics: first, they are either 'pro-religion', 'neutral-liberal' or 'multiculturalist' and in any event do not take a stand against religion as such. This is a 'content-related' problem. Secondly, they normally avoid interdisciplinary research. This would be a methodological deficit.

As to the 'content-related' problem, it appears that most publications in the field of law and religion argue for special protection for religious freedom and the religious conscience—and the list of examples is simply too long to be mentioned here. This is not a problem which is unique to legal scholarship. Pro-religious tendencies and biases amongst scholars of religion are common (though becoming less common) in other disciplines as well, such as sociology, psychology, philosophy and obviously theology.[1] Within legal and philosophical scholarship it is uncommon to find arguments according to which there is nothing special about religion, so that religion should not be singled out for special treatment.[2] Also uncommon are arguments that the liberal state should use its persuasive power (rather than its coercive power) in order to change religious beliefs that oppose 'the core values of free and equal citizenship'.[3] This book takes the 'religion is not special' position one step further. I will

---

[1] B Beit-Hallahmi, *Psychological Perspectives on Religion and Religiosity* (London, Routledge, 2015) 235.

[2] For a recent argument in this vein see B Leiter, *Why Tolerate Religion* (Princeton NJ, Princeton University Press, 2012).

[3] For a recent argument along these lines see C Brettschneider, *When the State Speaks, What Should It Say?: How Democracies Can Protect Expression and Promote Equality* (Princeton NJ, Princeton University Press, 2012) 143.

argue that religion is indeed special and that it should definitely be singled out—but for negative or less favourable treatment. This argument will hopefully breathe new life into an ancient debate, as contemporary academic publications offering explicit or implicit arguments about the need to not tolerate religion or about the links between religion and intolerance are surprisingly rare.

As to the methodological deficit, most of the literature in the field of law and religion, and certainly most of the literature that criticises various aspects of religion, does not engage with the relevant issues from an interdisciplinary point of view. There is and always has been widespread academic interest in issues pertaining to religion. Religion is studied from various points of view: legal, philosophical, psychological, sociological, theological and so on. Interdisciplinary research about religion, however, is still quite rare.[4] Some approach the issue from a relatively narrow (yet still very helpful) perception;[5] some mainly engage with philosophical arguments;[6] whereas others address the issue from a 'popular-philosophy' point of view.[7] Legal writing about law and religion often ignores philosophical questions regarding this issue. Philosophers who write about religion normally do not apply their views to highly relevant legal issues. Legal scholars and philosophers alike tend to ignore empirical findings about religion and religious people. This book aims to integrate these disciplines and to offer a more comprehensive approach to this issue. It aims to establish the argument for the need to not tolerate religion by putting together philosophical arguments, legal research and empirical findings.

The main arguments of the book are, first, that illiberal intolerance should not be tolerated in a tolerant-liberal democracy; secondly, that there are meaningful, unique links between religion and intolerance, and between holding religious beliefs and holding intolerant views (and ultimately acting upon these views); thirdly, that the religiosity of a legal claim is normally a reason, although not necessarily a prevailing one, to reject that claim. More

---

[4] For a recent attempt to combine insights from the legal and sociological studies of religion see R Sandberg, *Religion, Law and Society* (Cambridge, Cambridge University Press, 2014) and especially chapter 6. For an ongoing and interesting interdisciplinary approach to religion see the academic journal *Religion, Brain and Behavior*.

[5] D Richards, *Fundamentalism in American Religion and Law* (Cambridge, Cambridge University Press, 2010); A Guiora, *Freedom from Religion: Rights and National Security* (Oxford, Oxford University Press, 2013).

[6] N Bamforth and D Richards, *Patriarchal Religion, Sexuality, and Gender: A Critique of New Natural Law* (Cambridge, Cambridge University Press, 2008); R Audi, *Democratic Authority and the Separation of Church and State* (Oxford, Oxford University Press, 2011).

[7] S Harris, *The End of Faith: Religion, Terror, and the Future of Reason* (New York, WW Norton & Company, 2004); R Dawkins, *The God Delusion* (New York, Bantam Books, 2006); Christopher Hitchens, *God is not Great: How Religion Poisons Everything* (London, Atlantic Books, 2007).

specifically, and within the context of conscientious exemptions, it is argued that in most important cases accommodating religion by granting religious-conscientious exemptions is an expression of tolerance. Therefore, and if the limit of liberal tolerance is illiberal intolerance, the religiosity of one's conscience is normally a reason, although not necessarily a prevailing one, not to grant a conscientious exemption or not to tolerate the conscientious objection in other ways. The latter argument also applies to claims for accommodating religion by means other than granting conscientious exemptions.

These arguments are developed in the following way. Chapter two focuses on the principle of tolerance and suggests a few conceptual clarifications and a conceptual basis for the subsequent chapters. Following a perfectionist-liberal perception of the limits of tolerance, it is suggested in Chapter three that the limit of liberal tolerance is illiberal intolerance, or, in other words, that illiberal intolerance should not be tolerated by the liberal state. The limits of tolerance are described, inter alia, through the principles of reciprocity and proportionality. The former explains why intolerance should not be tolerated, whereas the latter prescribes how and to what extent it should not be tolerated. Chapter four explains what a 'tolerant-liberal democracy' is and differentiates it from other types of liberal democracy. Chapter five explores two main arguments. The first is an empirical argument according to which religious persons—because they are religious persons—are likely to be more intolerant than non-religious persons. The second is that there are meaningful, clear and unique theoretical links between religion, or, more precisely, certain types of religion, and intolerance. The theoretical links in fact explain why there are empirical links between religion and intolerance. Chapter six discusses the question 'Is religion special?' within the context of conscientious exemption. It asks whether religious-conscientious objections should be treated any differently from non-religious ones. It is helpful to divide the main approaches that address the issue of granting conscientious exemptions into five main categories: (1) neutral approaches; (2) 'equal-regard' approaches; (3) perfectionist-liberal approaches; (4) 'pro-religion' approaches; and (5) 'anti-religion' approaches. It is argued that the first four approaches should be rejected and that the fifth approach should govern the practice of granting religious-conscientious exemptions—and more broadly—the proper state response to religious claims for accommodation.

Two methodological caveats are required here: first, within the context of academic writing, when one argues for the validity of a certain argument, good practice would be to refute all or most other possible counter-arguments. Therefore, when I argue that the theoretical and empirical links between religion and tolerance provide a strong, sometimes compelling reason for not tolerating religion, I might be expected to fully address all possible reasons for tolerating religion—and to explain in detail why they sometimes or often do not outweigh the reasons for not tolerating religion. I am afraid this book fails to meet these expectations. Even though I am fully aware of the reasons for tolerating religion I will only discuss them in part since addressing and refuting them in full requires writing a second volume to this book. Thus, most parts of this book will make the case for not tolerating religion. The intelligent reader may also take into consideration the reasons for tolerating religion (and this is a well-researched subject)—and come to his own conclusion.

A second caveat concerns the writing style. This book cannot be easily classified. Parts of it use legal terminology that will be familiar to legal scholars, practitioners and students. Other parts assume prior knowledge in political and moral philosophy and will be more appealing to philosophers or to philosophy-minded readers, and thus possibly daunting to others. Some parts, however, deviate from what can be considered as classic academic writing and are aimed at intelligent readers who do not have any legal or philosophical background. Writing a book for lawyers, philosophers and intelligent people with no prior knowledge in law or philosophy requires a few compromises in terms of academic rigour, which hopefully have not resulted in compromising the overall quality of the arguments.

Lastly, throughout the book I refer to the third person as 'he'. After receiving worried comments from gender-minded readers, I should clarify that I have done this for brevity and consistency only and that 'he' encompasses also 'she'. Unless stated otherwise, all my arguments and observations, flattering and unflattering alike, apply to all sexes and genders equally.

2

The Principle of Tolerance

I. INTRODUCTION

A GOOD UNDERSTANDING of the principle of tolerance is fundamental in comprehending the notion of human rights and the related
issue of the limits of tolerance. The human rights regime is based,
inter alia, on the assumption that people have rights to engage in actions that
others may consider wrong. In other words, people have a right to tolerance.
In addition, we must fully understand what tolerance means in order to
address the critical question of the limits of tolerance, which implicates political, moral and legal issues alike. Issues pertaining to human rights can often be
dealt with as part of the issue of the limits of tolerance, as the limits of tolerance often describe the limits of human rights or the limits of the protection
granted to them.

Yet, just as it is critical to understand the principle of tolerance, so numerous disputes exist regarding how in fact to do so. This chapter aims to promote
an accurate understanding of the concept—or simply to clarify my understanding of the concept—as a starting point for further arguments.

Part II of this chapter suggests a basic definition for the principle of tolerance and discusses the meaning of having the right to be tolerated. Part III discusses the main elements of the principle of tolerance—namely the avoidance
of harm to another and the possible various reasons for harming another, or
avoiding such harm. Parts IV and V briefly describe the relationship between
tolerance and grudge, and tolerance and power, in order to further clarify the
scope and the nature of the principle of tolerance.

II. THE DEFINITION OF TOLERANCE AND THE RIGHT
TO BE TOLERATED

A. The Basic Definition

At its essence, tolerance means refraining from harming the 'object' that the
tolerant person considers to be negative, although the tolerant person has good

reasons (in his opinion) to harm it. In other words, the tolerant person makes an adverse judgement about another person, the adverse judgement provides the tolerant person with reasons to harm the other, but the tolerant person restrains himself and avoids harming the other. There could be two kinds of reason that justify harming the other: one kind is reasons pertaining to the values of the other, as articulated in, for instance, his behaviour, speech or lifestyle. The tolerant individual will find something negative in these expressions: danger, meanness, stupidity, immorality or irrationality, for example. The other kind of reason pertains mainly to inherent traits such as personality, looks, or the identity of the other person. These could be skin colour, gender, physical disability, nationality and the like. The tolerant person would find some negative, repulsive or detrimental features in these characteristics.

Tolerant behaviour could result from a number of reasons or motives. Tolerant behaviours can be identical in their outcome but the reasons underlying these behaviours may vary. Three main reasons for tolerance or three main types of tolerance can be noted: tolerance as a right, utilitarian-pragmatic tolerance and tolerance out of mercy or pity.

Tolerance as a right means that one has the right to be tolerated while others are under a duty to tolerate. If the tolerant person acknowledges this right, he refrains from harming what he considers negative, since he acknowledges the fact that the other person has a right to err or to behave negatively, or he acknowledges that the other person has a right not to be harmed despite the tolerant person's adverse judgement of the other's behaviour, opinions or identity.

The other kind of tolerance is utilitarian-pragmatic tolerance. Here, the tolerant person tolerates the other—although the tolerant person has reasons to harm the other—because he thinks that under the current circumstances, it is preferable for him or for society in general to tolerate the other person. According to the utilitarian-pragmatic tolerant approach, tolerance has no independent moral value. Generally, it is not viewed as something that one should aspire to or apply more widely. The main characteristic of this type of tolerance is its temporariness. The tolerant person opts for tolerance not out of a moral principle or acknowledgement of the other's right, but rather as the outcome of a risk assessment at a given time and place. Nonetheless, pragmatic tolerance should not be taken for granted. Despite its temporary nature, and although it does not depend on moral principles or rights, it is still preferable in certain cases to intolerance.

The third kind of tolerance stems from mercy or pity. For example, a convict may be granted a pardon due to his bad health, despite the authorities having reasons not to grant a pardon—reasons that are derived from the adverse judgement that the authorities make about the convict or his deeds. The prisoner does not have a right to be granted a pardon. There are not necessarily pragmatic reasons to justify the pardon. Mercy and pity explain tolerance in this case.

The three kinds of tolerance described above are not fully exhaustive. There are additional reasons for tolerance, and indeed some will be mentioned below. It seems, nonetheless, that these are the main kinds. The case of tolerance out of mercy and pity will not be discussed here. Also, pragmatic tolerance will be discussed almost exclusively in juxtaposition with tolerance as a right—the focus of the following discussion. Indeed, tolerance as a right is the most interesting kind of tolerance, as it poses the more complicated questions. There are three reasons for the special interest in tolerance as a right. First, unlike pragmatic tolerance, tolerance as a right relies on moral-principled reasoning that is circumstance-free. Secondly, again unlike pragmatic tolerance, in determining whether to harm the tolerated person or not, tolerance as a right requires that the tolerant person consider the other's interests, not just the tolerant individual's own interests or society's general interests. This requirement is not to be taken for granted. Thirdly, in tolerance as a right, one can find the most extreme contrast between the adverse judgement that the tolerant person makes about the tolerated person and the complicated acknowledgement that sometimes one has a right not to be harmed despite one's negative actions or wrong opinions.

B. Right to Tolerance—A Contradiction in Terms?

The term 'tolerance as a right' raises two main questions. First, aren't the terms 'tolerance as a right' or 'right to tolerance' inherently repetitious? Secondly, if there is a right to tolerance, how can it be justified?

The tolerant person acknowledges the right of the other to err or to behave badly, or he acknowledges the right of the other not to be harmed despite the adverse judgement that he makes about the other's behaviour, opinions or identity. However, one can argue that the concept of 'right' already contains the above-mentioned notion. In other words, rights exist in order to enable their holders to behave in a way that might seem to others to be wrong. Thus, it might seem that the difference between tolerance and respecting rights is non-existent or insignificant. However, there is in fact a significant difference between the two. Respect for or acknowledgment of the other's right applies more widely than the principle of tolerance. Any acknowledgement of the other's right to err or to behave negatively indeed reflects an attitude of tolerance (as a right). However, recognition of the other's right is not necessarily recognition of his right to err or to behave negatively. In other words, the principle of tolerance—and in fact the individual's autonomy as its primary justification—is one of many reasons to acknowledge the other's right. Thus, tolerance is not identical to respecting rights but it describes one specific motive to respect rights, or it describes what we do in certain cases when we respect rights.

There are indeed rights the main importance of which lies in the protection of the right-holder's freedom to behave in a way that might seem wrong to the state or other individuals. The importance of freedom of expression is known primarily in cases where the state or individuals have reasons to limit that expression—typically when the content of the expression or its consequences are viewed as negative. Freedom of association is important especially in cases where the state has reason to curtail associations, for example due to an association's wrong actions or values. Naturally, many other examples come to mind. In all of these, if someone who has reasons to harm another (due to an adverse judgement he makes about them) refrains from harming them, and if this refraining from harm is explained by the acknowledgment of a right, then the one who refrains from harming the other is indeed tolerant—and acknowledges the other's right to be tolerated. However, not all rights purport to enable their holders to behave wrongfully (in the eyes of others). Such, for example, is the right to be rewarded for work (as a moral or legal right). Its purpose is not necessarily to allow its holder to behave in a way that is viewed as wrong. Thus, whoever respects this right and acts accordingly—even if he has reason not to respect it—is not necessarily tolerant towards the right's holder. The right to leave one's country, for example, is not only justified through the protection of the right's holder to act in a way that is viewed as wrong. Let us assume that the state wishes to infringe this right for economic purposes by imposing a 'leaving the country tax'. The court is likely to abolish this tax based on an acknowledgement of the right to leave the country, but this acknowledgement will not necessarily be an expression of tolerance towards the holder of the right. Here, too, many other examples can be provided.

Thus, there is no repetition within the term 'tolerance as a right'. Not every recognition of a person's right is a recognition of his right to err or to act negatively, and therefore not every recognition of their right means that they have a right to be tolerated. Nevertheless, every acknowledgement of a person's right to err or to behave negatively means that they have a right to tolerance. Thus, tolerance does have an independent status. Tolerance describes a specific case of acknowledgement of another's right. One can even say that tolerance—and in fact, an individual's autonomy—provides a specific justification, with a specific value, to the acknowledgement of a right.

The primary justification for the existence of the right to tolerance lies in the importance attached to an individual's autonomy.[1] Autonomy, in this

---

[1] J Raz, 'Autonomy, Toleration and the Harm Principle' in R Gavison (ed), *Issues in Contemporary Legal Philosophy* (Oxford, Clarendon Press, 1987) 313.

context, is the freedom granted to an individual to be 'the author of his own life' and thus make decisions that seem to others meaningless, wrong or even damaging. Bernard Williams emphasises that in order to acknowledge tolerance as a value, as a virtue or as a right, we should acknowledge a certain 'good' that justifies tolerance as such and accept that that 'good', in the liberal view, is the individual's autonomy. Williams adds that since those who do not subscribe to liberalism do not necessarily acknowledge that autonomy has any particular value, they necessarily cannot recognise tolerance as a value or as a right.[2] Although we cannot take for granted the view that autonomy is a valuable thing, which as such justifies the principle of tolerance in general and holds tolerance to be an individual right, I do not intend to defend this position, since discussing it exceeds the scope of this chapter. Instead, the validity of this position will just be assumed. For the purpose of this chapter, suffice it to say that the principle of tolerance is based on the recognition of the importance of autonomy as expressed mainly in the liberal-perfectionist view of Joseph Raz, according to whom individual autonomy is the primary good that the state should advance, in acts and omissions alike.[3]

III. THE COMPONENTS OF TOLERANCE

As discussed above, tolerance means avoiding harming the 'thing' that seems negative to the tolerant person, although the tolerant person has reasons to harm it. In other words, the tolerant person makes an adverse judgement of a certain type about another, the adverse judgement gives the tolerant person reasons to harm the other, but the tolerant person restrains himself and avoids that harm. In this section the primary foundations of this definition will be clarified.

A. Tolerance and not Harming

Since tolerant behaviour means not harming the other, the meaning of 'harm' in this context demands clarification. Here I wish to suggest that first, the term 'harm' should be interpreted in the broadest way possible; secondly, a person is harmed as long as his condition is worsened according to his own perspective; and thirdly, harm to others might also be caused by omission.

---

[2] B Williams, 'Tolerating the Intolerable' in S Mendus (ed), *The Politics of Toleration* (Edinburgh, Edinburgh University Press, 1999) 65, 72–73.

[3] J Raz, *The Morality of Freedom* (Oxford, Clarendon Press, 1986) chapters 14, 15; J Raz, *Ethics in the Public Domain* (Oxford, Clarendon Press, 1994) chapters 3–5.

First of all, and for the sake of simplicity, the term 'harm' as applied here is significantly broader than its definition in John Stuart Mill's classical writing[4] and in the contemporary writing of Joel Feinberg.[5] Within the discourse of tolerance, and for the purpose of this book, 'harm' includes any negative behaviour towards another—and any limitations imposed on another's freedom. The harm can be emotional, mental, psychological, physical, economic or other. The harming behaviour might be expressed in condemning the other person, disrespecting him, physically or culturally estranging him, discriminating against him, avoiding his presence or physically harming him. Tolerant behaviour means avoiding harming the other person, regardless of the type of harm and its extent. Accordingly, classifying behaviour as intolerant does not depend upon the extent or type of harm (or indeed offence) that is inflicted upon another—or intended to be inflicted upon them. Intolerant conduct exists whenever there is any sort or extent of negative attitude directed towards another, assuming the negative treatment is the product of a negative judgement of them.

Secondly, a person is harmed as long as his condition is worsened according to his own perspective. In relation to the principle of tolerance, a person's condition can be worsened if he is forbidden to do something he wants to do (such as smoking) or if he is forced to do something that he does not wish to do (such as studying). Therefore, if I forbid someone to smoke because I have a negative view of smoking or smokers, I am intolerant towards that person. I will still be intolerant towards the smoker even if I forbid him to smoke because I am interested in his own good. My interest in his own good is the reason for my intolerant behaviour and may justify this behaviour, but that is irrelevant to the definition of my behaviour as either tolerant or intolerant. All that matters in classifying my attitude as intolerant is the fact that I harm others by limiting their freedom, and I do so because I have a negative view of their actions.

It is important to distinguish between classifying conduct as tolerant or intolerant and finding a justification for that conduct. This distinction is important for conceptual reasons but it has further implications regarding the one who is being tolerated (X) and the tolerant person (Y) alike. If we adopt X's point of view, then when Y limits X's freedom on account of an adverse judgement that Y makes about X's actions or values, it will be a double harm if this limitation will not only be permitted but also will not be classified as an expression of intolerance. If we adopt Y's perspective, then when he wishes to limit X's freedom because Y is seeking X's good and thinks he knows what this good

---

[4] JS Mill, *On Liberty* and *The Subjection of Women* (Ware, Wordsworth Classics of World Literature, 1996; first published in 1859 and 1869 respectively).

[5] J Feinberg, *The Moral Limits of the Criminal Law—Harm to Others* (Oxford, Oxford University Press, 1984).

is (and this is often one of the justifications for religious coercion and persecution, for example), Y must realise that he is being intolerant and acknowledge that by limiting X's freedom he in fact harms X—from X's own perspective. This acknowledgement is supposed to make the tolerant person work harder to justify his intolerance.

Thirdly, harm to the other might also be caused by omission.[6] A person's condition can be worsened in cases where I abstain from protecting him or helping him when (a) others prevent him from doing something or force him to do it, or (b) when he needs help for any other reason. Therefore, if I do not prevent Y from preventing X's smoking and if my sole motivation is an adverse judgement about smoking or smokers, I am being intolerant towards X (and perhaps, but not necessarily, tolerant towards Y). Accordingly, if I do prevent Y from preventing X's smoking, even though I make an adverse judgement about smoking or about smokers, I may be intolerant towards Y (depending on the causes for my action) but in any case I am being tolerant towards X. Moreover, and regardless of the existence of Y who wishes to harm X, X's condition can be worsened simply because I avoid helping him (for example, I refrain from donating money to him). If I avoid helping X only because I make an adverse judgement about him or about his values, characteristics or behaviours, I am being intolerant towards him. Accordingly, if I choose to help X despite my adverse judgement, I am being tolerant towards him.

Omissions in general pose an interesting case within the discourse of tolerance, since an omission can be an expression of intolerance and tolerance alike. An omission is an expression of intolerance towards another if he is worse off (or no better off) as a result and if the omission results from an adverse judgement about him. That would be a case of passive intolerance as opposed to active intolerance which finds expression in acting in a way that harms someone. The omission will be an expression of tolerance if the tolerant person avoids harming the other person despite the adverse judgement that he makes about the other. That would be a case of passive tolerance as opposed to active tolerance, which means acting in order to benefit someone despite the adverse judgement that is made about them.

To conclude, avoiding harming a person is a central component of the principle of tolerance. Understanding the elements of the term 'harm' is therefore critical for understanding what tolerance is really about. Here, the term 'harm' refers to any negative attitude towards the other. The harm might be caused by acts, as well as by omissions. It can be caused by forbidding a person

---

[6] And see Mill (n 4 above) 14: 'a person may cause evil to others not only by his actions but by his inaction, and in either case he is justly accountable to them for the injury'. Mill then added that 'to make any one answerable for doing evil to others, is the rule; to make him answerable for not preventing evil, is comparatively speaking, the exception'.

to do something or by forcing him to do it. As long as a person's condition has been worsened (or not improved) in his own eyes and as long as the harm caused to him is the result of an adverse judgement made about him (or about his values, characteristics or behaviour), we would say that that person is not being tolerated. Lastly, there may be cases in which Y will act or refrain from acting in order to harm X or to avoid helping him—as a result of Y making an adverse judgement about X—yet X will not be harmed (even in his own view). These rare cases are still examples of intolerance as acting with an intention to harm X alongside making an adverse judgement about X are the only necessary and sufficient conditions for seeing Y as intolerant. The actual infliction of harm is not a necessary condition in that respect.

B. The Element of Restraint

As previously noted, the tolerant person makes an adverse judgement about another. The adverse judgement gives the tolerant person certain reasons to harm the other person. The tolerant person has also other reasons not to harm the other. Acting according to the reasons not to harm the other is indeed tolerance.

The following example will clarify the importance of the element of restraint. Y might decide not to harm X, although X is a male who wears women's clothes outdoors. Y can decide not to harm X for a number of reasons. First, Y can think that X's behaviour does not provide even the slightest reason to harm him. Y might still think that men should not wear women's clothes in public, but if at the same time he does not think that this behaviour provides a reason to harm X, the element of restraint does not exist, and Y cannot be considered tolerant. Secondly, Y can think that even though he himself would never dare or want to wear women's clothes in public, it is simply charming that there are men who decide otherwise. Here too, Y cannot be considered tolerant. Thirdly, Y can be completely indifferent to the phenomenon of men wearing women's clothes. He has no opinion on the matter, either positive or negative. Here too, Y cannot be considered tolerant towards this phenomenon. Fourthly, Y can think that X's behaviour provides Y reasons to harm X. If Y has other reasons, of any kind, not to harm X, and if Y acts upon these reasons, and indeed does not harm X, Y can be considered tolerant.

In all the cases where the need to harm the other person is not even evoked, the element of restraint does not exist. It is important to distinguish between cases in which a person or the state has no reason to harm the other and cases in which such reasons do exist. The principle of tolerance reflects the second category. The first category involves other terms such as recognition, acceptance, understanding, approval and apathy, among others. Although these terms might be combined in the discourse of tolerance in certain contexts they do not explain the core meaning of the concept.

C. Reasons to Harm Another Person

The adverse judgement that the tolerant person makes about another provides the tolerant person with reasons to harm them. But the discourse of tolerance is not necessarily implicated in any case in which a person has reasons to harm another. The reasons to harm the other should stem from an adverse judgement about the other, and the adverse judgement should stem from the other's values, behaviour or identity. The other's identity here is comprehended very widely and includes innate and acquired identity, social and economic status, profession and personal characteristics. Not every reason to harm the other is a reason that stems from an adverse judgement of the other based on his values, his conduct or identity. Accordingly, not every reason to harm the other is necessarily also a reason for not tolerating him as opposed to simply harming him.

Let us assume that for some reason, a man is chasing me in order to harm me. Another man accidently blocks my escape route. If I have no other way to keep running but by pushing violently the man who blocks my way, I have very good reason to harm him by pushing him violently. Even if I do push him, it would be a mistake to classify my behaviour as intolerant, since my reason to harm him was not based upon an adverse judgement I made about his values, behaviour or identity. At most, I can be seen as inconsiderate of the other or disrespectful towards him, but not intolerant towards him. On the other hand, if I harm a person by pushing him violently as a reaction to something he had said or done, and especially when his speech or his acts that triggered my response reflect his values, then my behaviour could be classified as intolerant. Thus, a tolerant person is a person who has reasons of a certain kind to harm another, and avoids acting upon those reasons.

At this point another question can be asked: should the reasons to harm another be good reasons from a morally objective perspective? John Horton's influential view is that tolerance exists only when the other behaves wrongly from an objective moral perspective and therefore only when the tolerant person has good reason from an objective moral outlook to harm that other person.[7] Therefore, a person who does not have objectively valid moral reasons

---

[7] J Horton, 'Toleration as a Virtue' in D Heyd (ed), *Toleration: An Elusive Virtue* (Princeton NJ, Princeton University Press, 1996) 29. For a similar view see D Augenstein, 'Tolerance and Liberal Justice' (2010) 23 *Ratio Juris* 437, 444.

to harm the other cannot be perceived as tolerant even if that person refrains from harming the other. Thus, for example, if a Jewish racist is shocked when he finds out that his young son secretly married a Muslim woman, and that racist father refrains (for whatever reason) from harming his son following that, it would be wrong, according to Horton, to consider the racist father as tolerant. This is so because the racist father does not have valid moral reasons to harm his son in the first place.

It seems that Horton's view is problematic for a number of reasons. First, it leads to a very narrow definition of the principle of tolerance, and in fact of the tolerant person, making the concept nearly useless. Secondly, it turns the state's demands of those who hold immoral views into a 'nameless demand'. Thus, for instance, in the case of a homophobic view of a certain man, assuming that this view provides someone with a reason to harm homosexuals in some manner, what exactly is the content of the demand that the enlightened state should make towards the homophobe? The demand to respect the other (in the deepest and fullest sense of the term) or to consider him as equal is a proper demand but far-fetched for the homophobe, and therefore politically useless. This demand should not be looked down upon, but a more realistic demand should be added to it or perhaps precede it. Also a demand for apathy towards the other is not sufficient because it ignores the intensity of the values that make the homophobe what he is. A realistic and reasonable initial demand from the homophobe would be to avoid harming the other even though he has good enough reasons (from his perspective) to harm him. But how should we label this demand? It is not enough to use the words 'restraint' and 'self-control', since they are broader than the concept of tolerance, and apply to situations that have nothing to do with tolerance (thus, for instance, a man who needs to diet for health reasons needs to exhibit restraint and self-control, but not tolerance, in the face of the strong will to eat forbidden food). Moreover, the mere demand not to harm the other is not enough, since it is too narrow and overlooks the fact that the homophobe has good enough reasons in his eyes to harm the other—reasons which are based on deeply held values rather than more shallow ones such as greed or the wish to gain social appreciation. Tolerance is the only term that provides a title and a distinct content to the demand made of the homophobe. A good enough reason is required to refuse to apply the principle of tolerance to this kind of case, and it seems that such a reason does not exist.

Thirdly, Horton's view does not properly appreciate the one who avoids harming the other. Within the demand for tolerance lies a certain appreciation towards the one who accepts the demand, especially when the tolerant person acts upon moral reasons not to harm the other. If we follow the example above, demanding that the homophobe be tolerant applies a certain (yet very limited) understanding towards the homophobe. It appreciates the fact that the homophobe is required to make a sacrifice and to suffer, as the homophobe is required to rise above any good reason he might have in his view to harm the other and accept the other's right not to be harmed despite his 'wrong' way of life. Tolerance is a complex principle that suits a complex reality. In the above example, clearly homophobic views should not be accepted. These views and even their holders, under certain circumstances, should be condemned. At the same time, the homophobe does deserve some appreciation if, despite his reasons to harm homosexuals, he avoids harming them. He certainly deserves more appreciation than the homophobes who do act upon their immoral views. Perceiving the tolerant homophobe as tolerant both accurately reflects his attitude and expresses our very limited yet deserved appreciation of his constraint.

Fourthly, it seems that Horton's view confuses two different questions. It combines the conceptual questions of 'what is tolerance?' with the normative question, 'what is morally right and what is morally wrong?'. According to Horton, if the potential harmer's reasons to harm the potentially harmed are morally repugnant, then even if the potential harmer restrains himself and avoids acting upon the reasons to harm the other, we cannot consider him tolerant. Horton specifically states that any discussion of the meaning of toleration must also be a discussion of the things we value.[8] Yet it would seem worthwhile to differentiate between the analytical clarification of concepts— which should be 'morally neutral'—and normative arguments about the difference between good and bad, right and wrong. This is what we do when we engage with analytical philosophy. We differentiate between the definition of the rule of law, for example, and questions such as whether the rule of law has an inherent moral virtue or when it is justified to act against the rule of law. We differentiate between the definition of 'rights' and the question of when people should have rights. Similarly, we should differentiate between what tolerance in fact means—and questions such as which 'things' should not be tolerated, which things should be tolerated and which things should not just be tolerated but rather respected and accepted.

In sum, a tolerant person is one who avoids harming the other although he has reasons to harm him. In order for tolerance discourse to apply, the reasons to harm another must relate to the identity of that person, his behaviour or his values. Nonetheless, those reasons must not necessarily be morally good reasons. Suffice it that the holder of those reasons considers them as adequate justification to harm the other. The next question is which types of reason to avoid harming the other qualify for such avoidance to be defined as tolerance.

---

[8] J Horton, 'Three (Apparent) Paradoxes of Toleration' (1994) 17 *Synthesis Philosophica* 7, 14.

D. Reasons to Avoid Harming Another—Reasons for Self-Restraint

The previous paragraph professed that the reasons to harm another should be of a certain kind, namely reasons that stem from an adverse judgement of the other on account of his values, behaviour or identity. On the other hand, the reasons to avoid harming the other could be of any kind.

The assertion that the reasons to avoid harming someone could be of any kind contradicts what appears to be the common view, according to which tolerance only exists if the tolerant person has *moral* reasons not to harm someone (outweighing the reasons to harm them).[9] Those moral reasons normally collapse into one main reason, which is the need to respect the other person as an agent or the other person's autonomy (but not necessarily his values or behaviour). Thus, and according to this approach, tolerance exists only if the tolerant person avoids harming the other person out of respect for the other person's right to choose his way of life and to be an autonomous person. This approach has been called, as described above, 'tolerance as a right'. According to this approach, tolerance which exists only for pragmatic-utilitarian reasons is not tolerance at all, or is not tolerance in its true sense. Alternatively, tolerance that exists only for pragmatic-utilitarian reasons may be considered as a compromise or as a 'practice of tolerance' rather than 'genuine' or 'pure' tolerance.[10]

Reducing the principle of tolerance to only those cases in which not harming another is derived from moral reasons and not from utilitarian ones excludes from the tolerance discourse important and central cases. This includes cases in which someone is tolerant because not tolerating the other would be too costly; or because he is not powerful enough to act intolerantly; or the damage to society as a whole resulting from intolerance would outweigh the damage caused by that other person; or giving the power and the authority to the state not to tolerate the other person might lead to an exploitation of this power in unjustified cases, and so on. It seems right to see in all of these cases a special kind of tolerance, ie utilitarian tolerance (or at times tolerance out of necessity), rather than excluding these cases from the tolerance discourse utterly or classifying them as cases that do not express 'real' tolerance.

---

[9] L Green, 'On Being Tolerated' in M Kramer, C Grant, B Colborn and A Hatzistavrou (eds), *The Legacy of HLA Hart: Legal, Political, and Moral Philosophy* (Oxford, Oxford University Press, 2008) 277, 279; D Heyd, 'Introduction' in Heyd (n 7 above) 3; R Cohen-Almagor, *The Scope of Tolerance: Studies of the Cost of Free Expression and Freedom of the Press* (London, Routledge, 2006) 8, 27; B Leiter, *Why Tolerate Religion?* (Princeton NJ, Princeton University Press, 2012) 9.

[10] Leiter (n 9 above) 9–12.

To clarify this claim, consider the following example, derived from a similar example that Cohen-Almagor offered in another context.[11] Assume that a Muslim academic participates in an academic conference where the first speaker defames and insults Muslims wherever they are. The Muslim academic is the next speaker. He decides to overlook the speech of the racist who spoke before him. He can reach this decision for several reasons: fear of challenging the racist academic who enjoys a senior position in his field; the harmed academic's non-assertive personality, which avoids face-to-face confrontations; fear that condemning the racist speaker might lead to his counter-condemnation and diversion of the attention from the academic research he wishes to present, and so on. None of the above reasons is a moral reason to avoid condemning the racist. These reasons are not based on respecting the other as an equal fellow citizen or as a person. They are all utilitarian or related reasons. Still, it would be justified to depict the Muslim academic's non-reaction as a tolerant reaction. The Muslim academic made an adverse judgement about the racist, the adverse judgement gave him reasons to harm the racist (for example by condemning his words), but he chose to act upon the reasons to avoid harming. This is enough to make him tolerant.

To take another example, the authorities grant a licence for a racist demonstration and even make sure the occasion is given security. The common approach requires having moral reasons to avoid harming the other in order for the conduct to be classified as tolerant. Here, the authorities' behaviour will be classified as tolerant only if the authorities allowed the demonstration despite their objection to the messages conveyed there and if they did so because they believe that the racist speakers have a moral right to convey their message by holding a demonstration, despite the repugnant content of these messages. This indeed is tolerance. But what if the authorities think that the racist demonstrators do not have such a right and, moreover, in principle they do not believe that the speakers' dignity should be respected? Meaning, it is neither the demonstrators' opinions nor the demonstrators themselves who deserve respect, consideration or acknowledgement. The authorities might still allow the demonstration because they think that under the circumstances this is the most effective way to increase the public's awareness of the existence of racist opinions or because they deem that not authorising the demonstration might cause riots, the results of which would be worse than the harm to be caused by the mere existence of the demonstration. These are 'time and place'-based reasons, generated by the authorities' interest or the

---

[11] See Cohen-Almagor (n 9 above) 27.

public interest at a given moment and not the moral rights of the prospective demonstrators or respect for them as such. Nevertheless, it would be right to classify the authorities' behaviour as tolerant.

One can argue against including the above circumstances in the classification of tolerance, since it comprises too wide a definition of the term and might weaken it. Indeed, a conceptual-analytical discussion of the meaning of concepts and principles should be cautious of overly broad definitions. This holds true in the case of the term tolerance as well as concepts such as the rule of law, democracy, human rights, etc. A proper methodology would prefer a narrow and focused definition, at the price of leaving peripheral cases or unusual cases outside the boundaries of the concept. In this case, on the other hand, reducing the definition of tolerance to 'tolerance as a right' only, and excluding pragmatic-utilitarian tolerance entirely from the tolerance discourse would lead not only to excluding peripheral and unusual cases from the definition of tolerance, but also to excluding main, central cases. The core of tolerance is making an adverse judgement about another and restraining from acting upon this adverse judgement. The question of why this restraint is applied should not be a part of the definition of tolerance, but rather a criterion to classify types of tolerance. In the case mentioned above, where the authorities authorise a racist demonstration for utilitarian reasons only, it cannot be argued that the authorities were pluralistic or neutral towards the racists or that they accepted or respected the racists or their views. The authorities' response should be accurately understood as:

> we will allow you to demonstrate not because you have the right to do it, and despite the fact that we despise you and the values that you hold, and only because it currently serves the public interest or because it increases awareness of the existence of racism for the purpose of fighting it.

Here, the authorities are tolerant because they refrain from harming the demonstrators, although the adverse judgement that they make about them provides the authorities with reasons to harm them.

There is no other moral-political concept or principle that reflects this situation and this attitude, except for the definition hereby suggested for the principle of tolerance. Moreover, this is not a less-appreciated tolerance or a less authentic one. In certain cases, it would be the right response to acts of others. More specifically: in cases where the intolerant activity or the intolerant persons are not worthy of any respect but rather deserve condemnation and ostracising, an attitude of 'right to tolerance' would be morally wrong. Utilitarian tolerance might fit such cases better. There is no inherent value in perceiving tolerance as a right. Moreover, the modern perception of tolerance as it has evolved following the religious wars in Europe in the sixteenth century was utilitarian tolerance. The fundamental writings of that time did not discuss tolerance as a right, but only, or mainly, utilitarian tolerance.[12] In Locke's writings, one can find utilitarian justifications for the principle of tolerance (in addition to other justifications), which focus on the uselessness of forcing a belief on others and the lack of an appropriate governmental body for this purpose.[13] Excluding utilitarian tolerance from the concept of tolerance would ignore the roots of this concept and the paradigmatic circumstances that generated it.

Acknowledging the fact that tolerance can result from diverse reasons and motives gets us closer to a better understanding of a complex concept and allows us to use it more accurately to explain or justify behaviours—and the reasons for those behaviours.

IV. TOLERANCE AND GRUDGE

A common criticism of tolerance is that it is almost always accompanied by disapproval and exercised grudgingly. If tolerant behaviour is not based, at least in part, on a 'positive' state of mind (such as recognition, acceptance, openness or respect), then the tolerant behaviour might in fact offend the one who is being tolerated.[14] Indeed, it is unpleasant to be tolerated. People and groups wish to be recognised as equals. They wish or demand that their values and ways of life are recognised as equal and worthy of respect—rather than just being tolerated. On the one hand, this criticism of tolerance is indeed accurate, as it describes nicely the essence of the concept of tolerance. The tolerated person is a burden that lies on the tolerant person's shoulders. The tolerant person may even clarify this point to the tolerated person who indeed would have preferred that the equal treatment he receives would derive from recognition or respect rather than tolerance. On the other hand, the fact that tolerance is almost always exercised grudgingly does not indicate either a conceptual problem or a normative one. The concept of tolerance does not describe a desirable state of mind or a desirable attitude. It describes a

[12] Erasmus, 'On Mending the Peace of the Church' in JP Dolan (ed), *The Essential Erasmus* (New York, Plume, 1964 (1st edn 1536)) 288–327; Sebastian Castellio, *Concerning Heretics* (trans and ed by RH Bainton) (New York, Octagon Books, 1965) 104–6, 121–35, 141–54, 169–83.

[13] J Locke, *A Letter Concerning Toleration* (Indianapolis IN, Hackett Publishing Company, 1983; first published in 1689).

[14] Green (n 9 above); Augenstein (n 7 above) 437. See also MC Nussbaum, 'Radical Evil in the Lockean State: The Neglect of the Political Emotions' (2006) 3 *Journal of Moral Philosophy* 159, 160: 'All ... democracies ... have strong reasons to support an idea of toleration, understood as involving respect, not only grudging acceptance'. For a similar view that opposes the partial identification of tolerance with grudge, and offers to identify tolerance as 'recognition' see: AE Galeotti, *Toleration as Recognition* (Cambridge, Cambridge University Press, 2002).

behaviour that is accompanied by a state of mind, which may be but does not have to be justified. The behaviour is normally refraining from harming. The state of mind is that of self-restraint: not harming even though an adverse judgement that is made about another provides the tolerant person reasons to harm the other. There are cases, which are in fact quite common, in which a person makes an adverse judgement about another and nonetheless refrains from harming him for various reasons. 'Tolerance' merely names this state of mind and behaviour. There is no other concept that does it. Thus, from the conceptual point of view, there is no difficulty in the fact that tolerance is normally accompanied by a grudge. But is it a problem from the normative point view? Here, again, the answer would have to be 'no'.

Tolerance and grudge should not necessarily be avoided in favour of respect, acceptance, recognition or openness, nor should tolerance and grudge be perceived as the lesser evils. There are situations in which tolerance, precisely because of its disapproving nature, is the right response to people or behaviours that are not worthy of more. These are the cases where it is morally justified to make an adverse judgement about another, maybe even to denounce his behaviour or his values, yet still not to harm him in more meaningful ways. In the example given regarding the authorities granting a licence to a racist demonstration, it is neither the demonstrators' opinions nor the demonstrators themselves who deserve respect, consideration or acknowledgement. In this case the racist demonstrators deserve nothing more than (pragmatic) tolerance which may well be grudgingly exercised.

That tolerance is grudging and entails making an adverse judgement about others leads some scholars to consider tolerance as an 'interim virtue', which is positioned between persecution and indifference of some sort towards the other. This kind of indifference stems from the recognition that certain acts of individuals should not bother other individuals, but rather be perceived as private acts which should be respected as such. Bernard Williams, for example, claimed that in a liberal society the appropriate attitude towards certain matters, such as sexual tendency and religious belief, should be indifference mixed with acceptance of the fact that it is a private matter that society should not classify as good or bad.[15] But even here, the transition from persecution to tolerance and later on to indifference and even acceptance of the other is not an inherently morally desirable transition. The transition is desirable only when it relates to things that should be accepted or respected, or to things that we should be indifferent to. One should assume that even Williams would not

---

[15] B Williams, 'Toleration: An Impossible Virtue?' in Heyd (n 7 above) 18, 20–21, 26.

suggest applying a relaxed attitude of indifference towards those who severely harm the other with no justification, even within the private sphere.

Both Leslie Green, who is troubled by the link between tolerance and grudge, and Williams, who perceives tolerance as an 'interim virtue', are struggling with the complex meaning of tolerance. It seems that they perceive tolerance as a mixture of good and bad. Good—as tolerance results in 'not harming'. Bad—because of the grudge that accompanies the tolerant attitude. But perhaps we should perceive both elements of tolerance (not harming—and grudge) as neither good nor bad in themselves. Perhaps tolerance itself (much like intolerance) is neither good nor bad. Tolerance might be unjustified and even morally wrong if things that should not be tolerated are tolerated. Accordingly, intolerance might be justified and even morally necessary if things that should not be tolerated are indeed not tolerated. Therefore, classifying tolerance as a moral virtue, as an interim virtue or as a lesser evil—cannot be part of the concept of tolerance itself. At most, we can classify certain tolerant behaviours as morally necessary, morally allowed, lesser evils or morally wrong. The question of how we should decide which tolerant behaviour falls into which category is a normative and complex question that will be discussed in more detail in Chapter three. Suffice it to say that if the primary justification for the existence of the right for tolerance lies in the importance attached to the individual's autonomy.[16] If tolerance is a means to protect and promote an individual's autonomy and if the state has an obligation to protect and promote an individual's autonomy, then the state has to be tolerant. On the other hand, since intolerance means, inter alia, harming the other, then the same harm principle that allows the state to interfere with someone's liberty (or to harm him) in order to prevent him from unjustly harming another, allows the state—and sometimes requires that the state—be intolerant towards those who are unjustly intolerant towards others.

Be that as it may, the one point that should not be overlooked is the all-important necessity of making a distinction between the concept of tolerance and the practice or the value of tolerance. The mere fact that the concept of tolerance describes behaviour or state of mind that seems unattractive to some (mainly to neutral liberals or pluralist liberals—as opposed to perfectionist liberals) is far from being a sufficient reason, or indeed a reason at all, to alter the concept of tolerance altogether. Any discomfort regarding what tolerance is really about should be expressed in discussions about the practice of tolerance and its value, namely about the questions of when and why it is justifiable to tolerate others.

---

[16] Raz (n 1 above) 313.

V. TOLERANCE AND POWER

Tolerance, it is commonly argued, can only be exercised by the powerful towards the powerless.[17] If this is true, then the concept of tolerance is utterly useless when we ask ourselves what the powerless do, or what they ought or ought not to do, since the powerless can be neither tolerant nor intolerant of the powerful. This view is misguided as, in fact, the powerless can be both tolerant and intolerant of the powerful.[18] The powerless can be of two kinds: either those who are normally powerful but find themselves powerless under certain circumstances, or those who are normally and constantly powerless.

In the first case, the powerless may choose to tolerate another precisely because of their temporary lack of power. This would be a case of utilitarian-pragmatic tolerance, where the normally powerful cannot achieve their goals at all or effectively through intolerant behaviour, or cannot achieve their goals through intolerant behaviour without suffering a meaningful and harmful counter-reaction. To take one example, the state, which is normally the powerful party, may make an adverse judgement about the existence of discrimination against women in private educational institutions, which are operated by powerless communities. Despite this adverse judgement that provides the state with reasons to interfere and harm the powerless minority, and in fact to be intolerant towards the discriminatory practice, the state might refrain from forcing the abolition of the discriminatory practice, and by that to tolerate it. The state's tolerance may result from its lack of power. The state may believe that an intolerant reaction will be futile or that the harm that will be caused to society as a whole as a result of the state's intolerant response will outweigh the expected benefits. Normally, the state is the powerful party in this kind of confrontation, whereas the discriminating minority group is the powerless party. Nonetheless, the state may tolerate the normally powerless minority due to a lack of power to achieve its goals through an intolerant approach. Under these circumstances, the state is in fact the weaker party—and its weakness is the reason for its tolerance.

The second case in which the powerless can still be tolerant is the case where a person (or a group) is normally and continuously powerless. For conceptual clarity, it is important to note that when we talk about lack of power we do not mean a total lack of ability to harm another or offend him. In cases of a total

---

[17] See for example: J Derrida, 'Autoimmunity: Real and Symbolic Suicides' in G Borradori (ed), *Philosophy in a Time of Terror* (Chicago IL, The University of Chicago Press, 2003) 127–28; DD Raphael, 'The Intolerable' in S Mendus (ed), *Justifying Toleration: Conceptual and Historical Perspectives* (Cambridge, Cambridge University Press, 1988); PP Nicholson, 'Toleration as a Moral Idea' in J Horton and S Mendus (eds), *Aspects of Toleration* (London, Routledge, 1985).

[18] For a similar position, even if not explained in detail, see Williams (n 15 above) 18, 19.

lack of power the powerless clearly cannot be tolerant since the element of restraint from harming the other does not exist. Someone who cannot harm the other, in any way or to any extent, cannot be perceived as someone who restrains himself from harming the other and therefore cannot be tolerant. In these cases it can be said that not harming the powerful other is not an expression of tolerance but merely an act of surrender or acquiescence.[19] However, such cases are extremely rare and in any event it seems that the academic writing does not refer to these kinds of cases. The lack of power that is discussed here, and in the literature, refers to a situation where the powerless can harm the powerful, but the harm caused will be relatively marginal, will not achieve its goal (at all or only marginally) and most importantly might bring about a harsh counter-reaction of the harmed powerful or of a third party. Accordingly, the powerful are those who can harm another while taking the risk of suffering a marginal reaction, a reaction that will not achieve its goal (at all or only marginally).

In these circumstances, there are several cases in which the behaviour of the powerless can be classified as tolerant. The powerless (a person, a group or a community) may make an adverse judgement about someone powerful. This adverse judgement may provide reasons to harm that powerful person. If the powerless refrain from acting upon these reasons—that is, refrain from harming the powerful—the powerless are being tolerant. If the powerless would have refrained from harming the powerful even if they had the power to harm without suffering a non-marginal response, then the powerless are not only tolerant, but also recognise the other's right to be tolerated. If the powerless refrain from harming the powerful only because currently they do not have enough power to harm without suffering an undesirable counter-reaction, the powerless are still tolerant but for utilitarian reasons only.

In another example, two parties in a dispute could refrain from harming each other, although each of them has good reason to harm the other. In such a case they are mutually tolerant. The reason might stem from the fact that they are equally powerful and have an equal ability to harm each other. In this case, their equal ability to harm each other makes them powerless against each other. Their mutual tolerance is not generated from the acknowledgement that the other has a right to be tolerated. It relies on utilitarian reasons, and as such it is temporary and subject to varying circumstances.

As mentioned, it seems that the academic writing according to which the powerless or the weak cannot be tolerant does not relate to the rare and unimportant cases where the powerless cannot harm the other in any way. It seems that the situations at hand are those that depict substantial, at times ongoing,

---

[19] Augenstein (n 7 above) 443.

differences between the power possessed by the powerful and that of the powerless. This is the case in a relationship between a parent and child, the king and his subjects, the majority group and minority groups and so on. However, in all of these cases the powerless can still harm or offend the powerful. A child who thinks he has good reason to harm one of his parents can act upon these reasons and insult the parent, refuse to speak to him or cause damage to his parent's possessions. A subject who thinks he has good reason to harm or offend the king can act upon these reasons and publicly ridicule the king. Members of a minority group who think they have good reason to harm or offend the majority can condemn the majority's conduct, avoid the presence of members of the majority group, avoid trading with them or ask a third party to intervene and harm the majority. More often than not the intolerant act of the powerless will not be effective and will not achieve its goals. Their intolerant acts might be followed by a counter-reaction of the powerful which would make the powerless even worse off. Nevertheless, as long as the powerless act in order to harm the powerful because the powerless make an adverse judgement about the powerful, the powerless are intolerant of the powerful. Accordingly, if the powerless refrain from taking these actions because of any reason whatsoever, then the powerless restrain themselves and are in fact tolerant.

All the above cases and examples do not contradict the common view that the tolerant must be in a position to voluntarily decide not to use their power to harm another despite their capacity to do so.[20] According to this view, without the capacity to harm someone and without making a voluntary decision not to harm them, we are facing, yet again, not an expression of tolerance but merely an act of surrender or acquiescence. In all the above examples and cases the powerless do have the ability to harm the powerful, yet the powerless may voluntary decide to avoid harming the powerful because of various possible reasons.

The ability of the powerless to be intolerant towards the powerful and thus also to be tolerant towards them stems from the fact that intolerance, as well as tolerance, can be exercised to various degrees. Classifying certain behaviour as intolerant does not depend upon the kind of negative attitude shown towards the other or the extent of the harm inflicted on him. Any negative attitude towards the other is an expression of intolerance (if it results from an adverse judgement that was made about the other). The negative attitude towards the other can be expressed in relatively mild ways such as condemning the other, avoiding his presence or avoiding helping him. It could also be expressed in not such a mild way, by, for example, discriminating against someone, humiliating them or torturing them. All of these are expressions of intolerance to

---

[20] Augenstein (n 7 above) 443.

various extents. It is hard to imagine situations in the private sphere or in the public sphere in which the powerless cannot take even one action that expresses intolerance towards the powerful. When it is established that the powerless have the ability not to tolerate the powerful, it becomes clear that they could also tolerate the powerful.

Thus, there is no conceptual reason to argue that the discourse of tolerance cannot be applied to questions such as what the powerless do—and what they ought to do. No doubt the distinction between powerful parties and powerless parties is important regarding the normative question of the limits of tolerance. This is true whether we face a direct dispute between the powerful and the powerless or whether the state is required to intervene as a mediator in a dispute between the powerful and the powerless.[21] From the conceptual point of view, however, and in any of these disputes, tolerance can be required from the powerful and the powerless alike—and be exercised by the powerful and the powerless alike.

VI. CONCLUSION

The principle of tolerance can be used for the needs of various political theories and regimes. Different political theories would use it in various ways and for various goals. None of these contradict the possibility of reaching a common understanding of the concept of tolerance. The moral or political discourse can endure disputes with regard to normative questions such as the appropriate limits of tolerance. It is more problematic to endure disputes with regard to the meaning of the term tolerance itself. Such disputes hinder achieving a common conceptual basis to serve as the joint starting point for the normative disputes that follow. The goal of this chapter was not to offer a full and comprehensive understanding of the principle of tolerance, but rather to clarify some of the main components of the concept and to differentiate it from related concepts. I have argued that tolerance exists when the tolerant person makes an adverse judgement of a certain type about another, the adverse judgement provides the tolerant person with reasons to harm the other, but the tolerant person restrains himself and avoids harming the other—for whatever reason. It seems that this definition reconciles the need to clearly distinguish between tolerance and other principles or states of mind and the need not to leave central and important cases out of the discourse of tolerance.

---

[21] On the importance of the power gaps in such cases see for example: G Newey, 'Is Democratic Toleration a Rubber Duck?' (2001) 7 *Res Publica* 315, 326.

This definition of the principle of tolerance is morally neutral. Accordingly, engaging in normative evaluations is not required in order to identify the tolerant and intolerant. It follows that tolerance is not necessarily morally right and that intolerance is not necessarily morally wrong. Both tolerance and intolerance merely describe behaviours and their motives or reasons. Answering the question of when tolerance or intolerance is justified does require normative evaluations and should be discussed separately, and only after agreement is reached on what tolerance is really about.

3

The Limits of Liberal Tolerance

I. INTRODUCTION: PERFECTIONIST LIBERALISM AS A STARTING POINT

THE PERCEPTION OF the principle of tolerance that was suggested in Chapter two can be endorsed (or rejected) regardless of the kind of political theory one supports.

Things are different when one tries to prescribe the limits of tolerance and especially the proper response to intolerance. This is a normative issue and therefore any view concerning this issue must be viewed in light of a more general political theory. This chapter, as well as the whole book, derives from a substantive-liberal point of view (or 'value-based liberalism' as opposed to a procedural or neutral one), which is much closer to Raz's notion of perfectionist liberalism than to Rawls's neutral liberalism, Dworkinian liberalism or Kymlicka's liberal multiculturalism.[1] I suggest, without elaborating on this point, that substantive liberalism, autonomy-minded liberalism or a form of Razian-perfectionist liberalism is the best workable theory compatible with human well-being. Moreover, it offers more space to its competitive legitimate doctrines than any other workable doctrine.[2] Needless to say, I do not share Rawls's view that a value-based liberalism is just 'another sectarian doctrine'.[3] Thus, what I shall refer to as 'liberal tolerance' should be read as a value-based

---

[1] R Dworkin, 'Liberalism' in S Hampshire (ed), *Public and Private Morality* (Cambridge, Cambridge University Press, 1978) 113; J Rawls, *Political Liberalism* (New York, Columbia University Press, 1993); W Kymlicka, *Multicultural Citizenship: A Liberal Theory of Minority Rights* (Oxford, Clarendon Press, 1995). See also B Ackerman, *Social Justice and the Liberal State* (New Haven CT, Yale University Press, 1980); T Nagel, *Equality and Partiality* (Oxford, Oxford University Press, 1995); B Barry, *Justice as Impartiality* (Oxford, Oxford University Press, 1995).

[2] B Colburn, 'Forbidden Ways of Life' (2008) 58 *The Philosophical Quarterly* 618, 629.

[3] J Rawls, 'Justice as Fairness: Political not Metaphysical' (1985) 14 *Philosophy & Public Affairs* 223, 246. I will not elaborate on the criticism saying that neutrality itself is 'another sectarian doctrine'. A more specific and related argument is that not just Raz's notion of liberalism is a value-based one but also Nozick's and Kymlicka's, and therefore that all are culturally and religiously intolerant: J Chaplin, 'How Much Cultural and Religious Pluralism can Liberalism Tolerate?' in J Horton (ed), *Liberalism, Multiculturalism and Toleration* (Basingstoke, Palgrave Macmillan, 1993) 32.

liberal tolerance and ought not to be confused with neutral liberal tolerance, eg Thomas Nagel's rather vague notion of what he refers to as impartial liberal tolerance.[4] Accordingly, the limits of tolerance to be discussed below should be read as the limits of liberal tolerance even though some of the relevant arguments can apply to other variants of tolerance as well.

Neutral liberalism has come under increasing attack during recent decades. The first attack is 'external', from those who resent most or all of the substantive values shared—to various extents—by liberals, namely equality, freedom (as protected by the harm principle), individualism and autonomy. The second attack is 'internal', from those who embrace substantive liberalism but reject its aspiration to neutrality or its anti-perfectionism.[5] These attackers sometimes offer the principle of tolerance as a way to replace the undesirable or impractical aspiration to neutrality with a hierarchy of values.[6] However, neutral liberals do not always take this internal attack seriously. Some do not fully confront the nature of tolerance and do not fully explore it as an alternative to neutral liberalism or pluralism. Others ignore it altogether. Advocates of tolerance, on the other hand, sometimes fail to answer two of the main questions regarding tolerance, namely, the nature of its limits and the proper response to intolerance. I will offer initial answers mainly to the second question.

Following a perfectionist liberal-based perception of tolerance, I will argue that the limit of liberal tolerance is illiberal intolerance, or in other words—that the illiberal intolerant should not be tolerated by the liberal state. The limits of tolerance are described through the principles of reciprocity and proportionality. The former explains why intolerance should not be tolerated whereas the latter prescribes how and to what extent it should not be tolerated. The cumulative effect of these principles is that apart from on rare occasions illiberal intolerance should never be tolerated.

---

[4] T Nagel, *Equality and Partiality* (Oxford, Oxford University Press, 1991) 154–55.

[5] J Raz, *The Morality of Freedom* (Oxford, Clarendon Press, 1986); R Abel, *Speech and Respect: Hamlyn Lectures Series* (London, Sweet & Maxwell, 1994) especially chapter 4; G Sher, *Beyond Neutrality: Perfectionism and Politics* (Cambridge, Cambridge University Press, 1997); S Wall, *Liberalism, Perfectionism and Restraint* (Cambridge, Cambridge University Press, 1998); C Brettschneider, *When the State Speaks, What Should It Say?: How Democracies Can Protect Expression and Promote Equality* (Princeton NJ, Princeton University Press, 2012); S Macedo, 'Transformative Constitutionalism and the Case of Religion: Defending the Moderate Hegemony of Liberalism' (1998) 26 *Political Theory* 56, 58, 76; G Watt, 'Giving unto Caesar: Rationality, Reciprocity and legal Recognition of Religion' in R O'Dair and A Lewis (eds), *Law and Religion—Current Legal Issues*, vol 4 (Oxford, Oxford University Press, 2001) 45, 54.

[6] For a particularly attractive attempt to replace liberal neutrality with liberal tolerance see: SS Smith, 'The Restoration of Tolerance' (1990) 78 *California Law Review* 305.

II. THE LIMITS OF TOLERANCE: RECIPROCITY
AND PROPORTIONALITY

A. Introduction

Finding and defining the limits of tolerance is one of the greatest challenges of liberal democracies. Some liberals are torn between the notion that in some cases the liberal state can or even must limit expressions of some values and their commitment to neutrality or to pluralism. This chapter does not aspire to present a comprehensive guide to liberal tolerance but to offer some basic guidelines for a better liberal perception of the limits of tolerance, according to which illiberal intolerance should not be tolerated. Since any discourse regarding the limits of tolerance must be a value-based one, the suggested approach to the limits of tolerance can be adopted only by those who embrace substantive liberalism, autonomy-minded liberalism or some form of perfectionist liberalism. There is no point in trying to persuade non-liberals of a liberal-value-based approach to tolerance. As Bernard Williams correctly points out, if we defend tolerance as a value then its justifications will entail certain 'goods', particularly that of personal autonomy, which others do not accept as a good; therefore they do not accept tolerance or, more accurately, tolerance as a right.[7]

The general argument that illiberal intolerance should not be tolerated consists of two sub-arguments. First, the main guide to defining the proper response to illiberal intolerance is reciprocity. According to the principle of reciprocity the limit of tolerance is intolerance, or in other words the tolerant, as a starting point, should not tolerate anything that denies the justifications of tolerance and tolerance itself. The principle of reciprocity is valid regarding all possible expressions of intolerance: acts (discriminating against whites, for example), direct hate-speech (about whites and to whites), indirect hate-speech (about whites to a third party) and advocating intolerant views of others. The important differences between these examples can be taken into consideration while applying the principle of proportionality.

Secondly, I will argue for the principle of proportionality as a complementary principle to reciprocity. It is not sufficient to claim that one should not tolerate intolerance. One should also ask what nature and level of intolerance justifies a specific intolerant response and its degree.

---

[7] B Williams, 'Tolerating the Intolerable' in S Mendus (ed), *The Politics of Toleration* (Edinburgh, Edinburgh University Press, 1999) 65, 72–73; TM Scanlon, *The Difficulty of Tolerance: Essays in Political Philosophies* (Cambridge, Cambridge University Press, 2003) 201.

B. Reciprocity

Reciprocity can have different meanings. It may mean 'treat others as you would like to be treated' or better yet 'do unto others, wherever possible, as they want to be done by', or 'treat others as you would like to be treated, if you were them'. For the purposes of this chapter I suggest that reciprocity means acting contrary to what X initially requires towards those who act contrary to what X requires. Therefore, if X stands for 'respect for others', then reciprocity requires the state not to respect those who do not respect others. Accordingly, if X stands for 'freedom of religion', then reciprocity requires the state to limit the freedom of religion of those who use this freedom to curtail the freedom of religion of others. If we apply this notion to the harm principle or to the offence principle, for example, it would mean that the state or society is allowed, and normally is required, to harm or offend those who unjustly harm or offend others, or intend to do so.

Reciprocity can also require that with regard to X (certain values, principles and so on) one has to act contrary to what X requires towards those who infringe X (or act against it), in order to protect X itself. It is not merely 'tit for tat', as reciprocity does not necessarily require harming someone in the same way. This perception of reciprocity means, for example, that if the state takes freedom seriously it has to restrict A's freedom if A intends to limit unjustly B's freedom (or sometimes his own); if the state takes autonomy seriously it has to restrict A's autonomy if A intends to reduce unjustly B's autonomy; if the state takes free competition seriously it has to interfere with the free market and impose restrictions on monopolies and cartels in order to ensure free competition; and finally, if the state takes democracy seriously it has to limit some democratic rights of anti-democratic parties in order to protect democracy.[8] Since international law does take reciprocity seriously it can be found in almost all the important international documents regarding human rights.[9]

---

[8] For promoting reciprocity as a justification for banning undemocratic (and intolerant) political parties from taking part in the political process, see GH Fox and G Nolte , 'Intolerant Democracies' (1995) 36 *Harvard International Law Journal* 1, 14–16.

[9] For a few central examples see Article 8.2 of the European Convention for the Protection of Human Rights and Fundamental Freedoms (1950), which states that the right to respect for private and family life can be infringed in order to protect the rights and freedoms of others. Article 11.2 states the same regarding freedom of assembly and association. Article 5.1 of the International Covenant on Civil and Political Rights (1966) includes a general principle of reciprocity regarding the Covenant's protected rights; see also Article 22.2. For a general principle of reciprocity see also Articles 29.2 and 30 of the Universal Declaration on Human Rights (1948).

For an opinion that there is a right not to tolerate only those who infringe human rights see S Mendus, 'Introduction' in S Mendus (ed), *Justifying Toleration: Conceptual and Historical Perspectives* (Cambridge, Cambridge University Press, 1988) 5, 13; and DD Raphael, 'The Intolerable' in S Mendus (ed), *Justifying Toleration: Conceptual and Historical Perspectives* (Cambridge, Cambridge University Press, 1988) 147.

Reciprocity, as described above, does not have to be the sole justification for not tolerating the intolerant. The state can, and at times must, refuse to tolerate those who diminish unjustly the autonomy of others. Yet, it does not mean that by doing so the state necessarily diminishes the autonomy of the intolerant person. Put differently, it does not have to be the case that with regard to X (eg autonomy) the state acts contrary to what X requires towards those who infringe X, in order to protect X itself. The state can protect autonomy by not tolerating those who diminish it without diminishing the autonomy of the intolerant. In these cases, the justification for not tolerating the intolerant can be found in the importance of autonomy to human lives. To take one example, the state can decide not to grant tax benefits to religious schools that unjustly discriminate against pupils or teachers on the basis of sex, race or sexual orientation. The state may also deny any public funds to these institutions. This may be a justified liberal-intolerant response to anti-liberal intolerant behaviour, yet that response does not significantly diminish the autonomy of religious communities, institutions or individuals.

The principle of reciprocity regarding the limits of tolerance is recognised as a valid principle by a number of scholars, liberals and non-liberals alike, although sometimes in various versions of the principle or without naming it as such. Frequently, it is discussed inconsistently or not analysed thoroughly. Rawls, for example, said, without elaborating on that specific point, that 'it seems that an intolerant sect has no title to complain when it is denied an equal liberty'.[10] Bollinger's view on freedom of speech and tolerance also adopts, although only at times and not explicitly, the principle of reciprocity.[11] A stronger, sometimes overlooked, view in support of reciprocity can be found in Kymlicka's discussion of multiculturalism when he argues for the right of national minorities to maintain themselves as culturally distinct societies only if they are themselves governed by liberal principles.[12] Augenstein suggests that in the 'respect conception of tolerance' the parties tolerating each other respect one another in a reciprocal sense: they regard themselves and others as citizens of a state in which members of all groups should have equal legal and political status.[13] The inevitable question would then be: how can we tolerate those

---

[10] J Rawls, *A Theory of Justice*, Revised edn (Cambridge MA, Harvard University Press, 1999) 190. For a broader and slightly different sense of reciprocity see p 179. See also J Rawls, *A Theory of Justice* (Cambridge MA, Harvard University Press, 1971) 218, although in the broader context it is unclear whether Rawls argues for reciprocity or for a pragmatic approach to the limits of tolerance.

[11] LC Bollinger, *The Tolerant Society* (Oxford, Oxford University Press, 1988) 243.

[12] Kymlicka (n 1 above) 153. However, on pp 167–69 Kymlicka supports granting constitutional exemptions to non-liberal national minorities even at the cost of violating human rights within the minority's community.

[13] D Augenstein, 'Tolerance and Liberal Justice' (2010) 23 *Ratio Juris* 437.

who break this reciprocal relationship—and how can we do so in the name of tolerance itself? Finally, Mensching, in his comprehensive essay on religion and tolerance, justifies the principle of reciprocity regarding tolerance and specifically regarding freedom of religion—but does not elaborate on that point.[14]

Most, if not all, advocates of the principle of reciprocity do not explain exactly what justifies it. For some, this view seems so intuitively true that no elaboration is needed. Hammer, for example, briefly mentions 'the unavoidable quandary of a tolerant society that demands, by a simple definition of the term, a certain level of intolerance at least towards intolerant views'.[15] However, the best way to explain why the principle of reciprocity is required in order to define the limits of tolerance is to address it to the justifications of tolerance, ie to argue that whoever or whatever denies these justifications should not be tolerated. It is important to note that not every intolerant act necessarily contradicts all the justifications for tolerance and accordingly not every act that contradicts one or more of the justifications for tolerance can be seen as an intolerant act. Hence acting intolerantly and acting against the justifications for tolerance are two different cases that may or may not overlap.

The most coherent and comprehensive justification for 'tolerance as a right' is personal autonomy. The main advocate of this justification is Joseph Raz. According to Raz's perception of autonomy, which I fully embrace here, an autonomous person is a (partial) author of his life. People are autonomous when they are able to make their own choices and have an adequate range of valuable options from which they are able to choose.[16] By respecting the other's autonomy the tolerant put up with the other's wrong choices. In other words, the tolerant recognise the other's freedom to be wrong.[17] However, as Raz argues, the justification of autonomy has its limits and therefore tolerance itself has limits. According to Raz, 'autonomy-based toleration ... does not extend to the morally bad and repugnant ... autonomy is valuable only if exercised in pursuit of the good'.[18] Raz does not elaborate on what exactly is 'bad and repugnant' or 'good'.[19] Nevertheless, he does put forward one

---

[14] G Mensching, *Tolerance and Truth in Religion* (trans HJ Klimkeit) (Tucaloosa AL, University of Alabama Press, 1971) 168.

[15] LM Hammer, *The International Human Right to Freedom of Conscience* (Farnham, Ashgate Publishing Ltd, 2001) 73.

[16] J Raz, *The Morality of Freedom* (Oxford, Clarendon Press, 1986) chapters 14 and 15.

[17] By saying that, I do not necessarily mean that there is a moral right to do what is morally wrong, as opposed to J Waldron, 'A Right to Do Wrong' (1981) 92 *Ethics* 21; and D Enoch, 'A Right to Violate One's Duty' (2002) 21 *Law and Philosophy* 355.

[18] J Raz, 'Autonomy, Toleration and the Harm Principle' in R Gavison (ed), *Issues in Contemporary Legal Philosophy* (Oxford, Oxford University Press, 1987) 313, 326–27. See also on pp 322–23.

[19] For another helpful discussion of good and unacceptable ways of life yet without pointing out any detailed definition see J Raz, 'Free Expression and Personal Identification' (1991) 11 *Oxford Journal of Legal Studies* 303, 319.

unavoidable criterion: whoever or whatever denies autonomy or even fails to promote it should not be tolerated by the government.[20] This is not an example of applying the principle of reciprocity. This is a different kind of argument according to which those who act contrary to what underlies autonomy-based toleration, or simply contrary to what autonomy entails, should not be tolerated. This argument is based on the weight accorded to autonomy.[21] A similar, modified approach was suggested by Colburn, who argues that autonomy-minded liberalism must rule out—and therefore not tolerate—ways of life 'that could not develop under an autonomy-promoting education'.[22] Colburn's argument reminds us that even according to Raz, autonomy can be 'described without commitment to the substance of the valuable forms of life with which it is bound up'.[23] Therefore, autonomous people may decide to live a non-autonomous life. This is so because autonomous people can decide for themselves what is valuable and what a good life is. Colburn rightly suggests that 'this leaves wide open the question of what values might in fact be chosen by different agents, and certainly does not imply that the values need to include autonomy or freedom'.[24] Colburn's argument is only true under the condition that a person who chooses to live a non-autonomous life (eg a person who treats a religious leader as an absolute authority with regard to various aspects of his life) still possesses the mental and practical ability to change his mind and to choose alternative ways of life. Autonomy-minded liberalism cannot tolerate an irreversible and meaningful waiver of freedom and autonomy with regard to a wide range of aspects of one's life. Another pre-condition for the ability of autonomy-minded liberalism to tolerate ways of life that do not appreciate autonomy is that choosing such ways of life must result from being educated in a system that values autonomy. This leads Colburn to argue that 'any way of life will *de facto* be ruled out if it requires children to be raised in ignorance of possible courses their lives might take other than those approved by their parents'.[25] Thus, even Colburn's modified, moderate and autonomy-based perception of the limits of liberal tolerance

---

[20] Raz (n 18 above) 329, 331. See also J Raz, 'Comments and Responses' in LH Meyer, SL Paulson and TW Pogge (eds), *Rights, Culture, and the Law: Themes from the Legal and Political Philosophy of Joseph Raz* (Oxford, Oxford University Press, 2003) 253, 266–67. For a similar view see also F Raday, 'Culture, Religion and Gender' (2003) 1 *International Journal of Constitutional Law* 663, 701.

[21] The questions of why autonomy should be so highly considered and why it should gain precedence over other principles, values or 'goods' will not be discussed here. I will simply refer, with full consent, to Raz's views on these matters.

[22] Colburn (n 2 above) 624.

[23] Raz (n 16 above) 395.

[24] Colburn (n 2 above) 622–23.

[25] Colburn (n 2 above) 624. For a similar approach see M Rosen, 'The Educational Autonomy of Perfectionist Religious Groups in a Liberal State' (2012) 1 *Journal of Law, Religion & State* 16.

prescribes intolerance towards illiberal (and intolerant) educational systems and institutions and—in turn—ways of life.

The connection between tolerance and autonomy can lead us to two similar conclusions. First, if tolerance enables autonomy and if government has a duty to ensure and promote autonomy, then government has a duty to ensure and promote tolerance. Secondly, since intolerance is by definition harming others (or offending them), then the same principle that allows the infringement of autonomy in order to defend autonomy and promote it—or allows harming others in order to protect autonomy, allows not tolerating the intolerant in order to defend tolerance and promote it. This is the essence of the autonomy-based tolerance and a central part of the more general view of substantive liberalism.

Since autonomy can be considered as the ultimate justification for other human rights that relate to tolerance (eg freedom of expression, freedom of conscience and religion and so forth) or can be seen as a distinct human right that overlaps with these other human rights, and since all of the above can be used as a justification for tolerance, it is not far-fetched to describe the limits of tolerance in the following way: any behaviour that contradicts or diminishes the justifications for tolerance (or, in some cases, fails to promote these justifications) should not be tolerated.

Thus, tolerance demands that one should not tolerate illiberal intolerance. If we assume that Y does not tolerate X without sufficiently good reason, then assuming that the state takes tolerance seriously, it is committed to protecting X's right to be tolerated by not tolerating those who infringe that right. Allowing Y not to tolerate X in the name of tolerance is self-contradictory. Not tolerating Y's unjustified intolerance towards X is the only way to be committed to tolerance, or more accurately—to its justifications or to the values it protects. From the point of view of the intolerant person, it seems highly unsound to argue for the defence of tolerance while acting contrary to it at the same time.

The argument for reciprocity was brought forward in a very powerful and convincing way by Karl Popper. Unfortunately, too many liberal states and some liberal thinkers fail to accept, develop and apply this simple insight. Popper's initial argument is that:

> Unlimited tolerance must lead to the disappearance of tolerance. If we extend unlimited tolerance even to those who are intolerant, if we are not prepared to defend a tolerant society against the onslaught of the intolerant, then the tolerant will be destroyed, and tolerance with them.[26]

---

[26] K Popper, *The Open Society and its Enemies* (London, Routledge, 1945) 265.

The first part of Popper's statement is trivial. Few, if any, would argue for a general principle of unlimited tolerance. All agree that tolerance has to have its limits and the only significant question is about the nature of those limits. The second part, however, is more meaningful. Here Popper refers to the special case of tolerating—or not tolerating—the intolerant. No doubt unlimited tolerance towards the intolerant would result in the loss of tolerance and the victory of intolerance. Therefore, following Popper's argument, unlimited tolerance is specifically undesirable towards the intolerant, yet his further and most important argument is that:

> We should therefore claim, in the name of tolerance, the right not to tolerate the intolerant. We should claim that any movement preaching intolerance places itself outside the law, and we should consider incitement to intolerance and persecution as criminal, in the same way as we should consider incitement to murder, or to kidnapping, or to the revival of the slave trade, as criminal.[27]

Popper's view could be that there are cases where intolerance should not be tolerated—for the sake of tolerance itself. But Popper's view (or at least the logic of his argument) could also be interpreted in a broader manner, namely that intolerance should never be tolerated, for the sake of tolerance itself. Evidence that that has been Popper's intention can be found in his concluding remark that government should 'tolerate all who are prepared to reciprocate, i.e. who are tolerant'.[28]

Thus, it can be argued that adhering to the principle of tolerance provides a prima facie reason not to tolerate intolerance. Alternatively, it may be the case that adhering to the principle of tolerance does not provide a prima facie reason either to tolerate the intolerant or to refuse to tolerate the intolerant. This is so because our response to intolerance must take into consideration the values that ground the intolerant behaviour. We should not tolerate only unjustifiable intolerance. The question whether an intolerant behaviour is justifiable would have to be answered on a case-by-case basis—and the answer will depend on the kind of theory of justice or moral or political theory to which we subscribe. How exactly we should exercise this approach is governed by the principle of proportionality that will be described shortly.

C. Reciprocity and Pragmatic Justifications

One can hold purely pragmatic justifications for tolerance. One can also hold a more comprehensive notion of tolerance by not tolerating others according to the principle of reciprocity only when there is no pragmatic reason that

---

[27] Popper (n 26 above) 265.
[28] Popper (n 26 above) 266.

prevails and leads to tolerating the intolerable. This comprehensive approach can be called a pragmatic-reciprocity approach. For a better understanding of this approach I will discuss, albeit not in great detail, some pragmatic justifications in themselves and vis-à-vis the principle of reciprocity.

First, one can argue that there is no such thing as a false idea or, alternatively, that any idea can be right or wrong, and since there is no way of knowing which it is, all ideas and values should be tolerated. This argument must be rejected since when discussing tolerance we are rejecting, by definition, the notion that we do not know what is right and what is wrong as well as the odd idea that 'there are no false ideas'. Tolerance is to be understood as not harming another even though the tolerant person thinks there are good reasons for harming the other (because the other's values or way of balancing values as expressed in his behaviour, way of life or speech, seem to the tolerant to be 'wrong'). If this is indeed what tolerance means, then a tolerant person must assume that he knows which values are right and which are wrong. The tolerant person might be wrong in assuming that there are false ideas. If there are false ideas, the tolerant person might fail in identifying them, but this is all beside the point. The point is that when discussing pragmatic justifications for tolerance we cannot refer to justifications that are based on the idea that there is no such thing as a false idea, or on the notion that any idea can be right or wrong and that there is no way of knowing which it is. These ideas may justify pluralism, neutrality, respect for others and so on, but not tolerance.

Secondly, one can argue that even if there are false ideas the government should not decide on their falsity, since giving this power to government will eventually lead to its misuse. However, even those who embrace this argument are not denying the power of government to uphold certain limitations on some value-based practices and even speech.[29] Instead of arguing that government should never hold the power not to tolerate any opinion whatsoever, one should argue for pragmatic or principled reasons to oppose a government's intolerance towards specific opinions or ways of life. The argument that giving some power to the government to do something right (to restrict only ideas that need to be restricted) will result in its misuse to a degree that does not justify giving that power at all, has its problems. By adopting this line of argument we can equally argue that by refraining from giving government power that might be misused, we will end up denying government the power to do

---

[29] See for example PP Nicholson, 'Toleration as a Moral Idea' in J Horton and S Mendus (eds), *Aspects of Toleration* (London, Routledge, 1985) 158. On pp 163–64 Nicholson argues against intolerance since giving anyone the power to decide what to tolerate will result in mistakes and abuse of that power. Nevertheless, on p 170 he agrees that government can 'discriminate against one idea by giving extra aid to the opposite idea' and on p 172 he agrees that in some cases government should not tolerate the intolerant.

what it should do and what we want it to do. The argument against according excessive weight to the fear of abuse of governmental power is merely a specific implementation of a more general argument concerning the difficulty that exists within every modern democracy to find the right balance between defending human rights and limiting them—for the sake of the stability and continuity of the human rights regime itself. I suspect that all too often striking the wrong balance may be equally undesirable, whether the diversion from the right balance is towards over-protection of human rights or under-protection of them. It is wrong to assume that it is always better to grant over-protection to human rights than to allow others to harm them more than necessary. I suspect that various and changeable circumstances may lead to different answers in different cases. Therefore, a general presumption in this context will be implausible or at least undesirable.

Thirdly, the argument against not tolerating the intolerant can be read as a slippery slope argument. Giving the power to the government not to tolerate intolerance may result in having no stable boundaries to that power. It may therefore lead to uncertainty and create a 'chilling effect' that would deter people from taking lawful actions which, in their view, are dangerously close to the unstable and vague boundaries of the law. The slippery slope argument is generally not very appealing and is not very convincing in this case either.[30] The slippery slope problem is a regrettable yet sometimes inevitable side-effect of legitimate governmental powers. Moreover, at times, having unstable and vague legal boundaries is actually desirable and beneficial to the rule of law itself.[31] Suffice it to say that even if this argument poses a problem it could be regarded as the lesser evil when the alternative (always tolerating the intolerant) is considered.

Fourthly, one can argue that there are false ideas but allowing them to be heard is the best way to discover the truth and leads to a lively and strong perception of the truth. As the principle of reciprocity focuses on intolerant views and not merely on false ones, then the above argument can also be read more generally as an argument that supports tolerating the intolerant if and only if tolerance as a whole will benefit from it. This powerful argument does not contradict the principle of reciprocity. Since, according to the reciprocity principle, tolerance is our main concern, it seems coherent to argue that as a starting point we should not tolerate the intolerant unless our intolerant reaction will reduce significantly the total level of tolerance in society as a whole. Indeed, sometimes we should tolerate the intolerant as a lesser evil since, for

---

[30] For a general anti-slippery slope argument see D Enoch, 'Once You Start Using Slippery Slope Arguments, You're on a Very Slippery Slope' (2001) 21 *Oxford Journal of Legal Studies* 629.

[31] T Endicott, 'The Impossibility of the Rule of Law' (1999) 19 *Oxford Journal of Legal Studies* 1, 6, 7.

pragmatic reasons, we are not able to eradicate the intolerant views or behaviour without causing more harm to tolerance itself, or to other valuable values or interests. Nevertheless, when the principle of proportionality is explained I will argue that some level of intolerance towards the intolerant is possible and necessary in almost every case.

This argument of 'pragmatic reciprocity' can be found, although not in these words, in Rawls's writings. According to Rawls, any society that wishes to preserve its basic culture and social institutions must be intolerant towards certain ways of life.[32] In order to protect some fundamental liberal norms, namely respect for the other and not harming the other, society must set a limit to the scope of values it can respect or tolerate.[33] This is the reciprocity part of Rawls's argument, although it is not argued in great detail. But then, Rawls also argues that when an intolerant sect appears in a democratic society, tolerating it may persuade its members to believe in freedom, and thus, provided the sect is not strong enough to eliminate liberal democracy, 'it will tend to lose its intolerance and accept liberty of conscience'.[34] Therefore, according to Rawls, unless the group is strong enough to significantly harm the liberal state one should tolerate it and by persuasion 'liberalise' it. Only when the liberal society is in real danger, and only if tolerance as a whole will benefit from not tolerating the intolerant is an intolerant reaction justifiable.[35] This is the pragmatic part of Rawls's argument and as such it raises one important concern: Rawls's position that a liberal society should be in real danger before it refuses to tolerate intolerance and that tolerance as a whole will benefit from not tolerating the intolerant, are very nearly contradictory.

In some detail: while the pragmatic-reciprocity approach that I have offered supports, in principle, intolerance towards the powerless intolerant, Rawls's pragmatic-reciprocity approach supports tolerance towards the powerless intolerant, and intolerance towards those who are powerful. I suggested that intolerance should not be tolerated unless the intolerant response to intolerance will reduce significantly the total level of tolerance in society as a whole or will cause undesirable harm to desirable values or interests. This approach supports not tolerating powerless groups precisely because we wish to prevent them from gaining power. Rawls's approach, however, dictates tolerance until the point at which the tolerant group gains power. The obvious concern regarding Rawls's approach is that when the intolerant group gains sufficient power to threaten the liberal constitution and liberal society, intolerance towards that group is likely to be ineffective or too expensive and may result in

---

[32] Rawls (n 3 above) 225–30.
[33] Rawls (n 10 above) 192, 325.
[34] Rawls (n 10 above) 192–93.
[35] Rawls (n 3 above) 220. See also in Rawls (n 10 above) 192, 193.

harming the tolerance regime itself. Adopting Rawls's approach might result in a liberal majority (or an elite liberal minority) that is not powerful enough to face an overly powerful intolerant group.

It seems that Walzer follows a similar approach to Rawls. According to Walzer, the state should tolerate anti-democratic (and normally intolerant) groups or communities unless a political party is founded on the basis of the group's intolerant values, in which case the state could ban the party from participating in the political process. This ban, Walzer argues, is not intolerance but simply a matter of caution.[36] Although it is hard to understand why Walzer thinks that banning parties from the political process is not intolerance but only 'caution', the more important quandary relates to his distinction between the pre-political or ex-political and the political, according to which we should not tolerate the intolerant (or just be cautious) only when they enter the political sphere.

First, and much like Rawls's approach, Walzer is waiting too long before being intolerant towards the intolerant. Groups and communities might accumulate significant power and enter the political sphere with strong support that will make it harder, from a pragmatic point of view, not to tolerate them. Secondly, intolerant groups can cause significant harm to members and non-members alike, regardless of their participation in the political process. A socially organised intolerance can be as powerful and as harmful (or even more so) to individuals and to society as a 'formal' political one. Thirdly, once Walzer agrees that some ideas should not be entitled to gain political power or that democracy should prevent some ideas from gaining the majority's support, it can hardly be consistent to allow these ideas to take full part in the market-place of ideas in the public sphere. If a judgement is made that some ideas are not legitimate and steps should be taken to prevent them from gaining formal-political support, steps should also be taken to prevent them from gaining 'non-political' popular support. The state has a duty, in order to prevent harm to its citizens, not to tolerate any public expression or implementation of those ideas. Again, Walzer fails to recognise the importance of the public, yet informal and non-political, sphere.

D. Tolerance—A Moral Virtue?

The notion that one should not tolerate some values, ways of life and so on, either according to the principle of reciprocity or according to the 'pragmatic-reciprocity' approach, is rejected by some who perceive tolerance as a moral

---

[36] M Walzer, *On Toleration* (New Haven CT, Yale University Press, 1997) 9.

virtue and therefore find it hard to comprehend that intolerance is sometimes allowed or even necessary.

Therefore, it might be useful to clarify this point before we go on. Is tolerance always a good thing in the sense that one should always be tolerant, or are tolerance and intolerance neither good nor bad in themselves since one can be wrongly tolerant or rightly intolerant? Nicholson argues that toleration is always good for the reason that the alternative—intolerance—is always worse (the negative case for toleration), and because tolerance has an independent value (the positive case for toleration).[37] Nicholson argues that part of being moral is to give serious consideration to other people's ideas, and failing to do so means not just selfishness or making an illegitimate demand for a privileged position but also immorality. Therefore, 'since toleration is good, to be tolerant is a moral duty … and therefore the tolerator has no moral right not to be tolerant'.[38]

The first problem with this argument is that not all the ideas other people have deserve serious consideration[39] and that not all people deserve an equal amount of respect. Nicholson argues that '[the tolerator] must respect the personality of the holders of those opinions, and treat them as rational moral agents whose views can be discussed and disputed, and who are capable of changing their minds on rational grounds'.[40] Nevertheless, there are surely people who although in principle are 'capable of changing their minds on rational grounds', in fact rarely turn to rational grounds for formulating and changing their opinions. On what basis should such people be treated as what they are not (ie rational agents)? Here I share Bernard Williams's view (and criticism of Kant) that the concept of a 'moral agent' does and must have an empirical basis and should not be understood as a 'transcendental characteristic' of human beings.[41]

Thomas Scanlon presents a similar argument to Nicholson's. Scanlon does not tolerate the intolerant when he argues that we should not regard the views of the intolerant as entitled to be heard. But he then suggests that we must distinguish between intolerant opinions and their holders, and as a result 'it is not that their *point of view* is entitled to be represented but that *they* … are entitled to be heard'.[42]

---

[37] Nicholson (n 29 above) 164. For a similar approach of a negative case for toleration see Scanlon (n 7 above) 201.

[38] Nicholson (n 29 above) 166–67.

[39] And it seems that Nicholson himself is aware of that: (n 29 above) 165.

[40] Nicholson (n 29 above) 165.

[41] B Williams, *Problems of the Self: Philosophical Papers 1956–1972* (Cambridge, Cambridge University Press, 1973) 235.

[42] Scanlon (n 7 above) 197. For a similar argument see Williams (n 7 above) 73.

It is possible to understand and to criticise Scanlon's view in two ways. We can accept his claim that one should separate intolerant opinions from their holders, and that generally opinions should be separated from their holders. If that is true, then by banning an opinion we do not disrespect its holder but only his opinion. The person is still a fellow citizen who has an equal place in society, though some of his opinions do not. This argument is convincing only if we accept that there are views that are not entitled to be heard and that not respecting a person's view or, more accurately, a person's entitlement to express his view, is not equivalent to not respecting that person. These assumptions, however, are not very appealing, and clearly this is not what Scanlon is arguing for. Therefore, the following may offer a better understanding and evaluation of Scanlon's view.

By saying that there are opinions that are not entitled to be heard but their holders are, Scanlon does not separate opinions from their holders. If one's entitlement to be represented means that all one's views should be heard, then Scanlon does not offer any meaningful separation between opinions and their holders. According to Scanlon all opinions should be heard only because someone holds them, and accordingly, censoring an opinion because of its content denies its holder's equal citizenship. If that is the case, then in fact all views should be heard precisely because they are not separated from their holders. I do not think Scanlon meant to say that 'you are what you think', but he does argue for a strong connection between people and their opinions.

If we follow this line of argument we can reach two opposite results: the first is to allow intolerant views to be heard as a result of respect for their holders; the second—and the more desirable—is that we must disrespect a person by preventing him from promoting his intolerant views (or acting upon them) precisely because they are intolerant. The principle of reciprocity is valid here as well. If the illegitimate point of view disrespects others, it is fully justifiable to prevent this harm (or offence) or to respond to it by disrespecting not just the bigot's point of view but the bigot himself.

Up to now I have criticised Nicholson's (and Scanlon's) argument that all ideas other people have deserve serious consideration and that all people deserve an equal amount of respect by allowing them to express their views freely. The criticism of Nicholson's second argument is more fundamental. The argument that tolerance is a moral virtue and that therefore one must always be tolerant cannot be justified. Nicholson does not argue that because tolerance is good there is a prima facie reason to tolerate. His argument is that one must always be tolerant. But, if tolerance is indeed always good and if to be tolerant is a moral duty, then intolerance is always bad. Even then, and since one must always be tolerant according to Nicholson, it is never justifiable to take measures to confront intolerance. But if the principle of reciprocity is justified, then this categorical conclusion is clearly mistaken. Note that

Nicholson himself recognises the need not to tolerate the intolerant.[43] But one surely cannot claim that because tolerance is always good and intolerance always wrong, it is sometimes permissible not to tolerate the intolerant. This is simply self-contradictory.

Thus, the notion that tolerance is a moral virtue is either misguided or does not mean that one should always be tolerant. All it may mean is that one should be tolerant unless compelling reasons allow or demand an intolerant response to a wrong. It might be argued that it would be better to give up entirely an attempt to describe or to justify tolerance as good and simply to argue that tolerance and intolerance are not end-points on a spectrum of good and bad but can be either good or bad according to the circumstances. This is a point worth stressing since in contemporary liberalism toleration is seen as second-best and being intolerant is sometimes considered inherently wrong. These misconceptions lead some liberal thinkers to incorrect observations regarding the principle of tolerance.

For example, Scanlon, who sees tolerance as second best, argues that since religious groups and political movements would lose their point if they had to include just anyone, it is not intolerant of them to deny goods to those who do not share their values.[44] The correct conclusion should be that while this is intolerance, it might be justified. Scanlon also wrongly claims that it is not intolerance to oppose the creationists who wish to teach 'creation science' in public schools, and that it is not intolerance to enforce tolerance in behaviour and prevent the intolerant from acting on their beliefs.[45] In both cases the right observation is that, again, this is a justifiable form of intolerance. This is a form of intolerance because we make an adverse judgement about creationists and intolerant people and act upon our adverse judgements by denying creationists and intolerant people certain freedoms, benefits, opportunities etc. Leiter made a similar mistake when he argued that it would be compatible with the principle of tolerance to prohibit the teaching of religious explanations for the origin of human life in state schools whereas it would not be compatible with the principle of tolerance to prevent creationist and intelligent design proponents from publicly articulating their views.[46] However, both prohibitions are in fact an expression of intolerance. Prohibiting the teaching of religious explanations for the origin of human life in state schools harms or limits the freedom of religious teachers—because we make adverse judgement about their religious explanations. This is a paradigmatic case of intolerance. The only question is which intolerant response towards creationism can be

---

[43] Nicholson (n 29 above) 169–72.
[44] Scanlon (n 7 above) 194.
[45] Scanlon (n 7 above) 196.
[46] B Leiter, *Why Tolerate Religion* (Princeton NJ, Princeton University Press, 2012) 121.

justified or is proportionate. It is a question about the limits of tolerance rather than about compatibility with the principle of tolerance. There is nothing in the principle of tolerance as such that allows the exclusion of creationism from state schools or that does not allow silencing of creationists altogether. The principle of tolerance merely describes behaviours and states of mind. It does not, in and of itself, justify behaviours.

These examples remind us to properly differentiate between the analytical question of what tolerance and intolerance are—and the normative question of whether tolerance and intolerance are justified.

E. Tolerating the Intolerant: Who Carries the Burden?

It seems that some of the general disapproval of tolerance or the inconvenience that tolerance causes to some liberals lies not just in tolerance entailing an adverse judgement of the other but also in the notion that the state is the one that is likely to act intolerantly towards individuals and minorities, and to initiate such intolerance. Liberalism sees the paradigmatic case of intolerance as being one of an over-powerful state or orthodoxy unjustly eliminating individuals' and minorities' freedoms.

Such concerns can be found in the well-known criticism, by Herbert Marcuse, who claims that the concept of tolerance is often used to serve the powerful oppressor's goals.[47] Marcuse claims that all too often minority groups are the ones that are required to tolerate the powerful. In addition, political tolerance is exercised by the powerful majority towards sub-groups of the majority who harm minority groups. At best, Marcuse suggests, tolerance is demanded equally from minority groups who do not seek to harm each other but seek only to enjoy an equal voice in the public sphere—and from groups who promote hatred towards minority groups and wish to exclude them from the public sphere. This practice of tolerance is exercised in the name of an alleged objectivity or neutrality, even though it reflects the powerful oppressor's values. Marcuse's observation, which is accurate in itself, does not indicate any difficulties with the concept of tolerance. Rather, his argument indicates how the idea of tolerance is often misused by the oppressor. Yet, this provides liberals with even more reasons to use the concept of tolerance with reluctance, inconvenience or suspicion.

Either way, it is not always the case that intolerance is used by an over-powerful state or orthodoxy unjustly to eliminate individuals' and minorities'

---

[47] H Marcuse, 'Repressive Tolerance' in RP Wolff (ed), *A Critique of Pure Tolerance* (London, Jonathan Cape Publishers, 1969) 65. See also W Brown, *Regulating Aversion: Tolerance in the Age of Identity and Empire* (Princeton NJ, Princeton University Press, 2006) 4.

freedoms, and one might wonder just how commonly it is employed in this way. All too often intolerance is the practice of minority groups towards their weakest members (this can be found mainly but not solely in religious groups and in patriarchal cultures) and of members of powerful groups towards members of powerless groups. In these cases the liberal's unwillingness to allow state power to eliminate intolerance results in harm caused to the weakest in society.[48] The greater the state's unwillingness to impose tolerance, the greater is the burden of tolerance towards the intolerant that the powerless have to carry.

Thus, when intolerant minority groups aim their intolerance directly at the state or towards the powerful, an intolerant response, even if often justified, should be taken only after special serious consideration since here the risk of misusing the state's power is relatively high. Note that in this case avoidance of an intolerant response results in the powerful carrying the burden of tolerance. However, when intolerant groups or individuals aim their intolerance at powerless groups or individuals, avoidance of an intolerant response by the state results in the powerless carrying the burden of tolerance. Therefore an intolerant state response in these cases is less suspicious and no special considerations should be taken into account.

The last case might be misleading since the state's intolerant response to intolerance by third parties towards minorities will presumably be based on the values of the state or of the powerful. Moreover, in this case (as opposed to the first one) the burden of tolerance does not necessarily shift from the minority to the majority or to the state but from the minority to a third party, who may also be a minority or at least not part of the dominant powerful group. Nevertheless, in the second case the state's power is less likely to be misused, since no intolerance is aimed directly at it. The state may still be accused of imposing its values on minority groups, but this is only troubling if the state holds or imposes illiberal or wrong values.

F. Proportionality

Although it is a well-established principle in public law, most scholars ignore the principle of proportionality when discussing the limits of tolerance. Its absence leads to an unsatisfactory and incomplete approach to the limits of tolerance. Disregarding the principle of proportionality leads to a misleading dichotomy: one is regarded either as tolerant or as intolerant. Since some are unwilling to be identified as intolerant or unwilling to promote intolerance

---

[48] This harm is seen by some as a mental or a psychic tax imposed on the 'poorer', and therefore as a regressive, unjust tax: MJ Matsuda, 'Public Response to Racial Speech: Considering the Victim's Story' (1989) 87 *Michigan Law Review* 2320, 2322, 2376.

(mainly because they wrongly assume that intolerance is intrinsically wrong) tolerance is attached to many things that are very different from it (eg pluralism) and it is promoted even when it should not be.

The principle of proportionality reminds us that there are different kinds and degrees of tolerance and intolerance. It reminds us that the question is not just whether one is tolerant or not but also what kind and level of intolerance justifies a specific kind and level of intolerant response. As such, the principle of proportionality complements the principle of reciprocity. Intolerance can take the form of condemning another, insulting him, undermining his values, making him feel uncomfortable or unwelcome, avoiding his presence, discriminating against him, refusing to assist him, restricting his speech or behaviour, and so on. Similarly, an intolerant response to intolerance can also take the form of all the above.

According to the principle of proportionality one should match the nature and level of one's intolerant response to the nature and level of the intolerance one is facing. This general rule can be divided into three sub-rules.[49]

First, there should be a rational, logical connection between the nature of the original intolerance and the nature of the intolerant response. For example, an intolerant response to a racist speech in parliament should be connected to the political process and not to the MP's 'private' identity. Moreover, the rational connection test implies that an intolerant response should be effective or at least has to have—in principle—the potential of being effective.

Secondly, an intolerant response should eliminate or significantly reduce the effect of the original intolerance while causing the least amount of harm to human rights and interests. In other words, we should find the least harmful intolerant response that is still effective. For example, one's response to the emergence of a racist political party could be banning the party from the political process. This response has a rational connection to the intolerance we are facing. It can also be assumed that it is the least harmful means that can be taken in order to eliminate this political intolerance. On the other hand, putting the party's leaders and its members in prison may be effective but is certainly not the least harmful intolerant response possible.

Thirdly, the least harmful response to intolerance (which may still be harsh) and the consequences of such a response should be proportionate to the legitimate aim one is trying to achieve; that is, proportionate to the exact value, right or interest that should be protected from the intolerance we are facing. Assume that an intolerant religious group disrupts by demonstrations the

---

[49] For an in-depth discussion on the principle of proportionality, see: A Barak, *Proportionality: Constitutional Rights and their Limitations* (Cambridge, Cambridge University Press, 2012); M Cohen-Eliya and I Porat, *Proportionality and Constitutional Culture* (Cambridge, Cambridge University Press, 2013).

performance of a theatre play that offends its religious values. The police decision to arrest some of those causing the disruption and to forcibly keep the others at a reasonable distance from the theatre is both rationally connected to the nature and the level of the protestors' intolerance and can be seen as the least harmful intolerant response that is still effective (the latter is, obviously, a factual evaluation that depends on the circumstances of every case). However, if there is a high probability that this intolerant response to the religious intolerance will cause riots that result in the deaths of one or several innocent people or of many of the violent religious protestors then the least harmful yet effective response to the religious intolerance, or more specifically its consequences, is not proportionate to the legitimate aim we are trying to achieve (ie guaranteeing freedom of artistic speech) and therefore should be avoided.

However, and this is a crucial yet sometimes neglected point, although in some cases the least harmful intolerant (yet efficient) response should be avoided for pragmatic or moral reasons, that is not to say that the government and the public do not have a moral right to engage in an intolerant response to a lesser extent, even though it is not fully effective. In the example above the government can—and in my opinion should—condemn the religious intolerance and allow the public to freely and harshly criticise it. This is an important message that must be clear: we think you are intolerant and the only reason we do not take the necessary steps to eliminate your intolerance is not that we respect your values but that we do not want to expose society to an even more intolerant response.

Raz, however, argues that government must not condemn 'bad' speech, including 'attacking speech' (which is part of a good way of life).[50] Raz's argument is limited to freedom of speech and does not include acts. Nevertheless, it is well known that the boundaries between speech and acts are not always clear. Here, one can argue that hostile and intimidating speech towards a theatre audience that prevents them from attending a play or makes it extremely hard for them to fully enjoy the play is closer to an act than to speech. Moreover, even if we think that the religion that was offended by the play can form the basis of a generally good way of life, it is hard to agree that government must not condemn a specific intolerant expression of that way of life, especially when that expression denies the way of life of others and the legitimate implementation of their autonomy. In other words, one can say: we respect you, your religion and your way of life but we will not tolerate some aspects of your way of life if they reject the autonomy of others or unjustly harm them.

The possibility of expressing an intolerant response by condemnation is meaningful not only when the powerful state avoids, just for pragmatic reasons, what is in principle a justifiable response to intolerance, but also when a

---

[50] Raz (n 18 above) 318–20.

powerless group wishes not to tolerate the powerful. It seems that condemnation is one of the few ways a powerless group has of expressing its intolerance towards the powerful without risking an intolerant response, or at least not a major one.

The possibility of condemning the intolerant as part of the principle of proportionality may also solve the difficulty of Bernard Williams and others in appreciating tolerance. According to Williams, tolerance is impossible since it is required only for the intolerable, and more specifically liberal tolerance is impossible since it is required only towards those who deny personal autonomy as a good and as a basis of tolerance itself.[51] First, it could be argued that Williams' initial view is incorrect. Not all we should tolerate is intolerable, in the sense that not all we should tolerate denies the justifications for tolerance itself. We can tolerate the stupid, the irrational, the disgusting, the repulsive and so on. This has nothing to do with the denial of tolerance itself. Tolerance is required whenever a person makes an adverse judgement about another, and when the adverse judgement provides that person reasons to harm another. The adverse judgement does not have to be aimed at those who deny personal autonomy as a basis of tolerance itself. Secondly, even if we agree with Williams, the possibility of not tolerating the intolerable by condemnation, avoidance, refusal to assist and so on coincides with Williams' initial view (that we can only tolerate things that are intolerable) yet avoids harsh intolerance toward the intolerable and leaves it with most of its relevant and meaningful freedoms.

To conclude, the principle of proportionality—and especially its third element—is the core of the proposed pragmatic-reciprocity approach. It implies that one should not tolerate illiberal intolerance unless pragmatic reasons prevail, ie unless the intolerant response to intolerance (and the response to that) will cause disproportionate harm to human rights or to tolerance itself in society as a whole.

Lastly, the principle of proportionality offers a new approach to categorising our attitude regarding tolerance. Instead of the dichotomy between intolerance and tolerance, one can be seen as intolerant in some degree and therefore tolerant in another degree at the same time. When one chooses a proportionate response to intolerance, for example, one can be described as intolerant towards it—but only to some degree—and also as tolerant towards it—to some degree—because one avoids taking harsher and disproportionate measures as a response (provided one has reasons to take a disproportionate response). As part of his interesting and helpful discussion about various forms of latent and manifest tolerance, Cohen-Almagor gives the example

---

[51] Williams (n 7 above) 65, 73.

of walking out in protest as a reaction to an intolerable expression and won-ders whether it can still be considered as an act of tolerance.[52] The answer I suggest is that it is an act of intolerance since it intends to send a negative message to the speaker because of the content of his speech. However, it is also an act of tolerance to some extent as the one who chooses to walk out refrains from taking harsher measures regarding the speech or the speaker, although he might have good reason to take these measures—and because of what could be, but does not have to be, overriding moral reasons. Indeed, it appears that in most cases people are not merely tolerant or intolerant towards something or someone but actually tolerant and intolerant at the same time and to various degrees.

III. WHO IS THE TRUE INTOLERANT ONE?

According to the principle of reciprocity one has to identify the 'original' intolerance and decide on the proper response. However, it can be argued that there is no neutral way to decide who the original perpetrator of intoler-ance is. Therefore, the original perpetrator can and indeed often does argue that the liberal intolerant response towards him is not a response at all but the original intolerance itself, and that by forcing him to be tolerant in the liberal meaning, liberals themselves are being intolerant. This argument is misguided for two main reasons.

First, as was repeatedly stressed, tolerance discourse is by definition a value-based one and it seems awkward to accuse value-based liberalism of acting according to its values.[53] If rivals do not share a similar political or moral understanding of acceptable values, the discourse of tolerance will rarely be able to reconcile value-based arguments between them. More specifically, in order for the principle of reciprocity to be applied we need to determine the reasons for the intolerant act, which may or may not be justified, and not just the intolerant person's temporal position. Liberals and non-liberals can share similar perceptions of the principle of tolerance. They may agree about the definition of tolerance. They may even have the same view about the principled limits of tolerance. Both can agree, for example, that intolerance should not be tolerated. However, all too often they would not be able to reach the same answer to the question of when a certain intolerant act or tolerant behaviour is justifiable. Regarding that aspect alone, a theory of liberal toler-ance is quite useless. Nevertheless, it has great importance within the scope

---

[52] R Cohen-Almagor, *The Scope of Tolerance: Studies of the Cost of Free Expression and Freedom of the Press* (London, Routledge, 2006) 29–33.
[53] For the same argument regarding (Razian) pluralism see Raz (n 18 above) 322.

of liberalism. Those who do hold liberal values can employ the proposed approach about the limits of tolerance and more specifically, to agree about the criteria for identifying the true intolerant person and the unjustified tolerance that should not be tolerated.

Secondly and despite the above, there might be a partial solution to the problem of finding a neutral understanding of the limits of tolerance. When identifying the original intolerant person we can turn to two helpful tests. First, we should ask whether A intended to harm another or whether the harm was incidental to A's action or speech, and secondly, who first intended to harm the other—or, to put it in a more childish way, who started it?[54] In the following I will describe the 'intention to harm' criterion and the 'who started it?' criterion and will explain their relevance to the question of the limits of tolerance.

A. The Intention to Harm

It seems implausible to accuse someone of being intolerant unless that person has an intention to harm another. This is not to say that one's freedom can be restricted only when one has the intention of harming another. There are other reasons for restricting freedom: public order, paternalism, moral conventions, different perceptions of justice and so on. All I am arguing is that when the reason to restrict freedom is intolerance of another, an intention to cause harm must be proven.

One can argue that when the harm is unavoidable or highly predictable the actor is to be considered as intolerant if he does not refrain from the action. But the intolerant person, by definition, causes harm because he has a negative opinion of the other or because he believes he has good reason to harm him. I suggest that the categorisation of an act as intolerant should depend on the adverse judgement of the other being the primary reason or at least a reason that is necessary for committing the harmful act. When a negative opinion, for example, is one of the reasons for not avoiding an act that one would have done regardless of this opinion, the actor is not to be considered as intolerant but as inconsiderate or disrespectful.

Therefore it is not intolerance when one walks naked in one's neighbourhood if this is truly one's idea of a good life, ie if one would have walked naked outdoors in any other place (whether in a distant farm or on the high street). One is still not to be considered intolerant if one walks naked mainly because

---

[54] For the discussion of the limits of tolerance to be complete we should also refer to other considerations such as the measure of the harm, its frequency, the ability to avoid the harm (the captive audience question), the cost of such avoidance and so forth. These further considerations, however, are outside the scope of this chapter.

this is truly one's idea of a good life but also because one enjoys offending the feelings of the religious family down the street since one despises their basic values.[55]

Nevertheless, the 'intention to harm test' is not completely detached from the value-based approach. First, the term 'harm' itself cannot be wholly neutral, for some can disagree on what constitutes harm or, more frequently, on what weight should be given to what is agreed to be harmful. Secondly, the disagreement about what constitutes harm can reflect the question of 'who started it?' Assume that, according to one religion, a woman's face must be covered in public. The male religious believers may argue that no harm is intended or indeed caused: on the contrary, it is in the woman's interest to cover her face in public. Therefore any regulation aiming to eradicate this practice can be seen as a response to religious intolerance towards women that by definition harms women, or as an original intolerance towards religious practice that causes no harm and therefore is not intolerant. To refer to that problem more specifically we should turn to the question of 'who started it?'

B. Who was the First to Intend Harm?

The question is: who was the first to restrict (in the broadest sense possible) the freedom of the other because he has a negative opinion of the other or of his values? In the example of the religious face covering, we should find out exactly why women are required to cover their faces. Only if the motives for this demand relate to a negative opinion of women as such (or of their preferences) will it be justifiable to identify it as (the original) intolerance.[56]

An interesting example of trying to avoid the question of 'who started it?' and as a result to eliminate the distinction between acceptable and unacceptable values can be found in Michael McConnell's opinion on homosexuality. According to McConnell, both those who reject homosexuality and those who accept it are intolerant. The homophobic are intolerant as long as they intend to use the law to preserve or to strengthen restrictions on homosexuality as a way of life. The others are intolerant as long as they intend to use

---

[55] However, if a person refrains from walking naked in this case because he takes into consideration the fact that he has religious neighbours, he should be considered as tolerant. This is part of a more general argument that a person may do X without being considered as intolerant and may decide to refrain from doing X and as a consequence be considered as tolerant. This is so because the categorisation of persons as tolerant or intolerant depends not only on their acts but also on the reasons for their acts, as was discussed in Chapter two.

[56] It does not mean that if this demand is not intolerant it is justified. Acts do not have to be intolerant to be unjustifiable.

the law to change social conventions and to fully 'legitimise' homosexuality.[57] McConnell proposes that both views, seeing homosexuality as unnatural or even immoral behaviour and seeing homosexuality as 'healthy' and normal behaviour, should be respected by avoiding using the law to promote their perception of the good.

This attempt to equate homosexuality and homophobia and to consider both as intolerant is false. There is nothing in homosexuality as such that intends to deny the legitimacy of others, to condemn their way of life or to exclude it legally, socially and culturally. Homosexuality, as such, does not entail making adverse judgements about others. Equally, using the law to 'legitimise' homosexuality does not have to entail making adverse judgements about others, and having this judgement as a reason to harm them. However, the very essence of religious or conservative homophobia, when it is expressed openly, promoted in the public sphere or being used as a reason for formulating legal rules, is making an adverse judgement about homosexuals, condemning homosexuality as immoral and excluding it legally, culturally or even physically.

According to the intention criterion and the 'who started it?' criterion, any legislation that supports and promotes homosexuality cannot be regarded as intolerance, whereas any homophobic response to such legislation or to homosexuality in general is indeed the original intolerance. The latter should not be tolerated (in proportionate ways) unless one thinks that this original intolerance is morally justified, ie that homosexuality is immoral or harmful. In that case one should not argue that promoting homosexuality is intolerant but simply immoral or harmful.

Similarly, an indirect yet still incorrect dichotomy was suggested by Raz.[58] Raz argues that government should not criticise hostile portrayals of gays (published as a response to gays' demands to legitimise gay culture) or of Muslims (as a response to their demand to ban *The Satanic Verses*). The problem is that it is extremely hard to find resemblances between the two cases. The gays' demand does not intend to offend others or to limit their freedoms. It does not try to intimidate or to silence others. The Muslims' demand, however, does include all of the above.

If we connect the 'intention to harm' and the 'who started it?' criteria to the idea of proportionality and specifically to the possibility of condemnation, we find that on the same issue (condemning Muslims and homosexuals), Raz argues against the government's condemnation as opposed to public

---

[57] M McConnell, 'The Problem of Singling Out Religion' (2000) 50 *DePaul Law Review* 1, 43–44. Although the connection between tolerance and the status quo and between tolerance and using the law as a means to an end is not quite clear, I will not elaborate on this point here.

[58] Raz (n 18 above) 320.

condemnation because the former is the authoritative voice of society and as such should not be directed towards vulnerable minorities. There are two problems here. First, if, according to Raz, public condemnation of the Muslims' intolerance is or can be justified, one may argue that Raz's rejection of the government's condemnation is not a matter of principle but merely a matter of proportionality. Raz himself argues that on the one hand governmental condemnations 'cannot be justified' and that 'they are wrong in themselves' but that on the other hand extraordinary circumstances can justify them.[59] If this is true, and if the principle of autonomy dictates that government should not just avoid harming autonomy but should also promote it, then even Raz may agree that not only extremely intolerant attacking speech (which is still part of a good way of life) justifies governmental condemnation but also any other speech that diminishes personal autonomy.

Secondly, one can argue that by avoiding condemnation of attacking speech against gays, the government can be seen as sustaining such speech. It is not far-fetched to interpret non-condemnation as support, and while supporting (by not condemning) attacks on Muslims' intolerant response to offending literature coincides with the limits of liberal tolerance, supporting (by not condemning) attacks on gays fails to respond properly to intolerant views and results in harming the non-intolerant powerless.

One should also bear in mind the difference between attacking Muslims for their specific objection to a specific book (and I here assume that this is indeed the case) and attacking gays because of who they are. While the former is not necessarily an attack on Islam as a whole or on the identity of religious believers as such, the latter is an attack on certain people's identity.

To conclude, the 'intention to harm' criteria and the 'who started it?' criteria cannot be entirely value-free or uncontroversial but they do have some neutral aspects that can be accepted by non-liberals. Even if rejected by non-liberals they can surely serve the liberal when he has to decide the limits of liberal tolerance.

C. The Limits of the 'Who Started It?' Test

Consider the example of nudism. Presumably most people support the policy of not allowing nudism in public places. However, nudism as such does not have to contain an intention to harm others. The only reason for banning it is the view that it is obscene (or that because it is obscene, others might violate public order). But isn't banning nudism the original intolerance that, according to all I have said so far, should not be tolerated?

---

[59] Raz (n 18 above) 318.

As I already said, not tolerating intolerance is not the only justifiable reason for limiting the freedoms of others. All too often it is justifiable to be the original intolerant person; that is to employ an intolerant response to non-intolerant speech or acts. Thus, the 'who started it?' test can be useful only as a mechanism for shifting the burden of proof. When we have found who started it, he is the one who has to justify his intolerance. It is true, however, that his success in convincing us depends on whether we share the same or at least a similar perception of morality. This is an inevitable outcome of the non-neutral nature of any view concerning the limits of tolerance.

It appears that this conclusion brings us back to the starting point, at which I gave up any attempt to address my arguments to non-liberals but instead only to those who by and large 'speak my language' (drawing freely from Wittgenstein's terminology), ie to those who hold a non-neutral perception of liberalism or those who value the substantive values of liberalism.

IV. CONCLUSION

While it is plausible to argue for a neutral perception of the principle of tolerance, it is impossible to formulate a non-value-based perception of the limits of tolerance.

Relying on substantive-liberal values, mainly that of autonomy, I have argued that liberals should not tolerate, in a proportionate manner, anything that denies the justifications of tolerance or tolerance itself, unless this response would increase intolerance in society.

A lack of compliance with the principle of proportionality will constitute an abuse of power. A lack of compliance with the principle of reciprocity will justify the misguided criticism of liberalism, according to which liberalism is the opinion of those who have no opinion. The proposed limits of liberal tolerance remind us that liberalism contains meaningful and desirable values that should be protected, in proportionate and justifiable ways, from anti-liberal attacks. Upholding these proposed limits of liberal tolerance is one of the main characteristics of a tolerant-liberal democracy, which is the subject of the next chapter.

4

A Tolerant-Liberal Democracy

IN THIS CHAPTER I will describe in a deliberately sketchy way the meaning of a 'tolerant-liberal democracy' and how such a liberal democracy differs from a neutral or pluralist democracy. As the justifications for a tolerant-liberal democracy are spread throughout the book, the following discussion will be mainly explanatory, yet a few arguments about the shortcomings of the neutral-liberal state will also be brought forward. The chapter starts with a short description of the competing political theories, continues with a brief description of the shortcomings of neutral liberalism and ends with a clarification of the term 'tolerant-liberal democracy' vis-à-vis other forms of liberal democracy.

I. THE COMPETING POLITICAL THEORIES

The question of the limits of tolerance and the related question about the status that religion should have in democratic states cannot be answered in a satisfactory and coherent way without subscribing to one of three political theories: neutral liberalism, perfectionist liberalism or non-liberalism. This is not an exhaustive list of all possible political theories but it appears that these are the three main competing theories, at least with regard to the issues that are discussed in this book.

Neutral liberalism can be understood in various ways. For the sake of simplicity I will assume that it can be described in two main ways. First, it can be understood as a political theory that requires the state to avoid making adverse judgements about competing moral claims or to avoid evaluating competing ways of life. Here, neutral liberalism embraces a strong version of pluralism according to which there is no 'truth' or certain 'good', and therefore each moral claim and way of life should be treated equally. Thus, the state should not endorse, promote or restrict any value or way of life. This perception of neutral liberalism in fact endorses moral or cultural relativism. This is not, however, the common perception of neutral liberalism. The second, more common perception of neutral liberalism does not require the state to avoid making adverse judgements about competing moral claims or to avoid evaluating competing ways of life. It merely requires the state to pay equal respect to competing moral claims and ways of life. It requires yet again that the state should not endorse, promote or restrict any value or way of life, despite the fact that the state's authorities may believe that some values and ways of life are worth pursuing whereas others are not.[1] With regard to religion, a neutral or pluralistic state must treat equally citizens who act on religious beliefs and those who do not. It must also be 'neutral in relation to the different worldviews and conceptions of the good—secular, spiritual and religious—with which citizens identify'.[2]

There is no need to discuss here the similarities and differences between these two perceptions of neutral liberalism, since both perceptions support the same conclusion with regard to the limits of liberal tolerance. According to any perception of neutral liberalism, when the state decides whether to tolerate views, beliefs or 'conceptions of the good', it should ignore the values that ground the reasons for people's behaviour. The state can only take into account neutral considerations, such as the potential risk to public safety and the amount of harm that may be caused to the rights and interests of others. There are more moderate views of state neutrality according to which even a neutral-liberal state 'cannot remain indifferent to certain core principles, such as human dignity, basic human rights, and popular sovereignty'.[3] This view and similar others rely heavily on the Rawlsian concepts of 'overlapping consensus' and 'reasonable pluralism'.[4] These views will be discussed briefly when the case against neutral liberalism is made.

As opposed to neutral liberalism, perfectionist theories hold that the state has a duty or at least a right to promote well-being or human flourishing by supporting and protecting certain values and ways of life. This is true with regard to perfectionist liberalism and 'perfectionist non-liberalism' alike. Both theories demand that the state act—or to refrain from acting—in order to create and maintain legal and social conditions that best enable their subjects to pursue valuable and worthwhile lives, rather than any kind of life.[5] In a

---

[1] J Rawls, *Political Liberalism* (New York, Columbia University Press, 1993) 192–93; B Ackerman, *Social Justice in the Liberal State* (New Haven CT, Yale University Press, 1980) 11; R Dworkin, *Taking Rights Seriously* (Cambridge MA, Harvard University Press, 1977) 266, 273; R Dworkin, *A Matter of Principle* (Oxford, Oxford University Press, 1985) 191–92; R, Dworkin *Sovereign Virtue: The Theory and Practice of Equality* (Cambridge MA, Harvard University Press, 2000) chapter 6.

[2] J Maclure and C Taylor, *Secularism and Freedom of Conscience* (Cambridge MA, Harvard University Press, 2011) 9–10.

[3] Maclure and Taylor (n 2 above) 11.

[4] Rawls (n 1 above) 36–37, 153–54.

[5] S Wall, *Liberalism, Perfectionism and Restraint* (Cambridge, Cambridge University Press, 2007) 8.

nutshell, any perfectionist political or moral theory holds that some ideals of human flourishing are sound whereas others are not; that the state is justified in favouring the former; and that there is no general moral principle that forbids the state from favouring sound values, even when these values are controversial, as long as these values are indeed sound. This is true regarding any perfectionist theory and perhaps with regard to any ideology as such.[6]

Perfectionist liberalism normally holds that freedom and autonomy are distinct, sound values.[7] Perfectionist liberalism defends and promotes the liberal perception of autonomy and freedom either because continuous autonomy and freedom are inherently valuable or because they are necessary instruments for living a valuable and worthwhile life. Joseph Raz is widely considered as one of the prominent advocates of perfectionist liberalism. Raz claims that governments should help to make morally valuable options available to people and discourage them from pursuing empty, non-valuable or immoral ones. Accordingly, there are some options one is better off not having.[8] This leads Raz to conclude that 'it is the function of government to promote morality'.[9] One question that this view may give rise to is what makes Raz's view (or indeed liberal perfectionism generally) a liberal theory? How can a liberal theory advocate the claim that it is the function of government to promote morality? The answers to this query are twofold. The first answer lies in Raz's acceptance of the harm principle as a basis for restraining the exercise of coercive powers of the state. Although Raz, as opposed to Dworkin and Rawls, for example, sees moral ideals, eg autonomy, as legitimate reasons for political and legal actions, he excludes, in principle, legal prohibitions of immoral acts when these acts do not cause harm to others, and he does so also in the name of autonomy which is, after all, a liberal moral ideal. The second answer is more fundamental and relates to how we should define liberalism. It would be a mistake to equate liberalism with non-interference or with not taking a stand. Such a perception of liberalism would justify the criticism levelled at liberalism, according to which liberalism is the opinion of those who have no opinion, or the behaviour of those who do not act in accordance with their values.[10] Liberalism is first and foremost a theory that perceives autonomy, freedom and equality (as understood by liberalism itself) as goods. Since it is

---

[6]   See also S Fish, *There's No Such Thing as Free Speech—and it's a Good Thing Too* (Oxford, Oxford University Press, 1994) 137: 'any ideology … must be founded on some basic conception of what the world is like … it cannot legitimise differences that would blur its boundaries, for that would be to delegitimise itself'.

[7]   J Raz, *The Morality of Freedom* (Oxford, Clarendon Press, 1986) 19.

[8]   Raz (n 7 above) 410.

[9]   Raz (n 7 above) 415.

[10]   For a similar view see Fish (n 6 above) 134, 138.

a truism that these goods cannot be protected and promoted by continuous non-interference, liberalism in fact requires the state to interfere and at times to restrict autonomy and freedom in order to secure continuing autonomy and worthwhile freedom. Accordingly, the liberal state should not respect anti-liberal values and behaviour but tolerate them to a certain extent.

Perfectionist liberalism and non-liberal theories share quite a few characteristics. There are two main differences between perfectionist liberalism and non-liberal theories. The first difference is quite obvious. While perfectionist liberalism allows or demands that the state defends and promotes liberal moral ideals, non-liberal theories allow or demand that the state defends and promotes non-liberal or anti-liberal values, ways of life or opinions such as patriarchy, ethnocentrism, homophobia, nationalism or anti-liberal communitarianism. The second difference is of more importance. Perfectionist liberalism allows much more freedom and autonomy than non-liberalism does. Perfectionist liberals accept or tolerate a wide range of different ways of life as well as non-liberal behaviours and opinions unless these ways of life, behaviours or opinions are harmful or offensive beyond a certain extent. Non-liberals, on the other hand, will rarely accept or tolerate competing ways of life, behaviours and opinions. Put differently, even though perfectionist liberalism allows or even requires making adverse judgements about non-liberal ways of life, behaviours or opinions, only rarely will these non-liberal expressions be curtailed. In contrast, for perfectionist non-liberalism, the adverse judgement that is made regarding competing ways of life, behaviours or opinions, is all too often a sufficient reason for not tolerating them.

The fact remains, however, that perfectionist liberalism allows or requires not tolerating certain ways of life. One of the concerns of those who subscribe to neutral liberalism is that once the state starts excluding ways of life, behaviours and expressions due to their moral content we open the door to legal moralism.[11]

There are two responses to this concern. First, it can be argued that 'legal moralism' is used here as a scarecrow that is supposed to frighten all liberals, especially perfectionist liberals, and to convert them to radical neutral liberalism. Secondly, it can be argued that there is nothing wrong with legal moralism provided it is applied correctly and upholds moral-liberal values.

As to the 'scarecrow response', like a scarecrow, the threat of legal moralism is not quite real. Legal moralism (in the usual narrow sense) is preventing inherently immoral conduct whether or not such conduct is harmful or offensive to anyone. With regard to the limits of liberal tolerance, I argued that the

---

[11] L Alexander, 'Harm, Offense, and Morality' (1994) 7 *Canadian Journal of Law & Jurisprudence* 199; M Pinto, 'What Are Offences to Feelings Really About? A New Regulative Principle for the Multicultural Era' (2010) 30 *Oxford Journal of Legal Studies* 695.

tolerant-liberal state should not tolerate intolerant acts and expressions. By their definition, intolerant acts and expressions cause harm or offence to others. The principle applied by the tolerant-liberal state when it does not tolerate illiberal intolerance is not legal moralism but rather the harm principle and the offence principle. The harm principle allows the state to prevent unjustified serious harm to individual persons or groups, or unreasonable risks of harm. The offence principle allows the prevention of an unjustified offence (as opposed to injury or harm) to others. Both are the core of liberalism. They differ from legal moralism in meaningful ways. Legal moralism may result in prohibiting immoral but not harmful conducts (and perhaps even expressions) both in the private and in the public sphere whereas any form of liberalism would object to that. That was the crux of the famous Hart–Devlin argument. As indicated by Dworkin, Devlin in fact argued that 'if those who have homosexual desires freely indulged them, our social environment could change'.[12] This is not an argument that focuses on the offence caused by homosexuality. This is a different and more profound argument, which normally will not be used by liberals as a reason to curtail freedoms.

As to the 'there is nothing wrong with legal moralism' response—even if Larry Alexander is right to suggest that 'the Offense Principle … cannot be separated from Legal Moralism in any way that would justify criminalization of offensive conduct but not harmless immoral conduct'[13]—it does not follow that non-neutral liberalism or perfectionist liberalism should be rejected. Even if legal moralism and the offence principle may lead to similar results, it does not follow that the offence principle should be rejected. If one truly subscribes to liberalism (and not to non-interference or to neutrality) then one should acknowledge that legal moralism should be rejected when it is used to uphold illiberal values. It is less suspicious when it is used to uphold liberal values. Similarly, the offence principle should be rejected when it is applied in a 'neutral' way that is blind to the values of the offender and the offended. It should be endorsed in order to uphold liberal values. This is not anti-liberalism but rather perfectionist liberalism. This is best explained by Joseph Raz's accurate description of what perfectionist liberalism entails. Raz states that under perfectionist liberalism 'it is the function of government to promote morality'[14] and that 'it is the goal of all political action to enable individuals to pursue valid conceptions of the good and to discourage evil or empty ones'.[15] More importantly, Raz rejects the 'common conception which regards the aim and function of the harm principle as being to curtail the freedom of

---

[12] Dworkin 1977 (n 1 above) 246–47.
[13] Alexander (n 11 above) 206.
[14] Raz (n 7 above) 415.
[15] Raz (n 7 above) 133.

governments to enforce morality'.[16] Rather, Raz claims that the harm principle is a principle about the proper way to enforce morality.[17] If neutral liberals equate this liberal approach with legal moralism simply because it aims to enforce morality they will have to level the same accusation at John Stuart Mill himself. Mill's celebrated statement is that 'the only purpose for which power can be rightfully exercised over any member of a civilised community, against his will, is to prevent harm to others'.[18] Mill's lesser-known statement is that 'acts, of whatever kind, which, without justifiable cause, do harm to others may be constrained'.[19] The qualification of 'without justifiable cause' allows and in fact requires the state to evaluate the moral soundness of the reasons that one had for doing harm to others. There is nothing in Mill's writing that implies that this evaluation should only rely on 'neutral' considerations. Thus, attacking perfectionist liberalism by equating it to legal moralism is misguided. The next section in which the soundness of neutral liberalism is scrutinised complements the case for perfectionist liberalism.

II. THE CASE AGAINST NEUTRALITY

It has been argued that state neutrality is undesirable and in fact impossible.[20] If this argument is true, then the only possible liberal theory is perfectionist liberalism. The crux of the argument is that each state must make choices. While doing so, each state must make judgements about the conflicting conceptions of the good and must make value judgements about many aspects of its citizens' lives. Many of these judgements reflect moral choices and preferences of one set of values over another. Such is the case with regard to legal decisions about the mere existence of income tax and its rate; the existence of national health insurance and its extent; privatisation; abortions; euthanasia; criminalising hate speech; polygamy; anti-discrimination laws; sexual harassment laws; same-sex marriage laws; subsidising primary and higher education; subsidising cultural institutions and so on. Any legal or political decision regarding these is in fact a moral decision, at least in part. In order to make

---

[16] Raz (n 7 above) 415.

[17] Raz (n 7 above) 415.

[18] JS Mill, *On Liberty and The Subjection of Women* (Ware, Wordsworth Classics of World Literature, 1996; first published 1859) 13.

[19] Mill (n 18 above) 56.

[20] B Leiter, *Why Tolerate Religion* (Princeton NJ, Princeton University Press, 2012) 13–14, 115–30; A Bloom, *Closing of the American Mind* (New York, Simon & Schuster, 1987); R Niebuhr, 'The Return to Primitive Religion' (Winter 1938) 3 *Christendom* 5; S Smith, 'The Restoration of Tolerance' (1990) 78 *California Law Review* 305, 313–26; S Macedo, 'Transformative Constitutionalism and the Case of Religion: Defending the Moderate Hegemony of Liberalism' (1998) 26 *Political Theory* 56, 58, 76.

these decisions, the state has to embrace some values and reject others, or to accord greater weight to some values and less weight to others. Almost any political or legal decision distributes rights, duties, benefits, responsibilities and goods. Therefore, all states have to make moral decisions about how to apply a chosen version of distributive justice—and to justify that chosen version. Even legal positivists would agree that every so often the law reflects moral choices and as a result enforces morality. But there is more. Not only does every state make moral choices by enacting laws and applying public policies, but every modern state has to do it in order to enable its citizens to flourish, among other things. If we reject the Hobbesian model of a state or the radical night-watch model of a state, we must acknowledge that the state must give preference to certain values over others and that in fact every modern state does exactly that.

The impossibility of state neutrality is so obvious that it is difficult to comprehend how neutral liberalism is still being taken seriously. But since it *is* being taken seriously, an updated response to updated arguments for state neutrality is called for. One recent, impressive and representative defence of neutral liberalism elucidates nicely the shortcomings and the impossibility of state neutrality. Maclure and Taylor recently argued that the liberal state must be neutral in relation to the different worldviews and conceptions of the good with which citizens identify. At the same time, the neutral-liberal state should protect and reinforce 'core principles' such as human dignity, basic human rights, and popular sovereignty.[21] Maclure and Taylor admit that these values are not neutral but they are convinced that this does not raise any problems, as people with very diverse convictions can share and affirm these 'constitutive values'. Later in their book they set limits to freedom of conscience and argue that conscientious exemptions should not be granted when it will impinge on the rights and freedoms of others.[22] A few questions remain unanswered here: which rights and freedoms exactly? According to which political and moral theory should the content and limits of these rights be decided? Can questions about the existence of rights, their content and their limits be answered without subscribing to a specific political or moral theory (eg utilitarianism, Kantianism, Marxism, communitarianism or libertarianism)? Can such a theory be shared by people with very diverse convictions and enjoy an 'overlapping consensus'? I wonder. Maclure and Taylor then apply their approach to the case of the Jehovah's Witnesses who refuse to allow life-saving blood transfusions to be administered to their children because it contradicts their religious-conscientious belief. Maclure and Taylor decide against granting an exemption in this case because 'respect to the parents' rights was obviously

---

[21] Maclure and Taylor (n 2 above) 9–11.
[22] Maclure and Taylor (n 2 above) 101.

too great an infringement on the right to life of a minor'.[23] This is probably true but at the same time it is not a 'neutral' decision in any meaningful sense. Maclure and Taylor also object to exempting religious pupils from courses in sex education, ethics, religious culture or civic education, as it may compromise those pupils' ability to learn and gain skills that are necessary in a society with diverse beliefs and values.[24] This objection to granting exemptions can only be justified if we are not neutral in relation to the different worldviews and conceptions of the good with which citizens identify. This objection in fact expresses intolerance towards religious views because of their content and it does not do so in order to protect and reinforce what Maclure and Taylor define as 'core-constitutive principles' (human dignity, basic human rights and popular sovereignty). It does so in order to protect and reinforce values or interests that Maclure and Taylor (and I) perceive as valuable (gaining skills that are necessary in a society with diverse beliefs and values). It would be naïve, not to say arrogant, to claim that this view is neutral or that it can be shared and affirmed by 'people with very diverse convictions'. The fact is that religious pupils *do* seek exemptions from courses in sex education, ethics and religious culture. This alone proves that Maclure and Taylor's preferences are not in fact shared and affirmed by 'people with very diverse convictions'. 'State neutrality' and 'pluralistic liberalism' may sound attractive to some people and may have political appeal, but at the end of the day political and legal decision-makers must take a stand. Their decision may be a lot of things but certainly not 'neutral'.

Lastly, applying neutral discourse and neutral considerations instead of content-based ones, and escaping to the convenient, polite and politically correct non-judgmental nature of multiculturalism, pluralism and neutral liberalism may prove to be counter-productive in one interesting way. Multiculturalism, pluralism and neutrality are often aimed at inclusiveness and respect. Religious views will not be dismissed because of their content and nature—but by applying 'neutral considerations' that 'can be shared by all people'. Anti-liberal behaviours may not be accommodated, but not because they rely on repugnant values but rather because of 'neutral' constraints and difficulties. The implied assumption is that minorities and powerless groups (or individuals) would prefer their requests and demands to be rejected on neutral grounds rather than on content-based reasoning. This is a huge assumption. I dare to offer an opposite assumption according to which applying neutral considerations ignores the content of people's beliefs and values thus not respecting them as 'values-bearers'. Their views are not 'respected' as

---

[23] Maclure and Taylor (n 2 above) 101.
[24] Maclure and Taylor (n 2 above) 102.

they are not even considered. Expressing true respect towards people's views means referring to the values that ground their views, disagreeing with them and tolerating them—or not—based on their merits. Expressing true respect towards people's views does not mean ignoring the values that ground them, avoiding making adverse judgement about them and avoiding acting upon this judgement.

III. A PLURALISTIC-LIBERAL STATE OR A TOLERANT-LIBERAL STATE? THE RE-ESTABLISHMENT OF TOLERANCE

A liberal state should not and cannot be neutral. Should it be 'pluralistic'? What would be the difference between a pluralistic-liberal state and a tolerant-liberal state?

The term tolerance consists of two main elements: the first involves an adverse judgement towards another. The second is restraint. Restraint is expressed in refraining from harming the other even though the tolerant person believes that the adverse judgement that he makes upon the other provides reasons to harm him. These two elements clarify the difference between pluralism and tolerance. Indeed, the pluralist's behaviour can be absolutely identical to the tolerant person's behaviour, but their attitude will be entirely different. The true pluralist does not make an adverse judgement towards the other and thus does not need to exercise restraint. This is true whether we define pluralism widely ('there is no one truth or one good, and thus all views and ways of life are worthy of equal respect and existence') or narrowly ('there is—or can be—one truth; but in order to find it—if we are ever to find it, or in order to constantly examine our beliefs—every opinion and way of life should be treated with the same respect'). Surely these are not the only ways to define pluralism. Other definitions of pluralism may focus on the inherent value in respecting or allowing various and contradictory ways of life. Even so, any common definition of pluralism lacks the combination of an adverse judgement and self-restraint from acting upon it.

The distinction between tolerance and pluralism is well acknowledged. Nonetheless, there is still a need to further emphasise it, since confusion between these terms is still common, mainly in liberal writings.[25] Michael Sandel, for example, suggests two meanings for tolerance. The first is 'liberal-non-judgmental-toleration', which involves no moral judgement of the tolerated

---

[25] TM Scanlon, *The Difficulty of Tolerance: Essays in Political Philosophy* (Cambridge, Cambridge University Press, 2003) 187, 192; B Ackerman, *Social Justice in the Liberal State* (New Haven CT, Yale University Press, 1980) 162, 302; CL Eisgruber and LG Sager, 'Mediating Institutions: Beyond the Public/Private Distinction: The Vulnerability of Conscience: The Constitutional Basis for Protecting Religious Conduct' (1994) 61 *University of Chicago Law Review* 1245, 1315.

person, and the second is 'judgmental-toleration', which does involve such moral judgement.[26] Sandel is right to support 'judgmental-toleration' but is wrong to disregard the fact that 'liberal-non-judgmental-toleration' is not toleration at all but rather some kind of pluralism, neutrality or indifference. If tolerance is a principle of restraint and if the tolerant person makes adverse judgements about the tolerable or the intolerable, then 'non-judgmental-toleration' is self-contradictory. Michael Walzer, in his comprehensive discussion of tolerance, defines the idea in four ways.[27] The first ('simply a resigned acceptance of difference for the sake of peace') is actually a pragmatic tolerance. The second ('passive, relaxed, benignly indifferent to difference') is indeed indifference, not tolerance. In principle, an attitude of indifference can combine with negative judgements or repulsion. At times, adverse judgement or repulsion can be the reasons for an attitude of indifference. We may be indifferent to the suffering of others and we may not care about them, precisely because we make an adverse judgement about them. However, an attitude of indifference lacks the element of restraint that forms part of the suggested perception of the principle of tolerance. As Walzer himself claims, an attitude of indifference is relaxed and benign. Tolerance, however, entails burden and restraint, which cannot coincide with any relaxed attitude. Walzer's third way of defining tolerance ('a principled recognition that the "others" have rights even if they exercise those rights in unattractive ways') is indeed very similar to the proposed understanding of tolerance, which includes adverse judgement and restraint.[28] The fourth definition ('openness to the others; curiosity; perhaps even respect, a willingness to listen and learn' and even 'the enthusiastic endorsement of difference') is clearly a psychological attitude that has very little to do with the principle of tolerance as described above. Although Walzer's fourth definition cannot explain or describe the principle of tolerance in a satisfactory way, it does describe possible reasons for being tolerant. Y may have reasons to harm X, because of X's immoral behaviour. If Y refrains from harming X because he is curious about X's immoral behaviour, because he respects X's personhood and his right to be wrong, or because even though he perceives X's behaviour as immoral he is willing to learn more about it, Y is actually being tolerant towards X. It is important to appreciate that while openness to others, curiosity and a willingness to listen and learn are clearly not expressions of intolerance, it does not follow that they are necessarily expressions of tolerance.

---

[26] MJ Sandel, 'Judgmental Toleration' in RP George (ed), *Natural Law, Liberalism, and Morality* (Oxford, Oxford University Press, 1996) 107.

[27] M Walzer, *On Toleration* (New Haven CT, Yale University Press, 1997) 10–11.

[28] However, Walzer also calls this attitude 'moral stoicism' which, yet again, lacks the element of restraint.

Once the fundamental difference between tolerance and pluralism has been established, it is still unresolved why all too often the differences between the terms are completely blurred. Every answer to this question will probably be speculative, but even speculation is valuable as long as it is not easily refuted. One can claim that disregarding the difference between pluralism and intolerance merely results from a lack of attention to conceptual precision. This answer may very well be true in some cases. Another way to explain this mix of concepts is indeed clearly speculative, and I will intentionally describe it somewhat simplistically. Many of those who identify tolerance with pluralism (or respect and recognition) hold a neutral or pluralistic liberal political standing rather than a (genuine) tolerant one. The neutral-liberal discourse in its classical, full version does not make adverse judgements about contradicting, non-liberal ways of life or moral outlooks, as it does not acknowledge any hierarchy of values. Instead, it is very close to moral relativism, ie to a view according to which there is no valid way to evaluate the legitimacy and weight of different values. Therefore, the state should not morally evaluate various values, and accordingly it should not promote certain values and decline others. Tolerance, on the other hand, recognises that some values, beliefs and ways of life are desirable, others are less desirable, and others still are morally repugnant and illegitimate. Neutral liberalism does not subscribe to this view at all, or only in especially esoteric or extreme cases. Therefore, it is difficult for neutral liberalism to accept the definition of tolerance as proposed here. On the other hand, the principle of tolerance carries with it positive connotations. Over centuries, communities and nations were trained to believe, way before neutral liberalism, pluralism and multiculturalism took over parts of western political culture, that tolerance is mainly positive and that people should aspire to be tolerant. Neutral liberalism did not want or was not capable of determining that tolerance is a moral defect or an unfit treatment of the other. At the same time, neutral liberalism was also incapable of accepting the definition of tolerance that declines moral relativism. The solution was found in embracing the tolerance discourse but sterilising it from any content that implies the existence of a hierarchy of values, or from any content that entails an attitude that involves grudge, superiority and being judgemental. It has become politically and morally incorrect to imply that anti-liberal values and anti-liberal groups are inferior or plainly wrong. Thus, neutral liberalism embraced the outlook according to which tolerance is a moral virtue, but at the same time changed its definition and its essence to pluralism. Neutral liberalism's takeover of the political and legal discourse was performed, inter alia, by merging tolerance and pluralism into one concept the true meaning of which is pluralism—and juxtaposing it with intolerance. This is the dichotomy as described by neutral liberalism: you are either pluralist (and therefore tolerant according to neutral liberalism) or intolerant. Moral judgement, which is the core of true tolerance, was rejected.

Since too many scholars do believe that tolerance indeed means pluralism, recognition or respect, it is important to clarify why this attitude is problematic. In order to do so we first need to remind ourselves of the original meaning of 'tolerance', that was distorted without good moral or philosophical reasons but merely for 'political' reasons.

The origins of the term 'tolerance' are rooted in the Latin words tolerabilis, tolerare and tollere—the latter means carrying or lifting an object. Both 'tolerance' and its Latin ancestors linguistically imply the existence of a burden, originally a physical one and later on a mental one. It is common to see the wars of religion in Europe in the sixteenth and seventeenth centuries as the historical origins of the relatively modern concept of tolerance. More than a thousand years went by from St Augustine's position of extreme religious intolerance[29] until Christian religious tolerance emerged and, perhaps ironically, set the basis for secular liberalism, freedom of conscience and freedom from religion. In an almost evolutionary development, tolerance was first applied in the intra-Christian sphere,[30] then in the inter-religious sphere[31] and finally in the public-secular sphere.[32] Throughout this journey the understanding of tolerance as a burden that lies on the tolerant person's shoulders has not changed.

---

[29] St Augustine, 'Epistle to Vicentius' in P Schaff (ed), *St Augustine: The Confessions and Letters of St Augustine I* (1886, 1st edn 408) 382–89. St Augustine himself lived in the fourth and fifth centuries.

[30] Just before the wars of religion, an attempt to reconcile the Catholic and Protestant dispute was made by Erasmus in 1533, seen as one of the earliest calls for religious tolerance: Erasmus, 'On Mending the Peace of the Church' in JP Dolan (ed), *The Essential Erasmus* (New York, Plume, 1964, 1st edn 1536) 288–327.

[31] The most important and quite innovative promoter of religious tolerance at that time was Sebastian Castellio who, in 1554, more than a century before John Locke, acknowledged that coercion is not an effective means to determine people's beliefs and that humans are authorised to punish only diversions from the core of religion; that is a diversion from believing in (any) God: Sebastian Castellio, *Concerning Heretics, Whether They are to be Persecuted* (ed and trans RH Bainton), (New York, Octagon Books, 1965, first published 1554) 104–6, 121–35, 141–54, 169–83.

[32] JS Mill's *On Liberty* (London, JW Parker & Son, 1859) is unanimously considered as the milestone of modern liberal tolerance. This short survey is not exhaustive and does not describe recent developments in formal policies. Its only aim is to portray in very general lines changes in philosophical writings and thinking about tolerance. To take one example that does not fit into the rough chronology of tolerance as I have just described, the Catholic Church, before *the Second Vatican Council* (Vatican II), did teach that sometimes governments can and should tolerate non-Catholic manifestations of belief; but as recently as 1953 Pope Pius XII affirmed that religious error has 'no objective right' even to exist, much less to be propagated publicly: Address to Italian jurists, Ci Riesce, 6 December 1953. *Acta Apostolicae Sedis*, 45 (1953) 798. Only in 1965 at Vatican II did the Catholic Church formally state that 'the human person has a right to religious freedom' and that this right 'is based on the very dignity of the human person as known through the revealed word of God and by reason itself'. This declaration reflects a perception of tolerance as a human right, although mostly within the religious sphere.

Given the linguistic and historical origins of the concept of tolerance, the elements of adverse judgement and restraint are integral to the definition of tolerance. Indeed, linguistic and historical origins of a concept do not necessarily determine its present meaning. Yet, in our case, it appears that the historical and linguistic origins of 'tolerance' do help to understand its accurate meaning and to differentiate it from other concepts such as pluralism, neutrality, recognition and respect. More specifically, if the principle of tolerance does not include elements of adverse judgement and restraint, which political or moral principle does include these elements? If a tolerant approach is indeed a pluralist approach, which always celebrates diversity and does not entail making an adverse judgement towards another, how would one call the approach that does not always celebrate diversity and does entail making an adverse judgement towards another? There is no other concept to describe this approach, except for that of 'tolerance'. Since no other term exists to describe tolerance as is described here—and as it has been grasped for hundreds of years—identifying tolerance with pluralism might cause an unnecessary conceptual confusion and a conceptual lacuna. The distinction between cases in which an adverse judgement towards another and restraint from harming him exist, and cases in which these elements do not exist, is both morally and politically important. The distinction between pluralism (or openness and acceptance as a state of mind) and tolerance serves this purpose in the best way.

Differentiating between tolerance and pluralism and applying the true, original meaning of the concept of tolerance are especially important within the context of the relationship between religion and the liberal state. Augenstein describes nicely the current use of the term 'tolerance':

> it is quite common to claim that some liberal states treat their religious minorities more 'tolerantly' than others. What is implied here is not that these states are more willing to 'endure' or 'suffer' religious diversity. Rather, what we mean by qualifying them as 'tolerant' is that they have adjusted their interpretations of state neutrality and extended the reach of their equality norms to accommodate religious minorities.[33]

If we use the term 'tolerance' in that (misguided) way, how shall we describe secular-liberal states that indeed endure or suffer the mere existence of religion? How shall we describe atheists or anti-theists who also endure or suffer the mere existence of religion? Aren't they tolerant? If they are not—what are they? Surely they are not intolerant. But if they are tolerant, we cannot ignore the fact that they are not 'neutral' and that they do suffer and exercise

---

[33] D Augenstein, 'Tolerance and Liberal Justice' (2010) 23 *Ratio Juris* 437, 440.

restraint. They do not merely 'accommodate religion' or religious minorities by 'adjusting interpretations of state neutrality'.

Therefore, the only liberal alternative to the neutral-liberal state is the tolerant-liberal state. Because it is liberal it still values diversity and pluralism but does not perceive them as inherently valuable. Diversity and pluralism are only valuable within the limits set by liberalism itself. Beyond these limits diversity and pluralism (as a state of affairs) may or may not be tolerated—and to various extents—but will always be evaluated and treated according to the core values of liberalism.

5

The Theoretical and Empirical Links Between Religion and Intolerance

I. INTRODUCTION

THIS CHAPTER EXPLORES two main arguments. The first is that religious persons—because they are religious—are likely to be more intolerant than non-religious persons, not only concerning religion or 'religious matters' but in general. The second argument is that there are meaningful, clear and unique theoretical links between religion, or, more precisely, certain types of religion, and intolerance. These links explain why, as a broad generalisation, religious persons are likely to be more intolerant than non-religious persons.

It is suggested that the special links between religion and intolerance are the result of seven characteristics of religion: (1) religion perceives maintaining the unity of a distinct community and preserving its existence as one of its main functions; (2) religion aspires to gain formal control over its believers, other religious believers and heretics alike; (3) religion perceives its traditions, customs and symbols as sacred; (4) religion has a unique perception of the 'truth'; (5) religion is 'absolute' (6) religion prescribes unique links between religious faith, morality and the law; and (7) religion is almost always composed of intolerant values and beliefs.

The argument about the unique links between religion and intolerance is based on the fact that only religion possesses some of the characteristics described above, and on the fact that the other characteristics, which are not uniquely religious, have special ramifications when found within religions.

Although this chapter describes the links between religion and intolerance, it does not offer a definition of religion. It is often claimed that it is impossible to define religion and that any definition is likely to be satisfactory only to its author. Hood, Hill and Spilka argue that 'religion may encompass the supernatural, the non-natural, theism, deism, atheism, monotheism, polytheism, and both finite and infinite deities; it may also include practices, beliefs, and rituals that almost totally defy circumscription and definition'.[1] They also add that we distinguish religion from other aspects of our own culture, but that such a distinction may be invalid elsewhere, eg in most non-Western societies. Comprehensive, all-inclusive definitions of religion may be too broad and too vague, thus frustrating any attempt to make meaningful observations or normative judgements about religion as such. Narrow definitions will exclude unknown, non-popular or unique religions. Matters are even more complicated since, even if we do find a satisfactory definition of religion, there may be numerous possible ways of being 'religious'. Many have tried to define religion by applying a one-dimensional, general and overreaching criterion, eg religion as its believers' 'ultimate concern'[2] or religion as the ultimate meaningfulness of life.[3] Others have suggested lists of characteristics that have to exist in order for a belief to be 'religious'.[4] However, the best efforts of sociologists, legal scholars, anthropologists and philosophers of religion to define religion are frustrated at every attempt.[5]

Yet, we should not resort to the saying 'I do not know how to define it, but I know it when I see it', as in the case of pornography, for example. Although religion cannot be defined, at least not in a satisfactory way, sometimes it has to be defined. We cannot make normative evaluations about religion without knowing what religion is. In the legal world, the existence of freedom of religion as a legal, constitutional and international right requires us to define what religion is. Thus, religion cannot be defined but some characteristic marks can be given. It may be the case that 'religion' should be defined differently for different purposes or within different contexts. Within the context of the relationship between religion and intolerance and for the purpose of this book, I will refer to Judaism, Christianity and Islam as paradigms of religion and will address the following arguments to these religions and to any other religion that

[1] RW Hood, PC Hill and B Spilka, *The Psychology of Religion: An Empirical Approach*, 4th edn (New York, The Guilford Press, 2009) 7.

[2] P Tillich, *The Shaking of the Foundation* (London, SCM Press, 1948) 10–11.

[3] M Perry, *Love and Power: The Role of Religion and Morality in American Politics* (New York, Oxford University Press, 1991) 73.

[4] B Leiter, *Why Tolerate Religion* (Princeton NJ, Princeton University Press, 2012) chapter 2; SG Gey, 'When is Religious Speech Not "Free Speech"?' (2000) *University of Illinois Law Review* 379, 451; Y Dinstein, 'Freedom of Religion and the Protection of Religious Minorities' in Y Dinstein and M Tabory (eds), *The Protection of Minorities and Human Rights* (Boston MA, Martinus Nijhoff Publishers, 1992) 145, 147.

[5] For recent and less sceptical views see B Beit-Hallahmi, *Psychological Perspectives on Religion and Religiosity* (London, Routledge, 2015) 2–18; R Sandberg, *Religion, Law and Society* (Cambridge, Cambridge University Press, 2014) 28–52.

shares their common characteristics, as illustrated below.[6] I am well aware that there are meaningful differences within these three religions, differences that sometimes provide reasons for fanatical believers to start a religious war or carry out religious persecution. I will come back to this point before I discuss the theoretical links between religion and intolerance, but suffice it to say that these differences do not affect the strength of the general argument about the links between religion and intolerance.

The purpose of this chapter is to suggest that the argument about the principled and empirical links between religion (or religious orientation) and intolerance is not only a valid or possible argument but also a strong and convincing one. Its strength relies on a combination of principled arguments and empirical findings. If significant theoretical and empirical links between religion and intolerance do exist, it should lead to a rethinking of a wide range of legal and political issues, and ultimately to a re-evaluation of the proper place that religion should have in the legal and political sphere.

II. THE EMPIRICAL FINDINGS

A. Introduction: The Importance of Empirical Research

The empirical findings regarding the links between religion and intolerance are of great importance. Theoretical arguments about the link between religion and intolerance can be disputed; each example of religious intolerance can be answered by examples of religious tolerance, compassion and helping behaviour—either in religious scripts or in practice; each generalisation about religion or even about certain religions can be accused of suffering from significant inaccuracy, and so on. Religion indeed has some virtues that will not be addressed here. It might have been tempting to consider its virtues alongside the principled arguments regarding its intolerant nature and to decide which prevails or which arguments are simply more convincing. Here enters the empirical evidence. Its aim is to force opponents of the theoretical arguments to confront findings about how religion actually operates in real life and how it affects not only the views but also the behaviour of its adherents. Its further aim is to bridge the gap between political philosophy, legal arguments

---

[6] A similar approach was suggested by Kent Greenawalt, who argued that since there are no necessary or sufficient characteristics that should exist in order to identify a belief or a practice as 'religious', all we can do is to identify a belief which everyone agrees is 'religious' and to compare it to less paradigmatic cases. K Greenawalt, 'Religion as a Concept in Constitutional Law' (1984) 72 *California Law Review* 753, 766–67. See also GC Freeman, 'The Misguided Search for the Constitutional Definition of Religion' (1983) 71 *Georgetown Law Journal* 1519, 1548.

and empirical findings. Theory and practice must be closely linked in order for both descriptive and normative theories to be better established and more convincing.

Despite the importance and relevance of empirical findings it has not been common for legal or other philosophers to engage with them. During recent decades, however, there is a noticeable trend towards evidence-based legal studies. Various subjects within legal studies focus on analysing normative decision making. It is not surprising then that legal scholars choose to employ an interdisciplinary point of view, which involves social psychology, behavioural economics and so on. Whereas legal scholars (some of whom are engaged in what is sometimes called 'social-legal studies') turn to empirical findings for various reasons and motives, it is still hard to find empirically minded legal philosophers who make use of the sources of data presently being mined by legal scholars. This divide between legal philosophy and empirically oriented socio-legal studies is quite overwhelming.

It is plausible to detect in the writings of prominent legal and political philosophers some empirical referent or context, even in the most abstract arguments. Quite often, this is left implicit or simply without any empirical support, eg Dworkin's well-known argument that judges normally act as if there is one true legal answer to every legal question[7] (isn't it possible that many judges think there are a few, equally reasonable answers to a legal question?); Hart's famous view that committed participants in the legal system, mostly judges and other officials, regard the law as valuable or justified, at least in some respect;[8] and lastly, Waldron's assertion that the majority (or just the 'people') usually reaches its decisions not only by taking into consideration its specific interests; rather, it does so out of good faith, while applying relatively impartial opinion.[9] This assertion, which is not based on proved facts, leads Waldron to argue that there is no compelling reason to protect human rights from the will of the current majority by 'constitutionalising' them.

These are all descriptive, empirical arguments, at least in part, which are not supported by empirical findings (the same can be said of most classic political theories, eg those of Hobbes, Locke, Rousseau and others). At times, an empirical context is called forward by giving examples. In such cases the 'empirical' context does not strengthen the argument but merely exemplifies it. One clear example of what may be called 'empirical philosophy' can be found within American realism, which avoids the conceptual approach of the

---

[7] R Dworkin, *Taking Rights Seriously* (Cambridge MA, Harvard University Press, 1977) 22–44, 107–17; R Dworkin, *Law's Empire* (Cambridge MA, Harvard University Press, 1986) 225–56.

[8] HLA Hart, *The Concept of Law* (Clarendon Law Series), 2nd edn (Oxford, Oxford University Press, 1994) 238–76.

[9] J Waldron, *Law and Disagreement* (Oxford, Oxford University Press, 1999) 10–17.

positivists and naturalists in favour of an empirical analysis that seeks to show how judges really decide cases. This is, however, a rare and relatively narrow exception.

The call for philosophers to engage with empirical findings is not a novel development. Jeffrie Murphy refers to Karl Marx's well-known insight that 'philosophical theories are in peril if they are constructed in disregard of the nature of the empirical world to which they are supposed to apply'.[10] In an essay from 1927 (entitled 'Empiricism') John Anderson argued that 'realism, naturalism, materialism, pluralism, determinism and positivism … these are all, I should argue, connected with empiricism; it is on an empiricist view, and only so, that they can be maintained'.[11]

Daved Muttart expresses an unkind yet precise critique of contemporary jurisprudence, with which I completely concur. Muttart argues that

> jurisprudential theories are typically based on anecdote, superficial observation, and the undocumented impressions of individual authors … taken together, these short-comings constitute a serious empirical gap in jurisprudential scholarship … jurisprudential writing is too often characterized by allegation without verification, by idiosyncratic impression instead of rigorous research, by small and selective sample instead of systematic study … jurisprudence has been notoriously feeble in supporting its philosophical analysis with empirical research.[12]

Although Muttart focuses his criticism on theories of judicial behaviour, and mainly on the work of Hart and Dworkin, his criticism also applies to many other subjects of legal and political theory.

So what should legal and political philosophers do? They should, in appropriate cases, stop being legal or political philosophers and instead become interdisciplinary philosophers.[13] Indeed, any adequate social theory (including some aspects of legal philosophy) has to be simultaneously empirical, interpretive and critical.

There is little point in developing a normative theory of punishment without trying to find empirical connections between certain types of punishment and particular behaviours or social results; there is little point in developing a normative theory of democracy that, for example, opposes judicial review of legislation on the grounds that the judiciary does not represent the majority

---

[10] J Murphy, 'Marxism and Retribution' in J Waldron (ed), *Philosophy of Law* (Oxford, Oxford University Press, 1994) 59, 74.

[11] J Anderson, *Studies in Empirical Philosophy* (Sydney, Sydney University Press, 1962), electronic edition (2000) available at: setis.library.usyd.edu.au/anderson.

[12] D Muttart, *The Empirical Gap in Jurisprudence: A Comprehensive Study of the Supreme Court of Canada* (Toronto, University of Toronto Press, 2007) 3–4.

[13] RP Burns, 'The Tasks of the Philosophy of Law' (2007) 3, available at: ssrn.com/abstract=1016124.

will, before finding, also by turning to empirical research, whether an elected Parliament in fact represents the majority will; there is little point in formulating a theory of law without examining how the law works in practice. Lastly, there is little point in proposing a theory about the intolerant nature of some religions without examining the empirical links between religion and intolerance.

The scientific research about the connection between religion and intolerance has undergone significant changes during the last 70 to 80 years. I will divide this period into three main stages and conclude with contemporary studies and conclusions. The first two stages occur within the same period of time (both start in the early 1940s and end in the late 1970s), and differ only in terms of the research methods that were applied at this time. The third stage starts in the early 1980s and includes different research methods to those applied previously. What can be already revealed is the astonishing fact that regardless of date, research methods and specific research questions, the same conclusion was reached time and time again: on the whole, there is a strong and positive connection between religion and intolerance.

B. Empirical Findings—The First Stage

Many studies that were conducted from 1940 onwards proved a clear and direct connection between religiosity and holding intolerant views on various subjects. In 1993, Batson, Schoenrade and Ventis presented a comprehensive survey of 47 different studies conducted by different researchers between 1940 and 1990, among white, middle-class Christians in the United States (45 of these studies were conducted in the period up to 1972. The other two were conducted in 1987 and 1990).[14] The general question that was raised by Batson, Schoenrade and Ventis was a simple one: 'When persons are more religious are they less prejudiced, more prejudiced, or is there no difference?'[15] More specifically, the studies aimed to establish

> the relationship between one or more of three indices of amount of religious involvement (church membership or attendance, positive attitudes towards religion, and orthodoxy or conservatism of religious beliefs) and one of four types of intolerance or prejudice (ethnocentrism, racial prejudice, anti-Semitism, and other prejudice).[16]

---

[14] For a short description of the 47 studies, see: CD Batson, P Schoenrade and WL Ventis, *Religion and the Individual: A Social-Psychological Perspective* (Oxford, Oxford University Press, 1993) 296–302.

[15] Batson, Schoenrade and Ventis (n 14 above) 296.

[16] Batson, Schoenrade and Ventis (n 14 above) 296.

The findings were as follows:

> Overall, thirty-seven of the forty-seven findings show a positive relationship between amount of religious involvement and amount of prejudice. Eight findings show no clear relationship; most of these were conducted in the northern United States. Only two findings indicate a negative relationship … one can see that the pattern of results is highly consistent regardless of how religion or prejudice is measured. The pattern is also highly consistent over the years.[17]

Batson, Schoenrade and Ventis's conclusion was clear: 'At least among white, middle-class Christians in the United Sates, *religion is not associated with increased love and acceptance but with increased intolerance, prejudice, and bigotry*'.[18]

C. Empirical Findings—The Second Stage

The studies conducted during the first stage suffered from two flaws. First, they used direct questionnaires to identify and rate religiosity. Furthermore, they did not differentiate between different types of religious believers. The assumption that all religious believers, even those who are equally or similarly religious, are of the same kind, was criticised and promptly revised.

In 1966, Gordon Allport suggested two types of religious believers or two ways in which religious believers can perceive religion. Allport differentiates between 'extrinsic religion' and 'intrinsic religion'. In the former case, religion is merely a means to self-serving ends, such as feeling secure, being part of a community, achieving or preserving one's social status and so on. In the latter, religion is an end in itself. It is what Allport called 'the master motive' in the believer's life.[19] On the basis of this distinction, Allport claimed that a positive connection will be found only between 'extrinsic religion' and prejudice.[20] Others suggested alternative ways of assessing religious orientation, eg by measuring the amount of religious activity people take on, when the higher amount indicates holding an 'intrinsic religious' view, whereas a low amount

---

[17] Batson, Schoenrade and Ventis (n 14 above) 302.

[18] Batson, Schoenrade and Ventis (n 14 above) 302.

[19] G Allport, 'Religious Context of Prejudice' (1966) 5 *Journal for the Scientific Study of Religion* 447, 447–57.

[20] To put this claim to the test, a method should be found to differentiate between 'extrinsic believers' and 'intrinsic' ones. The most popular way to do so was suggested by Allport himself and Ross. See G Allport and J Ross, 'Personal Religious Orientation and Prejudice' (1967) 5 *Journal of Personality and Social Psychology* 432, 432–43. The assessment was based on both direct and indirect questionnaires. In this article Allport and Ross further developed the intrinsic–extrinsic distinction by offering a third type of religious persons: those who score highly both on the intrinsic and the extrinsic scale, also referred to as 'religious muddle-headedness'.

indicates holding an 'extrinsic religious' one.[21] This strategy is an objective-quantitative one as opposed to the subjective test of Allport and Ross.

Thirty-two studies that produced forty-one findings were conducted between 1949 and 1990 (only one of which was conducted after 1977), according either to the Allport and Ross 'religious orientation scale' or to the religious activity quantitative test.[22]

The findings were clear and exactly as predicted by Allport. In 39 out of the 41 findings, those classified as 'intrinsic believers' scored lower on prejudice, however measured, than those classified as extrinsic believers. These findings, alongside substantial deficiencies in the only two studies that found no difference, led Batson, Schoenrade and Ventis to the conclusion that 'it is difficult to conceive of obtaining stronger evidence that the way one is religious affects the religious–prejudice relationship'.[23] Indeed, from the mid-1960s to the late 1980s, the conclusion that extrinsic believers are relatively more prejudiced than intrinsic ones was reaffirmed in numerous studies and widely accepted among psychologists of religion.

It is interesting to note that, in several of these studies, as well as in Allport and Ross's ground-breaking study of 1967, it was found that the more intrinsic believers were less prejudiced than those with extrinsic religious orientation, who, in turn, were less prejudiced than those who scored high on both the intrinsic and the extrinsic scales. Most of the studies, however, limit their scope to examining only extrinsic and intrinsic religious orientations and chose to ignore the third type suggested by Allport and Ross, ie those who may score high on both extrinsic and intrinsic scales.

The revised conclusion is, therefore, that 'although being more religious correlates with being more intolerant and prejudiced, this is true only among those who have emasculated the more profound claims of their religion and are using it as an extrinsic means to self-serving ends'.[24] This revised conclusion coincides with Allport's early observation that religion makes and unmakes prejudice,[25] ie everything depends on one's attitude towards one's religion, which may be either extrinsic or intrinsic (or, following Allport's earlier terminology, immature or mature).

However, this is neither the final conclusion nor the end of the changes in the strategies and methods for finding the relationship between religion and intolerance. Although the above conclusion was widely adopted at first, probably also because it was less radical and troubling than the previous

---

[21] See Batson, Schoenrade and Ventis (n 14 above) 303–4.

[22] For a short description of the studies see Batson, Schoenrade and Ventis (n 14 above) 304–11.

[23] Batson, Schoenrade and Ventis (n 14 above) 304.

[24] Batson, Schoenrade and Ventis (n 14 above) 310.

[25] G Allport, *The Nature of Prejudice* (New York, Basic Books Publishers, 1954) 444.

one, an increasing number of scholars started to have doubts about both the assessment of prejudice and the methods of identifying extrinsic and intrinsic religious persons.

Regarding the accuracy of the assessment of prejudice, concerns have been raised about the problem of self-presentation.[26] Batson, Schoenrade and Ventis referred to studies that showed that, when answering direct questionnaires, people attempt to appear less prejudiced than they actually are.[27] They stated that 'there are several reasons to believe that individuals classified as intrinsically religious are likely to be more concerned to present themselves as tolerant and unprejudiced than are individuals classified as extrinsic'.[28] Another difficulty arises from the intrinsic–extrinsic distinction and its relevance to the existence of prejudice: earlier studies (until the early 1980s) investigated the link between intrinsic and extrinsic religious orientations and holding prejudice, but not just any prejudice. The main focus was on racial and ethnic prejudice. Within this narrow scope, intrinsic religious persons were found to be more tolerant than extrinsic ones. However, as more recent studies prove, this is not the case regarding other targets of prejudice.

Regarding the accuracy of identifying extrinsic and intrinsic religious persons, some scholars have suggested that the extrinsic and intrinsic scales failed to measure what they were supposed to measure, that they should be abandoned and that the sizeable literature based on them should be ignored.[29]

Therefore, the conclusion that being more religious correlates with being more intolerant and prejudiced but only amongst extrinsic believers is open to criticism and re-evaluation, as indeed occurred in the third stage of the studies.

D. Empirical Findings—The Third Stage

The justified criticism of the methodology of previous studies has led to a new generation of studies that changed the ways of classifying religious believers into different types and the ways of finding and measuring prejudice and intolerance amongst religious persons.

---

[26] A similar concern was raised by B Spilka, RW Hood Jnr, B Hunsberger and R Gorsuch, *The Psychology of Religion: An Empirical Approach*, 3rd edn (New York, The Guilford Press, 2003) 461.

[27] Batson, Schoenrade and Ventis (n 14 above) 311, and see especially S Gaertner and J Dovidio, 'The Aversive Form of Racism' in S Gaertner and J Dovidio (eds), *Prejudice, Discrimination and Racism* (Orlando FL, Academic Press, 1986) 61–89.

[28] Batson, Schoenrade and Ventis (n 14 above) 313. The writers adds that 'several studies have found that individuals who report being highly devout and committed to their religion present themselves especially positively when asked about their behaviour in others areas of life'. For more evidence, see p 315 fn 3.

[29] For specific examples see Spilka, Hood Jnr, Hunsberger and Gorsuch (n 26 above) 462.

In 1976, Batson suggested a new classification of religious attitudes that was embraced by most psychologists of religion.[30] The new classification remains relatively popular and has been used in many recent studies on the link between religion and intolerance. The new classification consists of three types of religious attitude: the first is 'religion as a means', which is similar to Allport's 'extrinsic religion'; the second is 'religion as an end', which is similar to Allport's 'intrinsic religion'; and the third and new one is 'religion as a quest'. The person who perceives religion as a quest will approach moral questions and questions about the meaning of life from a religious point of view but will reject dogmatic and one-sided answers. Such a person perceives religion as a quest or a way of finding the truth rather than as the truth itself. He also acknowledges that he might never learn the truth about highly important matters that are at the heart of every religion.[31] This type of religious person can be called a 'critical believer'. As the quest orientation involves a questioning and flexible approach to religious issues, it is theoretically associated with a more tolerant attitude.

Alongside this new perception of the various types of religious belief, a new methodology has evolved for measuring prejudice and intolerance amongst religious believers. From the late 1970s onwards, several studies started to apply one of two methods: using questionnaires that assess prejudice that the respondents' religious community does not clearly condemn; or using covert and behavioural measures of prejudice. Both methods aim to avoid the problem of self-presentation, as discussed above.

In 1993, Batson, Schoenrade and Ventis summarised six different studies that were conducted between 1985 and 1990. These took into account Batson's classification of religious believers and used questionnaires that assessed prejudice that the believers' community did not proscribe.[32] The findings of

---

[30] CD Batson, 'Religion as Prosocial: Agent or Double Agent?' (1976) 15 *Journal for the Scientific Study of Religion* 29, 29–45. See also Batson, Schoenrade and Ventis (n 14 above) 315–16 for a comparison between the proposed classification and Allport's, and 373–76 for a more detailed account of this classification. For a revised quest orientation scale, which is probably the most popular in recent studies, see CD Batson and PA Schoenrade, 'Measuring Religion as Quest: 1. Validity Concerns' (1991) 30 *Journal for the Scientific Study of Religion* 416; CD Batson and PA Schoenrade, 'Measuring Religion as Quest: 2. Reliability Concerns' (1991) 30 *Journal for the Scientific Study of Religion* 430.

[31] For an excellent example of the 'religion as quest' dimension, see the description of Ghandi's perception of religion, God and truth: SE Nepstad, 'Religion, Violence, and Peacemaking' (2004) 43 *Journal for the Scientific Study of Religion* 297, 299–300. For a description of Paul Tillich's perception of religion as 'religion as quest' (without using this terminology) see: JM Perry, *Tillich's Response to Freud: A Christian Answer to the Freudian Critique of Religion* (Lanham MD, University Press of America, 1988) 46–48.

[32] For a description of these studies, see Batson, Schoenrade and Ventis (n 14 above) 317–21. These studies were conducted in several parts of the United States, the Virgin Islands, Venezuela and South Africa.

these six studies were utterly different from those achieved in the second stage, as described above. Actually, they were reversed:

for nonproscribed prejudice, the extrinsic, means dimension shows no clear relationship to prejudice in seven of eight findings; the intrinsic, end dimension shows a positive relationship to prejudice in eight out of nine findings. Only the quest dimension shows evidence of a negative relation to prejudice when the prejudice is not clearly proscribed by the religious community (five of seven findings).[33]

These findings show that the intrinsic believer is not free from prejudice, as Allport claimed, but instead he confines his tolerance only to those groups or views that are accepted or tolerated by his religion's writings, teachings and community. This conclusion is supported by the following findings. Four of the six studies also examined, by questionnaire, the prejudice that the believers' community does proscribe (racial prejudice). The results were as follows:

the extrinsic, means dimension correlated positively with proscribed prejudice against blacks in two of three findings (no relation in the third); the intrinsic, end dimension was not reliably correlated with proscribed prejudice against blacks in four out of four findings.[34]

However, it should be kept in mind that these findings are not immune from the self-presentation problem. As the methodology of these studies was that of answering questionnaires, there are still doubts about the possible gap between one's real views and the way in which these views are presented. The next studies that used behavioural measures of prejudice were likely to solve this problem and bring us closer to a final conclusion about the relationship between holding a religious belief and intolerance.

One example of using the covert, behavioural method of measuring prejudice is sufficient to demonstrate the advantage of this method over the methodology of answering direct questionnaires. A study from 1974 produced these fascinating results:

white incoming college freshmen reported little concern about the race of their future roommate on an attitude questionnaire … but other incoming freshmen from the same group, responding to the same question on a housing office application, reported a definite preference for a white rather than a black roommate.[35]

---

[33] Batson, Schoenrade and Ventis (n 14 above) 321. For further studies that indicate a controversy regarding the role of social desirability or self-presentation in the relationship between intrinsic religiousness and prejudice, see Spilka, Hood Jnr, Hunsberger and Gorsuch (n 26 above) 463.

[34] Batson, Schoenrade and Ventis (n 14 above) 322.

[35] B Silverman, 'Consequences, Racial Discrimination, and the Principle of Belief Congruence' (1974) 29 *Journal of Personality and Social Psychology* 497, 497–508; as cited in Batson, Schoenrade and Ventis (n 14 above) 323.

These findings, as many others from similar studies, exemplify the weakness of all the studies we have examined thus far. Accordingly, these findings support, even if indirectly, the conclusions of the later studies—if only regarding the accuracy of their methodology.[36]

The findings regarding the correlations between the three religious dimensions and prejudice, as examined by the *overt* questionnaire, were as follows: a low positive correlation for the extrinsic-means dimension; and negative correlations for both the intrinsic-end dimension and the quest dimension. Identical results were achieved for the extrinsic-means dimension and the quest dimension using the *covert* behavioural technique, but the correlation for the intrinsic-end dimension with racial prejudice became significantly more positive.[37] This led Batson, Schoenrade and Ventis to conclude that 'the intrinsic end dimension is associated more with a desire to avoid *appearing* racially prejudiced than with genuine reduction of prejudice'.[38]

After reviewing all the above studies from the three different stages of research, Batson, Schoenrade and Ventis summarised their revised and final conclusion regarding the relationship between religion and prejudice in the following way:

> The extrinsic, means dimension is related to increased prejudice, but only when prejudice is proscribed. The quest dimension is related to decreased prejudice, both proscribed and not. The intrinsic, end dimension is related to the appearance of relatively low proscribed prejudice, but only the appearance. It is related to increased prejudice when the prejudice is not proscribed by the religious community.[39]

This complex conclusion was reached in more recent studies and it seems that most scholars accept it as accurate.[40] Nevertheless, this line of research, together with the above conclusion, does leave a few questions remaining. First, it is not always clear whether the intrinsic believers conceal, when they answer overt questionnaires, their prejudice and intolerance that exist to similar degrees in non-religious persons. Secondly, it is also unclear, as Batson,

---

[36] For more details, see Batson, Schoenrade and Ventis (n 14 above) 324–28. See also (for the first study): CD Batson, SJ Naifeh and S Pate, 'Social Desirability, Religious Orientation, and Racial Prejudice' (1978) 17 *Journal for the Scientific Study of Religion* 31. For more details for the second study, see: CD Batson, 'Religious Orientation and Overt Versus Covert Racial Prejudice' (1986) 50 *Journal for the Scientific Study of Religion* 175.

[37] Batson, Schoenrade and Ventis (n 14 above) 325–26.

[38] Batson, Schoenrade and Ventis (n 14 above) 326.

[39] Batson, Schoenrade and Ventis (n 14 above) 329. The same results about the role of proscription and non-proscription in the relationship between religious orientation and prejudice were achieved by RJ Duck and B Hunsberger, 'Religious Orientation and Prejudice: The role of Religious Proscription, Right-Wing Authoritarianism and Social Desirability' (1999) 9 *International Journal for the Psychology of Religion* 157.

[40] Spilka, Hood Jnr, Hunsberger and Gorsuch (n 26 above) 466.

Schoenrade and Ventis noted, whether the quest dimension is a source of increased acceptance and tolerance or merely a symptom of it. In other words, it is unclear whether because people perceive religion as a quest they are more tolerant, or whether people who are more tolerant, for various reasons, are also more likely to hold the quest dimension of religion.[41] Thirdly, the ratio between extrinsic, intrinsic and quest religious believers is unclear—in various religions and in different times and places. This was not the research question in any of the above studies yet it is a significant one if one wishes to draw meaningful generalisations about contemporary religions. Finally, researchers emphasise the distinction between proscribed and non-proscribed prejudice. Yet, it is not always clear how we make this distinction.

These quandaries do not affect, however, the strength of the revised and final conclusion reached by Batson, Schoenrade and Ventis. Their conclusion, and indeed a more radical one, was reaffirmed in a uniquely comprehensive study from 1983, in which McClosky and Brill presented a summary of three different studies, all of which aimed to examine the same question. The research question was: 'to what extent does religious identification as such presently serve as a force to strengthen or weaken respect for civil liberties in the United States?'[42] Religious identification was defined in the simplest and most direct way, ie by asking the question 'what is your present religion, if any?'. The research group consisted of 261 non-religious people, 44 Jews, 488 Catholics and 1,134 Protestants (including Episcopalians, Baptists, Lutherans and so on)—1,927 people overall. The religiosity of those who declared themselves as religious was also measured and classified.[43]

As supporting most civil liberties is very closely related to being more tolerant, I will use the phrases 'supporting civil liberties' and 'being tolerant' indiscriminately.[44] The general result concerning the relationship between religion and tolerance was clear and achieved repetitively in the three different studies. It was found that

> three groups stand out as scoring higher than average in their support for civil liberties—Jews, Episcopalians, and most of all, those who claim to have no religious identification at all … Baptists score lowest on the civil liberties scale … when all the Protestants are combined into a single category and compared with Jews and

---

[41]   Batson, Schoenrade and Ventis (n 14 above) 330.

[42]   H McClosky and A Brill, *Dimensions of Tolerance—What Americans Believe about Civil Liberties* (New York, Russell Sage Foundation, 1983) 404. For a detailed description of the research, see pages 403–14.

[43]   McClosky and Brill (n 42 above) 406. On measuring the amount of support for civil liberties, see pp 278–88.

[44]   In fact, the connection between tolerance and supporting civil liberties can also be found in the title of McClosky's and Brill's book (*Dimensions of Tolerance—What Americans Believe about Civil Liberties*).

Catholics, the Jews turn out to be the most libertarian by a significant margin, and Catholics prove on the whole to be more libertarian than Protestants. The Catholic-Protestant differences, however, are not large.[45]

It should be added that both the Catholics and Protestants scored significantly lower than average on their support for civil liberties.[46] Another clear result was achieved regarding the relationship between tolerance and degree of religiosity. It was repeatedly found that, as religiosity increases, support for civil liberties declines.[47] Moreover, McClosky and Brill found that the two groups, ie the highly religious and the non-religious 'differ sharply in their orientation toward civil liberties even when they have similar amounts of schooling'.[48]

It is highly reasonable that the overwhelming difference between the Catholics and the Protestants, on the one hand, and non-religious people, on the other, can only be explained through the religiosity of the former. The strong support for civil liberties amongst Jews can easily be explained as a clear case of pragmatic tolerance or simply lack of power. Being a relatively powerless religious minority, yet a minority which is well integrated in American society, it is unsurprising to find that Jews in the United States generally support the high protection of civil liberties and tolerance (as well as the separation of Church and State). As will be shown shortly, things are utterly different for religious Jews in Israel where they have the power to execute religious intolerance or, at least, have no prevailing reason to conceal it.

E. Empirical Findings—The 1990s and Beyond

The last study mentioned as part of the third stage of research was conducted in 1986 (following the survey by Batson, Schoenrade and Ventis). Therefore,

---

[45] McClosky and Brill (n 42 above) 404.

[46] Perhaps specific numbers will give a more precise impression of the clear relationship between religion and intolerance. Strong support for civil liberties was found amongst 69% of the non-religious people, 55% of the Jews, 30% of the Catholics and 25% of the Protestants. Little support for civil liberties was found amongst 8% of the non-religious people, 14% of Jews, 33% of Catholics and 41% of Protestants.

[47] In the three studies, the percentage of strong support for civil liberties amongst the deeply religious ranged between 14% and 16%. The percentage of low support ranged between 46% and 53%. Amongst those who scored low for religiosity, the percentage of high support for civil liberties ranged between 55% and 60%. The percentage of low support ranged between 12% and 20%. As a reminder, strong support for civil liberties was found amongst 69% of the non-religious people, whereas low support was found amongst only 8% of them.

[48] McClosky and Brill (n 42 above) 407. It should be noted that the average percentage difference in supporting civil liberties between the religious and non-religious groups differed for each and every civil liberty. To take a few examples, the average percentage difference between the religious and non-religious regarding issues relating to sexual freedom was 46%, to censorship of obscenity 36%, to homosexuality 29%, to women's roles 21%, to privacy 6% and to the death penalty 2%.

we need to address newer developments and findings regarding the relationship between religion and tolerance. The discussion below will be divided into two parts. First, recent conceptual and methodological developments will be addressed and evaluated. Then, a description of further empirical findings will follow.

*(i) Conceptual and Methodological Developments: The Concept
      of Religious Fundamentalism*

As mentioned above, the first studies that examined the relationship between religion and intolerance or prejudice ignored possible differences between different religious orientations. In the 1950s and '60s, Allport suggested that there was a distinction between intrinsic and extrinsic religion, and was the first to acknowledge that not all kinds of religious beliefs or attitudes share the same characteristics, ie that persons can be religious to the same degree but in different ways. In the 1970s, Batson added a third orientation—the quest religious orientation—that proved helpful in appreciating the complexity of the relationship between religion and intolerance. In the late 1980s, and especially in the 1990s, two new concepts were added to the equation: religious fundamentalism (RF) and right-wing authoritarianism (RWA). This was supposed to shed new light on the relationship between religious orientation and intolerance.[49]

Altemeyer and Hunsberger suggested a description of what religious fundamentalism actually means, and it seems that most recent studies have adopted their approach. Though Altemeyer and Hunsberger's perception of religious fundamentalism may not be without its problems, for the purposes of this chapter, I will accept it as it stands. According to their proposal, religious fundamentalism is

> the belief that there is one set of religious teachings that clearly contains the fundamental, basic, intrinsic, essential, inerrant truth about humanity and deity; that this essential truth is fundamentally opposed by forces of evil which must be vigorously fought; that this truth must be followed today according to the fundamental, unchangeable practices of the past, and that those who believe and follow these fundamental teachings have a special relationship with the deity.[50]

---

[49] Other studies offer a different classification of religious orientations, in which the 'extrinsic' dimension is divided into the 'extrinsic-personal' dimension and 'extrinsic-social' dimension. See, for example: LA Kirkpatrick, 'A Psychometric Analysis of the Allport-Ross & Feagin Measures of Intrinsic-Extrinsic Religious Orientation' in M Lynn and D Moberg (eds), *Research in the Social Scientific Study of Religion* (Greenwich, JAI Press Inc, 1989) 1.

[50] B Altemeyer and B Hunsberger, 'Authoritarianism, Religious Fundamentalism, Quest, and Prejudice' (1992) 2 *International Journal for the Psychology of Religion* 113, 118. Altemeyer and Hunsberger developed a 20-item religious fundamentalism scale (and a 16-item quest scale) that has been adopted in many studies ever since: Spilka, Hood Jnr, Hunsberger and Gorsuch (n 26 above) 466.

It is clear that religious fundamentalism is utterly different from the quest orientation and, in some respects, it is the complete opposite. It is also important to note that religious fundamentalism is distinct from religious orthodoxy, since the latter focuses on the content of the religious belief whereas the former focuses on the way in which the religious belief is held. Therefore, and as expected, Altemeyer and Hunsberger found strong and clear-cut correlations between a religious fundamentalist orientation and being prejudiced in a variety of ways (eg against homosexuals, racial minorities and more), and between quest orientation and low prejudice. These findings led Altemeyer and Hunsberger to state the following regarding the answer to the question 'are religious persons usually good persons?': 'It appears to be "no", if one means by "religious" a fundamentalist, nonquesting religious orientation, and by "good" the kind of nonprejudiced, compassionate, accepting attitudes espoused in the Gospels and other writings'.[51]

A long series of studies from the 1990s onwards repeatedly reached the same conclusions: first, the religious fundamentalism and the quest scales were strongly negatively correlated; secondly, high religious fundamentalism scores were significantly and positively correlated with prejudice and authoritarianism aggression; and, finally, high quest scores were significantly negatively associated with the same prejudice measures.[52] Even though recent studies apply this relatively new category of religious fundamentalism, one conceptual-methodological problem remains unanswered. It appears that when we try to identify and explain the links between religiosity and holding intolerant views, the common definition of RF is called into question. When RF is defined as an attitude according to which the essential religious truth is fundamentally opposed by the force of evil, which must be vigorously fought, it appears that the very definition of RF includes a meaningful intolerant attitude (which does not exist within the definitions of intrinsic and extrinsic religion, for example). A similar observation can be made with regard to defining 'religion as quest', which explains why 'religion as quest' is almost a mirror image of RF. In other words, finding that religious people are less (or more) tolerant because they are religious is interesting and meaningful. Finding that those who are categorised as 'religious fundamentalists' are intolerant is very close to being a tautology. Thus, presumably new concepts are required in order for newer studies on the links between religious and intolerance to shed more light on this complex issue.

---

[51] Altemeyer and Hunsberger (n 50 above) 125.

[52] For the list of studies see Spilka, Hood Jnr, Hunsberger and Gorsuch (n 26 above) 466, 472; Hood, Hill and Spilka (n 1 above) 417–21; B Hunsberger and LM Jackson, 'Religious, Meaning and Prejudice' (2005) 61 *Journal of Social Issues* 807, 810.

Recently, a few studies have examined the link between religion, prejudice and right-wing authoritarianism. However, being a relatively recent development with unclear and disputed findings, I will refrain from evaluating it here.[53]

(ii) The 1990s and Beyond—Further Findings

The purpose of the following survey is to exemplify the kinds of religious intolerance and prejudice that were found in relatively recent studies, or, in other words, to illustrate how earlier findings are repeatedly found in recent studies as well, and hence have not lost their validity. Some recent studies also offer new insights about the link between religion and intolerance. I will start by discussing recent findings about Judaism in Israel and will then move on to describe and analyse findings with regard to Christianity and other religions.

In a comprehensive study that was conducted in Israel between 1991 and 1995, the researchers tried to map Israeli public opinion about procedural democracy, human rights and tolerance.[54] The target group consisted of 2,400 respondents. They were divided into non-religious and religious people. The latter were divided into three sub-groups according to their religiosity: low/medium-religiosity believers (in Hebrew—*Masorteem*); high-religiosity believers (or, in the study's term—religious people); and extremely high-religiosity believers or simply orthodox believers (in Hebrew—*Haredim*).[55] The amount of tolerance of the respondents or the degree of their commitment to human rights was measured by scaling their answers to direct questionnaires. The questions dealt with four issues: political and social equality; voting rights of members of unpopular minority groups; unpopular and minority groups' rights to be elected to Parliament; and Israeli-Arab citizens' rights to be elected to Parliament.

The results were as follows: amongst the respondents as a whole, 59 per cent scored high for tolerance, whereas 41 per cent scored low. Amongst the non-religious people, 66 per cent score high for tolerance, with 52 per cent of the low/medium and the high religiosity believers, and 30 per cent of the orthodox religious believers. The level of commitment to democracy was measured by questions regarding the following: rating two options—a democratic government that holds contradictory views to those of the respondent, or a

---

[53] For this recent development, see Spilka, Hood Jnr, Hunsberger and Gorsuch (n 26 above) 467–470; Hood, Hill and Spilka (n 1 above) 165–66, 418–21.

[54] Y Peres and E Yuchtman-Ya'ar, *Between Consent and Dissent: Democracy and Peace in the Israeli Mind (Rights & Responsibilities)* (Lanham MD, Rowman & Littlefield Publishers, 2000).

[55] For the methodology of the research see Peres and Yuchtman-Ya'ar (n 54 above) 39–41, 79–81.

non-democratic government that holds the same views as the respondent; the relationship between the democratic and the Jewish nature of the state of Israel; the kind of response to a majority decision to pull out from the occupied territories; and the position regarding whether a slight threat to national security justifies limiting 'democratic rights'. It is clear that some of these questions are not confined to procedural democracy. Rather, they are related to attitudes towards human rights and, naturally, tolerance. The results are striking: amongst the respondents as a group, 58 per cent showed a commitment to democracy, and this was found amongst 71 per cent of the non-religious people, 51 per cent of the low/medium-religiosity believers; 26 per cent of the high-religiosity believers, and 10 per cent of the orthodox believers.

This research clearly shows a strong positive relationship between religiosity and a lower commitment to human rights, tolerance and democracy. Moreover, as Peres and Yuchtman-Ya'ar indicated, religiosity was proven to be the most influential variant in every study, far more than any other variant, such as schooling, economic status, place of residence and so on. Recent and numerous surveys and findings in the Jewish-Israeli context also show a continuous and clear strong positive relationship between religiosity and a lower commitment to human rights, tolerance and democracy. A comprehensive survey from 2010, for example, found that 49 per cent of Jewish citizens in Israel oppose granting equal rights to Palestinians who are also Israeli citizens (approximately 20 per cent of Israeli citizens are Palestinians). It was found that 33.5 per cent of non-religious Jewish citizens oppose the 'equal rights approach', 51 per cent of the low/medium-religiosity believers; 65 per cent of the high-religiosity believers, and 72 per cent of the orthodox believers.[56] Similar results were found with regard to issues such as equality in resource allocation between Jewish and non-Jewish citizens; equality between men and women; giving preference to the 'Jewish nature' of Israel over its democratic features; and willingness to live near non-Jews and homosexuals.[57] With regard to all these issues a strong positive relationship was found between religiosity and a lower commitment to human rights, tolerance and democracy.

As to Christianity, a series of studies from the 1990s indicate that the relationship between religiosity and unfavourable attitudes towards minority rights still exists amongst Christians in the United States.[58] Other studies (up until 2013) found correlations between 'religious devoutness' and bigotry, authoritarianism, dogmatism and anti-humanitarianism.[59] Other studies

[56] A Arian et al, *Auditing Israeli Democracy—2010: Democratic Values in Practice* (The Israel Democracy Institute, 2010) 18 (in Hebrew).
[57] Arian (n 56 above) 18, 76, 100, 125.
[58] Beit-Hallahmi (n 5 above) 143–44.
[59] Beit-Hallahmi (n 5 above) 145–46.

(up to 2010) found strong correlations between religiosity amongst Christians and anti-Semitism and racism generally.[60]

A relatively specific study that was conducted in the United States in the late 1990s examined the connection between religious orientation and anti-homosexual sentiments among Christians.[61] It was found that intrinsic faith is associated with a rejection of prejudice against anti-homosexual sentiment, even though homosexual behaviour was still regarded as a moral problem. Extrinsic motives, however, correlated positively with anti-gay indices. A similar, yet more extensive, study was conducted in the United States in 2001,[62] which examined attitudes towards lesbians, gays and bisexuals in relation to religion. The target group was asked two kinds of question. The first kind examined principled views about lesbians, gays and bisexuals (eg, whether homosexuality is morally wrong, and whether it is a normal part of some people's sexuality). The second kind concerned equal rights (eg, whether lesbian, gay and bisexual couples should be protected from discrimination in terms of employment, housing, social security benefits and the like). As to the first type of question, a high degree of intolerant views was found among the Evangelicals; a medium degree among non-Evangelicals and Catholics; and a low degree among those who were not affiliated to any particular religion. As to the second type of question, an extremely high resistance to legal equality was found among the Evangelicals; a certain support (around 60–65 per cent) was found among the non-Evangelicals; and stronger support (around 75 per cent) was found among the Catholics and non-religious people alike. These studies, and many more, led scholars to conclude that 'the link between religion and negative attitudes towards homosexuality is well established'.[63]

Numerous other studies during the 1990s reached the following more general and compatible conclusions: Catholics in the United States are more tolerant than most Protestant denominations (especially Southern Protestants); Evangelicals are less tolerant than other religious Americans; and high religious involvement is positively connected to high intolerance towards new religions. Some studies found that religious attendance and commitment are

[60]   Beit-Hallahmi (n 5 above) 147–48.

[61]   AS Fulton, RL Gorsuch and EA Maynard, 'Religious Orientation, Antihomosexual Sentiment, and Fundamentalism Among Christians' (1999) 38 *Journal for the Scientific Study of Religion* 14; and see also Spilka, Hood Jnr, Hunsberger and Gorsuch (n 26 above) 197.

[62]   Spilka, Hood Jnr, Hunsberger and Gorsuch (n 26 above) 198.

[63]   See Spilka, Hood Jnr, Hunsberger and Gorsuch (n 26 above) 464 and Hood, Hill and Spilka (n 1 above) 383–84 for a list of studies from the 1980s onwards. This conclusion was reinforced in more recent research that investigated covert, implicit prejudice against homosexuals among religious believers: WC Rawatt, 'Associations Between Religious Personality Dimensions and Implicit Homosexual Prejudice' (2006) 45 *Journal for the Scientific Study of Religion* 397, and see p 398 for a survey of other recent studies that reported similar results. See also: J Tsang and WC Rawatt, 'The Relationship Between Religious Orientation, Right-Wing Authoritarianism, and Implicit Sexual Prejudice' (2007) 17 *The International Journal for the Psychology of Religion* 99.

positively connected to high intolerance, whereas others found such a connection only with regard to atheists or amongst theological conservatives. Some studies found different types of intolerance towards different groups amongst extrinsic and intrinsic religious persons. Most of the newer studies indicate a connection between extrinsic-political religiosity or what is sometimes called 'theocratic orientation' and intolerance.[64]

Surprisingly, only a few studies have investigated prejudice and intolerance amongst religious persons towards members of other religions and atheists. The few studies that did examine this issue have produced similar results.[65] First, all kinds of religious orientation (ie fundamentalist, intrinsic, extrinsic and quest) were associated with more favourable attitudes towards the members of the group (in these studies—Christian believers) and greater intolerance towards members outside the group (atheists); secondly, high scores on the intrinsic and fundamentalism scales were found to be strongly correlated with religious group identification; thirdly, intrinsic and fundamentalist religious persons hold pervasive prejudices against religious persons outside their group; fourthly, religious group membership can contribute to inter-group prejudice, especially the intolerance of religious members outside the group; and, finally, people who identified themselves as atheists or non-believers did not show the same degree or pervasiveness of 'out-group' negativity towards religious groups. More generally, these findings are consistent with the social identity theory, according to which identification with a social group often produces noticeable in-group and out-group biases.[66]

A helpful review and evaluation of the empirical studies that have been conducted since the 1990s has been made by Hunsberger and Jackson.[67] Their initial observation was that

if one simply examines the 'total box score' for each religious orientation, it would appear that Intrinsic, Extrinsic and Religious Fundamentalism scales are associated

---

[64] For some of the studies that produced the above results see: SG McFarland, 'Religious Orientations and the Targets of Discrimination' (1989) 28 *Journal for the Scientific Study of Religion* 324; C Wilcox and TG Jelen, 'Evangelicals and Political Tolerance' (1990) 18 *American Politics Quarterly* 25; CG Ellison and MA Musick, 'Southern Intolerance: A Fundamentalist Effect?' (1993) 72 *Social Forces* 379; DA Gay and CG Ellison, 'Religious Subcultures and Political Tolerance: Do Denominations Still Matter?' (1993) 34 *Review of Religious Research* 311.

[65] Spilka, Hood Jnr, Hunsberger and Gorsuch (n 26 above) 475–76. The studies were reported in 1999 and 2003. For similar results, see also: WC Rawatt, LM Franklin and M Cotton, 'Patterns and Personality Correlates of Implicit and Explicit Attitudes Toward Christians and Muslims' (2005) 44 *Journal for the Scientific Study of Religion* 29.

[66] MA Hogg, 'Social Identity' in MR Leary and JP Tangney (eds), *Handbook on Self and Identity* (New York, The Guilford Press, 2003) 462; H Tajfel, 'Social Psychology of Intergroup Relations' (1982) 33 *Annual Review of Psychology* 1.

[67] Hunsberger and Jackson (n 52 above). The survey was of 16 studies conducted between 1990 and 2003 (see pp 810–11).

with intolerance (remember, the Intrinsic scale is usually thought to be associated with just the opposite—increased tolerance). Quest is generally associated with increased tolerance.[68]

However, Hunsberger and Jackson were quick to add that we should note that 'this simple tabulation of relationships hides important trends for different targets of prejudice'.[69] Their revised and up-to-date conclusion is that:

> The target of prejudice is important when considering prejudice-religious orientations relationships. The Intrinsic scale was consistently *negatively* related to the self reported racial/ethnic intolerance, but it was *positively* related to intolerance of gay men and lesbians and possibly to authoritarianism and intolerance of communists and religious outgroups though there are few relevant studies. The extrinsic orientation was sometimes positively related to racial/ethnic and gay/lesbians intolerance. Quest showed a weak tendency to be associated with tolerance for racial groups; a much stronger effect appeared for gay/lesbian as targets. Finally, RF was consistently related to increased prejudice against gay/lesbian persons, women, Communists and religious outgroups, as well as authoritarianism, but its relationship with racial/ethnic intolerance is less clear cut.[70]

A recent and important development in the psychological and sociological studies about the relationship between religion and intolerance concerns the scope of these studies in terms of geographical spread and religious affiliation. Until the late 1990s most of these studies were conducted in the United States (a few in Canada), and mainly amongst Christians. Now we have more (though not quite sufficient) findings that reinforce the empirical links between religion and intolerance. A comprehensive study from 1999, which was conducted amongst 16,604 people from 15 countries, found that the religiously affiliated and those who attended church more often were more prejudiced than the non-affiliated. It was also found that the effects of individual religiosity were stronger in more religious countries and weaker in more secularised countries.[71]

An exceptional comprehensive survey of almost 150,000 people (mostly Catholics, Protestants, Jews, Muslims, Hindus and Buddhists) in more than 60 countries found that the relation between religion and intolerance seems to be present in all religious denominations, based on both religious upbringing and

---

[68] Hunsberger and Jackson (n 52 above) 811.
[69] Hunsberger and Jackson (n 52 above) 811.
[70] Hunsberger and Jackson (n 52 above) 812.
[71] P Scheepers, M Te Grotenhuis and F Van Der Slik, 'Education, Religiosity and Moral Attitudes: Explaining Cross-National Effect Differences' (2002) 63 *Sociology of Religion* 157.

attendance at religious services.[72] It was also found that all religious denominations are associated with a more conservative attitude towards women.[73]

F. Empirical Findings—Conclusions

The conclusions that can be drawn from the extensive psychological and sociological studies about the relationship between religion and tolerance are two-fold. The first conclusion would be that people's responses to measures of religion and intolerance are closely related. The second conclusion would be that the first conclusion should be qualified and treated with caution.

The first conclusion finds expression in Wulff's observation, who, after reviewing the relevant literature up to 1997, stated that

> using a variety of measures of piety—religious affiliation, church attendance, doctrinal orthodoxy, rated importance of religion, and so on—researches have consistently found positive correlations with ethnocentrism, authoritarianism, dogmatism, social distance, rigidity, intolerance of ambiguity, and specific forms of prejudice, especially against Jews and blacks.[74]

Numerous other studies concluded that 'as a broad generalization, the more religious an individual is, the more prejudiced that person is'.[75]

As to the need to qualify the first conclusion, there are a few suggested qualifications that should be rejected or at least not be given much weight, whereas other qualifications do appear to help in formulating a more accurate conclusion about the relationship between religion and intolerance. Some of

---

[72] L Guiso, P Sapienza and L Zingales, 'People's Opium? Religion and Economic Attitudes' (2003) 50 *Journal of Monetary Economics* 225, 228, 263. It was also found that the only exception is Buddhists, who are more tolerant than non-religious people. Hindus and Muslims are the least tolerant towards immigrants and other races, followed by Jews, Catholics and Protestants.

[73] Guiso, Sapienza and Zingales (n 72 above) 264. It was also found that that effect is twice as strong for Muslims than for any other religion.

[74] DM Wulff, *Psychology of Religion: Classic and Contemporary Views*, 2nd edn (New York, John Wiley & Sons, 1997) 223, as mentioned in Spilka (n 26 above) 458. Similar conclusions were suggested by other scholars who reviewed the literature about the empirical link between religion and prejudice. For a recent description of these reviews, see: Hunsberger and Jackson (n 52 above) 808.

[75] For a list of these studies, see Spilka, Hood Jnr, Hunsberger and Gorsuch (n 26 above) 458. See also D Canetti-Nisim, 'Two Religious Meaning Systems, One Political Belief System: Religiosity, Alternative Religiosity and Political Extremism' in L Weinberg and A Pedhazur (eds), *Religious Fundamentalism and Political Extremism* (London, Routledge, 2004) 35, 40: 'It is well known that the degree to which believers are orthodox in their beliefs and practices has a role in the shaping of their approach to political attitudes'; and 46: 'there is little doubt regarding the association between religious orthodoxy and anti-democratic political attitudes and actions … common religious devotees are more intolerant, militant and exclusionist in their political attitudes'.

the qualifications and reservations were mentioned throughout the discussion. I will refer here to a few of the central ones.[76]

First, some research qualifies the conclusion that the more religious an individual is, the more prejudiced and intolerant he is, in terms of a possible curvilinear relationship. At least when church attendance was the measure of religiousness, it was proposed that 'those who do not attend church are relatively unprejudiced; that those attending infrequently to moderately frequently are the most prejudiced persons; and that active church members are among the least prejudiced in society'.[77] However, today it is widely agreed that

> given the problems with early studies that purportedly showed the curvilinear effect, the lack of recent studies to confirm such an effect, and the existence of some studies that looked for but could not find a curvilinear effect, it is questionable today whether such an effect does indeed exist.[78]

Secondly, other studies have suggested, as already shown, that the general conclusion about the relationship between religion and intolerance should be qualified in terms of religious orientation or religious dimension. However, the still popular classification, according to which religious orientation can be either extrinsic or intrinsic, carries with it significant difficulties. Spilka concluded that 'the relationship between prejudice and the I-E {intrinsic-extrinsic} dichotomy … is at best tenuous and difficult to interpret. At times it seems that the I-E distinction … has … led us into a psychometric and empirical morass of confusion'.[79] The quest orientation, as proposed by Batson, seems more promising, as there is a wide agreement about the positive correlation between this dimension and tolerance or low prejudice. Moreover, the religious fundamentalism orientation, of itself and together with the quest orientation, proved to be relatively productive in explaining the relationship between religion and intolerance. Both orientations emphasise the way in which religious belief is held and the willingness of religious people to re-examine and change their views.

---

[76] For the argument that 'religion has *indirect* influence on political tolerance wherein increased religious commitment and increased doctrinal orthodoxy both lead to increase *in*tolerance via other variables', see: MA Eisenstein, 'Rethinking the Relationship Between Religion and Political Intolerance in the US' (2006) 28 *Political Behaviour* 327, 338.

[77] For a list of the studies that reached this conclusion, see Spilka, Hood Jnr, Hunsberger and Gorsuch (n 26 above) 458–59.

[78] Spilka, Hood Jnr, Hunsberger and Gorsuch (n 26 above) 459.

[79] Spilka, Hood Jnr, Hunsberger and Gorsuch (n 26 above) 464; Hood, Hill and Spilka (n 1 above) 412–13. Hood et al also suggest that the I–E distinction may have a protestant bias: 382–83. For an argument according to which the religious means and end orientations are not mutually exclusive and that any religious orientation could be classified as either a means-extrinsic orientation or end-intrinsic one, see: KI Pargament, *The Psychology of Religion and Coping: Theory, Research, Practice* (New York, The Guilford Press, 1997) chapter 3.

Thirdly, it is widely accepted that the distinction between proscribed and non-proscribed prejudice is important in appreciating the relationship between religion and intolerance or prejudice. To take an example, it has been repeatedly argued that intrinsic believers may be inclined to be relatively tolerant when the prejudice is proscribed by their religion but intolerant when it is not. In other words, and more generally, it has been shown that different religious orientations can entail various degrees of prejudice towards different target groups.[80]

Fourthly, although the relationship between religion and prejudice and intolerance has possibly generated more research than any other domain in the psychology of religion,[81] most of these studies were conducted in North America and mainly amongst Christians.[82] This is unfortunate, as we should expect that the kind and degree of intolerant tendencies among religious people may be, at least to some extent, culturally and geographically specific. Until recently, the studies outside North America, which examined religious prejudice and intolerance among non-Christians, were too few and too often suffered from methodological flaws (with the exception of the numerous studies in Israel, which have produced consistent findings over the years). Therefore, they could not indicate meaningful and reliable relevant findings.[83] This regrettable fact could have raised doubts about the ability of using the North-American studies as a basis for creating general arguments about religion as such. Nevertheless, the relative consistency of the results in these studies over time; the relevant resemblance between Christianity, Judaism and Islam; and the fact that the description of religious fundamentalism is potentially applicable to at least these three religions, are strong reasons to believe in the applicability of former findings and their conclusions, at least to Christianity, Judaism and Islam, and perhaps to other similar religions as well. Recent comprehensive studies that were conducted amongst thousands of religious believers worldwide reinforce this assertion.

---

[80] For further discussion on the distinction between proscribed and non-proscribed prejudice see Hood, Hill and Spilka (n 1 above) 413–14.

[81] Spilka, Hood Jnr, Hunsberger and Gorsuch (n 26 above) 457.

[82] Spilka, Hood Jnr, Hunsberger and Gorsuch (n 26 above) 470 referred to a few studies from Europe, which also examined Christians, and that by using 'very different measures of religiousness, authoritarianism, and prejudice, have found links among these measures that are quite consistent with the findings reported above' (ie in studies from North America). See also a relatively recent study conducted in Belgium, which found a strong and positive link between religious orthodoxy and holding anti-democratic, conservative, nationalistic and racist political views: B Duriez, P Luyten, B Snauwaert and D Hutsebaut, 'The Importance of Religiosity and Values in Predicting Political Attitudes: Evidence for the Continuing Importance of Religiosity in Flanders (Belgium)' (2007) 5 *Mental Health, Religious and Culture* 35.

[83] For more details, see Spilka Hood Jnr, Hunsberger and Gorsuch (n 26 above) 470–71, Hunsberger and Jackson (n 52 above) 813–14.

Fifthly, empirical examinations of religious attitudes and empirical studies within the field of religious psychology are to be found only from the second half of the twentieth century. Moreover, a few decades had passed before consensus (or at least wide agreement) was reached within the scientific community regarding the reliability of certain research methods and the untrustworthiness of others. Therefore, most if not all of the reliable empirical findings and conclusions are limited not only in terms of the target group (mostly Christians) and geographic area (mostly North America) but also the relevant era (late twentieth century).

Sixthly, empirical research and, in turn, empirical findings and conclusions can always be exposed to critical, not to say suspicious, views concerning their reliability and methodology. Questions can be raised regarding two main subjects. The first concerns 'internal' problems, ie the research methods applied. The second is 'external' possible problems, ie whether and how the empirical study and findings were influenced by the identity of the researchers, their own beliefs, their sources of funding and so on. As to the internal problem, as stated before, there is wide agreement among leading scholars and scientists about the reliability of certain research methods and the deficiencies of others. The implications of this were discussed earlier and there is little point in questioning the current scientific consensus here. As to the external problem, since there is no evidence in the literature that such a problem exists, especially not with regard to the authoritative and comprehensive texts that survey and analyse a great number of relevant studies, it seems unnecessary to raise this issue here.

Lastly, it should be taken into consideration that, apart from the above qualifications and reservations, there is also good reason to believe that a considerable proportion of the studies conducted to date actually failed to describe how intolerant and prejudiced religious people really are. It is very likely that religious people are even more intolerant and prejudiced than as described by many studies. This is because most of the studies, even recent ones, have used 'pen and paper' instruments that examined self-reported prejudice, rather than using behavioural instruments to measure prejudice. In other words, most studies examined the relationship between religious orientation and overt forms of prejudice. Spilka and others remind us that this methodology 'suffer(s) from such problems as weak or unreported psychometric properties, the fact that they are obviously tapping prejudice, social desirability effect, and so on', and therefore 'more subtle measures may be necessary to identify prejudice against targets that tend to be protected by religious or other social standards'.[84]

---

[84] Spilka, Hood Jnr, Hunsberger and Gorsuch (n 26 above) 473.

III. THE THEORETICAL LINKS BETWEEN
RELIGION AND INTOLERANCE

Most of the literature on religion and intolerance indicates the empirical links between religious orientation and intolerance. However, the reasons for the links between religion and intolerance are rarely explored in depth. Spilka and others rightly stated that 'little work has addressed the issue of *why* religion and prejudice are associated'.[85]

This section offers an initial attempt to explain why religion and intolerance are associated. I suggest that the special empirical links between religion and intolerance are the result of seven characteristics of religion: (1) religion perceives maintaining the unity of a distinct community and preserving its existence as one of its main functions; (2) religion aspires to gain formal control over its believers, other religious believers and heretics alike; (3) religion perceives its traditions, customs and symbols as sacred; (4) religion has a unique perception of the 'truth'; (5) religion is 'absolute'; (6) religion identifies morality and law with the divine, hence generally it rises above human criticism and reform; and (7) the content of religious values and beliefs. Before approaching the principled arguments, a few caveats should be borne in mind.

First, even if the argument that all religions are intolerant by their very nature can survive scrutiny,[86] for the purpose of this chapter, the principled arguments about the link between religion and intolerance should be read with regard to Judaism, Islam and Christianity, as well as with respect to any religion that shares similar characteristics to those presented above. Limiting the scope of the argument about the principled link between religion and intolerance to these three religions does not diminish its importance, as these religions play a central role in the world's history and in contemporary culture and politics. Limiting the argument to these religions is also possible and sensible, as the differences that may exist between them (and between various denominations within them) do not affect the validity of the principled argument regarding each and every one of them. Moreover, some of the main features that these religions share are also the reasons for regarding them as intolerant religions. Cohn, for example, argued that:

> Judaism, Christianity and Islam ... have several distinctive marks in common: they postulate the belief in and worship of God; they each have holy scriptures and

---

[85] Spilka, Hood Jnr, Hunsberger and Gorsuch (n 26 above) 475.

[86] HH Cohn, 'Religious Intoleration and the Law' (1966) 12 *New York Forum* 257. For the possibility that there are (or were) religions that are not intolerant in nature and for the true meaning of such a claim see on p 269: 'There were, it is true, in many places (e.g. in ancient Greece, India and China) and at several periods in history, more or less "tolerant" religions which succeeded in suppressing any such atavistic urges and civilizing their adherents; but these urges existed, before they could be suppressed'.

other canonical texts and vest authoritative interpretations or applications thereof with binding force; each designates a class of officials or functionaries to preserve and propagate the faith; each seeks to imbue its religious, ethical and legal norms into the daily lives of individuals and communities, and none suffers dissidents from within. In addition there are, at least in Christianity and Islam, certain fundamental dogmata (for example, The Holy Trinity in Christianity, the divine prophecy of Muhammad in Islam) which everybody is duty-bound to believe.[87]

Although Judaism, Islam and Christianity will be treated as paradigmatic cases of intolerant religions, it is reasonable to assume that many other religions share similar characteristics to these three. The greater the similarity between other religions and Judaism, Islam and Christianity, the more we are able to apply the argument about the link between religion and intolerance to those religions as well.

Secondly, not all religions share all the characteristics that lead to the principled argument about the link between religion and intolerance. Nevertheless, not all of the following characteristics have to exist to a similar extent or at all in order for a specific religion to be intolerant. Both quantitative and qualitative careful examination is needed in order to reach this conclusion. This is not to say that a pure case-by-case examination is needed, since, as argued before, most of the well-known, popular and powerful religions do share these characteristics. A careful examination may be required, then, regarding less well known or new religions, or for evaluating new developments in old religions or in certain denominations of old religions.

Thirdly, it should be clear from the outset that the argument about the unique link between religion and intolerance is based on the fact that only religion possesses some of the characteristics that will be presented shortly, and on the fact that the other characteristics, which are not uniquely religious, have special ramifications when found within religions. Therefore, the argument that there are non-religious ideologies, beliefs or views that share one or more of the following characteristics does not imply that religion is not unique. It is indeed true that there are non-religious ideologies, beliefs or views that are also intolerant, yet the nature of the link between these ideologies and intolerance differs from that between religion and intolerance. I will return to this point later when discussing some of the characteristics of religion that may be shared by non-religious ideologies, beliefs or views.

Fourthly, the argument that there is a special, strong link between religion and intolerance and that, on the whole, religious people are more likely to be intolerant than non-religious ones should be read in the light of the previous

---

[87] HH Cohn, 'The Law of Religious Dissidents: A Comparative Historical Survey' (2000) 34 *Israel Law Review* 39, 40.

discussion on the concept of tolerance in Chapter two. Some may argue that holding any moral view is inherently intolerant, as it distinguishes between right and wrong and consequently leads to treating the right and the wrong differently, or, more specifically, it requires the application of some kind and degree of intolerant attitude towards the moral wrong. Therefore, one might say that the only difference between holding religious and non-religious moral beliefs finds expression in what these beliefs do or do not tolerate, rather in the fact that one belief is more tolerant than others. The previous discussion about the nature of tolerance can answer this query. Earlier, I suggested that tolerance is to be understood as not harming others, although the tolerant person thinks that there are good reasons for harming others because (a) others' values, expressed through their behaviour, way of life or speech, appear to the tolerant as 'wrong', ie dangerous, evil, immoral, unjust, useless, irrational and so forth, *or* (b) because others' personal characteristics (colour of skin, sex, manners, physical appearance, physical disability and so forth) seem to the tolerant to be repulsive or disgusting, or these characteristics imply the inferiority of others in the eyes of the tolerant.

I have also suggested that, when there is a right to be tolerated or a correlative duty to tolerate, this right or duty is generated from the principle of autonomy, which means, in short, that sometimes one has a right to do the wrong thing or to make wrong choices. Alternatively, the right to be tolerated is the right not to be harmed, even though one is doing the wrong thing or making wrong choices. Therefore, there is an important difference between not tolerating someone who unjustly infringes the autonomy of or harms others and not tolerating someone for other reasons. When we do not tolerate someone who unjustly infringes the autonomy of or harms others, we are being intolerant but, more importantly, we are, at times, responding to an act of intolerance (assuming, of course, that the infringement of the autonomy or the harm caused are the result of one having a negative view about the other, his values and so on). In other cases, when we, again, do not tolerate someone who unjustly infringes the autonomy of, or harms, others, we are doing so to protect the rationales of tolerance or its justifications (in this case—autonomy). However, when we do not tolerate others for other reasons we are actually the original intolerant persons. Here, we cannot claim that we are not tolerating others in order to protect tolerance itself. Consequently, this response is more suspect and requires a special kind of justification.

In this chapter, the argument that someone is intolerant means that he is the original intolerant person, ie that the reason for his intolerant attitude is any reason whatsoever, apart from the need to respond to the unjust infringement of a person's autonomy or to an unjust harm or risk of harm (and, again, when they are the result of one having a negative view about the other, his values and so on). This type of intolerance should usually not be tolerated, as it is only rarely justified, and because it undermines the justifications and the rationale of the principle of tolerance.

To sum up this argument, since autonomy justifies tolerance, the truly intolerant person is one who unjustly infringes the autonomy of others or unjustly harms or offends others, because he has a negative view about the other's values, way of life, identity and so on. Without attempting to justify this view here, I will simply suggest that autonomy is unjustly infringed, and harm or offence unjustly caused when it is not done in accordance with a perfectionist-liberal perception of the harm principle, a perception which is similar yet not identical to Raz's perception of the harm principle, as already discussed in previous chapters about the principle of tolerance and the limits of tolerance.

Therefore, to take an example, G may not tolerate X, ie may harm or offend X because X does not share G's moral beliefs, or acts contrary to what G perceives as moral commands or prohibitions (which, we have to assume, do not uphold tolerance, as understood above). In turn, the state (or other third parties) may not tolerate G because of G's beliefs and behaviour. It would be a mistake to perceive G and the state as equally intolerant. It is indeed true that both G and the state are acting intolerantly but the state's intolerance is no more than a response to an unjustified intolerance. We may say that, in this case, G is the truly intolerant person and that only G should be condemned or punished for his acts.

For this reason, the argument that religion is strongly and uniquely linked to intolerance and that religious people are more likely than non-religious ones to be intolerant can also be interpreted as meaning that religion is strongly and uniquely linked to unjustified infringements of others' autonomy or to harming and offending others, not in accordance with the harm principle, and, accordingly, that religious people are more likely to unjustly infringe others' autonomy or to harm or offend them, not in accordance with the harm principle.

Lastly, some of the arguments or characteristics that will be discussed below might appear too sketchy. Indeed, some of the following assertions and generalisations rely on the assumption that these generalisations are, by definition, mostly true or generally accurate; that the cases to which they do not apply are marginal exceptions which do not affect the strength of the generalisation itself; and that they reflect accurate, common and shared perceptions of their subject-matter, and therefore need no further elaboration.

Bearing these clarifications and caveats in mind, I will now examine the common characteristics of most monotheistic, communal, ethnic or political religions, which are also the reasons why these religions are closely related to intolerance.

A. The First Reason: The Communal Nature of Religion

Religion perceives maintaining the unity of a distinct community and preserving its existence as one of its main functions. Some claim that this is the main reason for the link between religion and intolerance.[88] Mensching, in his ground-breaking research, called it 'formal intolerance', since it does not necessarily result from disagreements about beliefs or about different perceptions of the truth or the good, but merely from the will to protect the unity of the community and to keep it separate from other communities.[89] A clear example of such 'formal intolerance' is religious dietary requirements (eg Halal food in Islam and Kosher food in Judaism). Despite partial attempts to rationalise religious dietary requirements the truth is that they have no intrinsic rationale. There is no rational reason for Jews, for example, to avoid eating pork or seafood, or to avoid eating dairy products together with or shortly after eating a meat product. Religious dietary requirements are mostly arbitrary and do not reflect different perceptions of the truth or the good. Their only purpose is to protect the unity of the community and to keep it separate from other communities. They prevent members of one religion from dining with members of other religions (especially at their homes) and they require the establishment of institutions that will supervise and regularise the ways in which these dietary requirements are kept.

According to the argument on the communal nature of religion, religion and society are interrelated. Religion is a public and cultural matter and sometimes a matter of state or of the ruler himself. The individual believer is not important as such, but more as part of his ethnic-religious community. If a religion is practised within race then the links between religiosity or religious teaching and ethnocentrism or racism are inevitable.[90] The communal characteristic of religion can be found not only in ethnic religions but in every 'public' religion, as opposed to 'private' ones. The Catholic Church, for example, especially when it dominated the world, took all necessary measures to maintain communal unity: denying the idea that a religious believer (or anyone for that matter) can be independent of God and the Church; establishing

---

[88] G Mensching, *Tolerance and Truth in Religion* (trans HJ Klimkeit) (Tuscaloosa AL, University of Alabama Press, 1971) 100–113; CL Eisgruber and LG Sager, 'Mediating Institutions: Beyond the Public/Private Distinction: The Vulnerability of Conscience: The Constitutional Basis for Protecting Religious Conduct' (1994) 61 *University of Chicago Law Review* 1245, 1249: 'It is the group identity of the faithful that mobilizes pity, distrust, or even hatred for those who are not believers'.

[89] Mensching refers to Judaism as an ethnic religion in which this function is more dominant than in other religions: Mensching (n 88 above) 103.

[90] Beit-Hallahmi (n 5 above) 147.

authoritative and single-minded leadership; maintaining harsh censorship of literature; condemning and excluding non-Catholics, and so on. Similar measures with similar ends can be found in Judaism and Islam.

Wellman and Tokuno described well the connection between the communal feature of religion and its intolerant nature when they argued that

> religion has always functioned to shape individual and social identities and inspire group formation … it is a part of the nature of religious communities to gain their identity through conflict and tension with out-group cultures. Conflict, in this sense, is socially functional.[91]

Wellman and Tokuno also argued, more specifically, that the communal nature of some religions best explains their tendency to intolerance. From their work on Western and Eastern religious traditions, past and present, they suggested that

> there are patterns within religion that tend toward conflict and even violence. Thus … *[t]he symbolic and social boundaries of religion (no matter how fluid or porous) mobilize individual and group identity in conflict, and sometimes violence, within and between groups.*[92]

Batson and Burris also stress the relation between the communal nature of religion and intolerance. They argue that

> all too often, it seems, religion functions not as a prophetic voice calling the faithful to shed their intolerance and bigotry, but as a mighty fortress of ingroup superiority, one that justifies elitism, ethnocentrism, oppression, and even destruction of those who are different.[93]

The same argument can be applied to almost every view that values the existence and preservation of distinct communities for any reason. Almost every communitarian view or every view that values various aspects of communitarianism is indeed an intolerant view—but only to a very limited extent. This is mostly a descriptive argument. Yet, it is also a normative argument, since regarding a certain view as intolerant means that reasons should be provided in order to explain why the intolerant view is justified. The reasons that can justify a communitarian-intolerant view are of a special nature. In short, a communitarian-intolerant view can be justifiable if it aims to preserve or nourish a community which is, on the whole, liberal or at least not anti-liberal.

---

[91] JK Wellman Jnr and K Tokuno, 'Is Religious Violence Inevitable' (2004) 43 *Journal for the Scientific Study of Religion* 291, 292, and see throughout their article for numerous examples.

[92] Wellman and Tokuno (n 91 above) 291.

[93] CD Batson and C Burris, 'Personal Religion: Depressant or Stimulant of Prejudice and Discrimination?' in MP Zanna and JM Olson (eds), *The Psychology of Prejudice* (Hillsdale NJ, Lawrence Erlbaum Associates, 1993) 149.

It should be a community that values autonomy or at least enables it and does not diminish it. Put simply, it should be a group or a community that is at least not anti-liberal, that does not tolerate unjustified intolerance, and that rejects illiberal attacks on its values and ways of life. This type of community may still be intolerant—but only towards those who diminish tolerance and its rationales.

Even though the above argument concerning the intolerant nature of communitarian religions applies in similar ways to religion and to any other view that values communitarianism, there is still something special about religion in this context. While religion and non-religious cultures or non-religious communitarian views share a similar 'communitarian nature', religion also has other features—some of them unique—that create a special and stronger link between religion and intolerance. The existence of these features means that religious communities are different from other communities. This means that the intolerant nature of almost every communitarian view is enhanced when it comes to religious communities because of features that will be discussed shortly and that are, in part, uniquely religious.

There is another aspect to the relationship between the communal nature of some religions and their tendency towards intolerance. The communal nature of religion is intertwined with religious group identification, which, in turn, may promote the self-glorification of the group on the one hand and the derogation of other groups or simple non-members on the other hand, as a means of enhancing the self-esteem of the group members. Hunsberger and Jackson referred to the communal nature of religion in terms of 'social identity' and connected this notion to other features of religion, which will be discussed shortly (namely, the claim to a monopoly on 'the truth' and the uniqueness of religious morality). They argue that

> maintaining a belief that one's religion teaches absolute truth, or is a unique source of morality, may contribute to ingroup preference (and enhance self-esteem), but may also generate prejudice against members of other religions. The desire for a positive social identity may also foster other forms of prejudice.[94]

A belief that one's religion teaches absolute truth, or is a unique source of morality, cannot but entail an intolerant state of mind concerning heretics and those who believe in the wrong religion. Whether this intolerant state of mind finds expression in an actual attitude is a different question, the answer to which depends on various and changeable circumstances.

Naturally, religion is not only interested in preserving the unity and existence of a community. It also plays a role in competing with other communities

---

[94] Hunsberger and Jackson (n 52 above) 818.

over non-religious, earthly benefits and resources. Hunsberger and Jackson concluded that

> [r]eligion-based intergroup tensions and prejudice toward outgroups are likely to be intensified if members perceive themselves to be in conflict with other religious or non-religious groups for valued resources … and these resources give additional meaning to individuals (e.g., political representation, voting power or economic benefits). Some recent evidence indicates that prejudice against people from different religions may arise from perceived competition on nonreligious dimensions.[95]

It is safe to assume that the members of a religious group normally perceive themselves as being in conflict with other religious or non-religious groups for valuable resources. The exact nature and magnitude of this conflict may vary but its existence, or at least the strong potential for its existence, is a social fact which is created, inter alia, by the communitarian nature of religion. It is also safe to assume that there are cases in which religion serves as a cynical mask for 'pragmatic' intergroup conflict over 'earthly' resources or simply power. Using religion as a mask in these cases would have been, of course, of little use if religion were not intolerant by nature to begin with.

Another factor that may ignite intergroup conflict is differences in power between counterpart groups. A recent, comprehensive study reached interesting findings in this context.[96] It was found that groups with power and resource advantages are more conflictual towards their lower-power counterparts and that groups with values incompatible with one another are more conflictual. This is not surprising nor is it surprising that religious infusion (ie the extent to which its rituals and discourse infuse private and public life) also predicts greater intergroup conflict. The more interesting finding was that

> highly religiously infused groups engaged in the more extreme forms of conflict— individual violence (assaults/murders/rapes), group violence (riots/police actions), and symbolic acts of aggression (e.g., desecration of graves, bombing of holy sites)— despite lacking political power and tangible resources.[97]

In other words, the intolerant nature of communal religion is so dominant that members of highly religiously infused groups may be relatively insensitive to the tangible costs potentially imposed by their high-power counterparts.[98]

---

[95] Hunsberger and Jackson (n 52 above) 818–19. See also Beit-Hallahmi (n 5 above) 147.

[96] S Neuberg, C Warner, S Mistler, E Hill and A Berlin, 'Religious Infusion and Intergroup Conflict: Results from the Global Group Relations Project' (2014) 25 *Psychological Science* 198. The researchers used data from the Global Group Relations Project to investigate 194 groups (eg, ethnic, religious, national) at 97 sites around the world.

[97] See also S Neuberg, C Warner, S Mistler, E Hill and A Berlin, 'Religious Infusion and Intergroup Conflict: Results from the Global Group Relations Project', APSA 2011 Annual Meeting Paper, available at: ssrn.com/abstract=1901492.

[98] Neuberg et al (n 97 above) 2.

The communal nature of religion—when it exists—can also explain the interesting case where members of a religious group show more tolerance towards members of other religious groups and less tolerance towards dissenters from their own group.[99] This is so as in many cases 'internal dissenters' pose a greater risk to the unity of a community than 'external others'. External attacks on religious communities may strengthen their unity and sense of solidarity. Internal dissent however may result in unwelcome changes in the nature of the community or in creation of 'sub-communities' which follow different versions of a certain religious faith.

The communitarian nature of religion is not a sufficient explanation for the links between religion and intolerance. Communitarianism almost always reflects an intolerant attitude but only to a very limited extent. Nevertheless, when put together with other characteristics of religion, it does contribute to establishing the link between religion and intolerance. The magnitude of intolerance is usually greater and its nature unique when the intolerant attitude relies on communal characteristics such as religion, race and nationality. The links between a 'personal religion' and tolerance are quite different than the links between a 'communal religion' and tolerance. The same thing can be said about the ramifications of these links.

B. The Second Reason: The Religious Aspiration to Gain Formal Control

The argument in this section is not that religions are intolerant *because* they wish to gain political or state powers over both believers and heretics. Rather, the argument is that religions wish to apply their intolerant content, which finds its clearest expression in the idea of salvation, by gaining political power over their believers, other religious believers and heretics. Therefore, first, we need to acknowledge that religions do aspire to gain political power and control. Since a mere aspiration to gain power does not constitute intolerance, we should then ask what the motivation behind this aspiration is, and what the implications of succeeding in gaining such power are.

---

[99] For a comprehensive study that reached such findings within Arab-Muslim countries, see: Ani Sarkissian, 'The Determinants of Tolerance in Arab Societies', APSA 2011 Annual Meeting Paper, available at: ssrn.com/abstract=1901491). It was found that 'while most Arabs agree that non-Muslims deserve the same political rights as Muslims, many Arabs do not show the same amount of tolerance toward converts away from Islam. Religiosity and support for political Islam are strongly associated with intolerance of Muslim converts, while religiosity is not associated with intolerance of non-Muslim minorities'.

As to the religious aspiration to gain state power, Mensching stated that

> a basic motive for [religious] intolerance is the claim to rulership as it is often raised
> by religious institutions and organizations, which even form alliances with earthly
> powers in order to accomplish their goals ... the sacred organization's claim to com-
> plete authority is ... [a] motive for intolerance.[100]

The religious aspiration to gain formal control or perhaps 'state powers' may
be concealed or postponed but only for pragmatic reasons.[101] When, however, religious institutions gain sufficient power, they do not limit themselves
to being intermediaries between God and their believers. At this point, they
usually aim to influence the public and the political sphere, either by taking
part in the political decision making, by being formal players in the political
sphere and process, or by becoming the sole political power, ie by establishing
and maintaining a theocracy.

Judaism, for example, was established as, and still aspires to be, a theocracy. Christianity, even though it started as a 'private' religion that focused on
individual salvation and was indifferent towards the earthly rulers, developed
consistently until the Church became a political power that had to regulate its
status vis-à-vis the Christian state. The aspiration to gain political power or to
design state authorities according to religious guidelines is no stranger to Islam
either. The common religious aspiration to gain state powers results from the
religious demand of absolute loyalty. As a matter of efficacy, absolute loyalty
can be better achieved by holding 'earthly' powers.

There is, of course, a close connection between religious orthodoxy, believing in the efficiency of religious persecution, having the power to persecute
and religious intolerance.[102] Surely there is nothing inherently wrong or intolerant in a mere aspiration to gain political or state power. However, when
this aspiration arises from religions that, by and large, adopt the complex and
troubling religious idea of salvation, it becomes clear why religions aspire to
such power and what would be the result of their success. Cohn expressed this
idea in a blunt yet accurate way when he said that

> it is the Motive of Salvation which is the most characteristically religious among all
> the various motives of religious intolerance ... The underlying theory is, of course,
> that the true faith must be imposed on unbelievers even by force ... There can be no

---

[100]   Mensching (n 88 above) 113.

[101]   R Niebuhr, *The Children of Light and The Children of Darkness*, 1st edn (Chicago IL, University
of Chicago Press, 1944) 127.

[102]   J Hall, *Law, Social Science and Criminal Theory* (Publication of the Comparative Criminal
Law Project, vol 14, 1982) 69–71. Cohn went even further than that when he argued that 'The
protection accorded by the laws and customs to religion as such extends automatically to religious intolerance': Cohn (n 87 above) 258.

human right, no worldly concern, that would be entitled to recognition or protection as against the need or the desire for religious salvation.[103]

There is also a close link between the religious perception of the truth (which will be discussed shortly), the idea of salvation, and intolerance. Hall asked 'whether it is possible for persons in power who believe that their religion is the only true religion to be genuinely tolerant when their "ultimate concerns", their most precious values are at stake'.[104] His answer, with which I concur, is that 'if the ultimate value of the believer, eternal salvation, is at stake why should that believer hesitate to employ any means, including torture, to protect that value?'[105] John Stuart Mill also noticed the central and destructive role the idea of salvation plays when he said that 'the notion that it is one man's duty that another should be religious, was the foundation of all the religious persecutions ever perpetrated, and if admitted, would fully justify them'.[106]

Naturally, the aspiration to gain earthly powers or the related aspiration to influence the public sphere does not have to be linked to the idea of salvation. It could be derived from a mere aspiration to religious exclusivity. Barry pointed out that

> the demand that the public arena should be suffused by religion is not, of course, a demand that it should be suffused by religion in general. Rather, it is a demand that one particular set of doctrines, or one particular religious authority, should be granted a privileged position ... the intention as well as the effect is unequal treatment.[107]

The implications of aspiring to religious exclusivity were also acknowledged by Dworkin who suggested 'polar attitudes' or two models that we can adopt as ideal types to follow in confronting concrete issues concerning religion in a liberal democracy. The first is that of a religious nation that tolerates non-belief. The second is that of a secular nation that tolerates religion.[108] Dworkin claims that 'people who support a tolerant religious society might be

---

[103] Cohn (n 87 above) 262. Cohn also notes that the idea of salvation can be found in almost all religions. It exists not only in popular religions that aspire to universalism but also in local or tribal ones. See also Hall (n 102 above) 77. For a more subtle argument, according to which 'no really religious man can pass the unbeliever by and do nothing', when only the nature or the extent—but not the existence—of the help that should be given to the unbeliever can be disputable, see: S Runciman, *The Medieval Manichee* (Cambridge, Cambridge University Press, 1947) 1.

[104] Hall (n 102 above) 77.

[105] Hall (n 102 above) 77–78.

[106] JS Mill, *On Liberty and The Subjection of Women* (Ware, Wordsworth Classics of World Literature, 1996, first published in 1859) 90.

[107] B Barry, *Culture and Equality: An Egalitarian Critique of Multiculturalism* (Cambridge, Polity Press, 2001) 28.

[108] R Dworkin, *Is Democracy Possible Here?* (Princeton NJ, Princeton University Press, 2006) 56.

tempted to declare the right of religious freedom to be sui generis, a special right reflecting the special importance of religion', and adds that

> they might therefore be tempted to a very narrow view of that right: that it encom-
> passes only the freedom to worship a supernatural being under one description
> rather than another, or in one church dedicated to such worship rather than
> another.[109]

Dworkin does not argue that religion is intolerant by its nature but one may wonder why anyone who would support a model of a tolerant religious society would be tempted by this narrow, unacceptable and indeed intolerant percep-tion of freedom of religion if not because of the intolerant nature of reli-gion itself? In fact, Dworkin's view is similar to Barry's argument, mentioned above, according to which the attempt to describe society in religious terms or the claim to shape the public sphere in the light of religious beliefs is actually a claim for the dominancy of a certain religious belief.

Whatever the exact motives for the religious influence on the political sphere may be, the results of such an influence are well known. Spilka et al said that

> psychologically, the infusion of faith into [the] public domain often functions to
> control thinking and stifle debate. The high valuation of religion introduces a 'stop-
> thinking' quality ... This conveys a moral essence that is not to be questioned. The
> topic in question is now endowed with a sacred quality, and it is strongly implied that
> we must correct what is religiously wrong.[110]

One of the implications of the argument about the link between religion and intolerance is the exclusion of religion from the public sphere, or at the very least, from the political sphere.[111] As this is not the topic of this chapter, I will limit the following discussion to a slightly different argument, ie that all who argue for the exclusion of religion from the public sphere appreciate the great potential of religion to realise its inherently intolerant nature when it has the power to do so. In other words, almost every argument for excluding religion from the political sphere, and I will not try to outline them here, is also an argument about the meaningful links between religion and intolerance, even if only implicitly. Walzer correctly argues that 'the point of separating church and state in the modern regimes is to deny political power to all religions authorities, on the realistic assumption that all of them are at least potentially intolerant'.[112] Bollinger holds a similar view. In trying to explain why religion

---

[109] Dworkin (n 108 above) 60.
[110] Spilka, Hood Jnr, Hunsberger and Gorsuch (n 26 above) 201.
[111] See, for example; W Stark, *The Sociology of Religion* (London, Routledge, 1967) 377: 'every-body will have to acknowledge that, where the principle of toleration reigns supreme, religion can no longer be an integral element in the inclusive culture'.
[112] M Walzer, *On Toleration* (New Haven CT, Yale University Press, 1997) 81.

should be excluded from the public sphere, he stated that 'a large part of the answer, I think, lies in the tremendous potential of religious belief to produce divisive, even explosive, intolerance'.[113] Even Michael McConnell, one of the leading 'pro-religion' scholars in the United States, wrote in two different places that 'Religious competition can be extraordinarily bitter, divisive and destructive, especially when religion is mixed with, and used as an instrument of political struggle';[114] and that 'official state alignment with a single religion was very frequently a source of discord, persecution and even civil war'.[115] Although McConnell cannot be suspected of supporting the argument about the intolerant nature of religion, he offers no other explanation—and I suspect there is none—of the danger of allowing religion into the political sphere or of establishing a state religion.

Iannaccone and Berman applied an interesting economic approach to the issue of excluding religion from the political sphere. Their argument is closely related to the argument regarding the link between religion and intolerance. They made the following comment:

> so why should we worry about political-religious parties? First ... sectarian religious groups enjoy a comparative advantage in certain forms of organised violence. The moment a sect enters the political arena, the stakes associated with winning and losing become much higher, and hence its incentive to employ violence increases ... Second, because religious groups almost always use their political power to repress religious competitors, political activism on the part of *some* groups virtually guaranties the mobilisation of *all* religious groups, further increasing the odds that at least some will resort to violence.[116]

The argument that religions aspire to win control over believers and heretics through gaining political power may support not only the rejection of the establishment of a state religion but also the exclusion of all religions from the political sphere. In a more radical fashion, it may also support not aiding any religion rather than aiding all religions equally. At the very least, it supports what Hume called 'philosophical indifference' to all religions. Hume's argument is that

> if he (a magistrate) admits only one religion among his subjects, he must sacrifice, to an uncertain prospect of tranquillity, every consideration of public liberty, science, reason, industry, and even his own independency. If he gives indulgence to several

---

[113] L Bollinger, *The Tolerant Society: Freedom of Speech and Extremist Speech in America* (Oxford, Oxford University Press, 1986) 188.

[114] M McConnell and RA Posner, 'An Economic Approach to Issues of Religious Freedom' (1989) 56 *University of Chicago Law Review* 1, 4.

[115] M McConnell, 'The Problem of Singling Out Religion' (2000) 50 *DePaul Law Review* 1, 22.

[116] LR Iannaccone and E Berman, 'Religious Extremism: The Good, the Bad, and the Deadly' (2006) 128 *Public Choice* 109, 121.

sects, which is the wiser maxim, he must preserve a very philosophical indifference to all of them, and carefully restrain the pretensions of the prevailing sect; otherwise he can expect nothing but endless disputes, quarrels, factions, persecutions, and civil commotions.[117]

Hume in fact required more than just 'philosophical indifference'. Suffice it to quote, with total agreement, his clearly rhetorical question: 'Is there any maxim in politics more certain and infallible, than that both the number and authority of priests should be confined within very narrow limits, and that the civil magistrate ought, for ever, to keep his *fasces* and *axes* from such dangerous hands?'[118] Hume did not argue, of course, for the separation of the Church and State but for state-funded established religion, yet his view relied on the need to supervise and control the intolerant nature of religion, or, more accurately, on the need to prevent or minimise competition between religions that would increase sectarianism, extremism and violence.[119]

C. The Third Reason: Sacred Traditions, Customs and Symbols

Mensching argued that an important reason for religious intolerance is religion's tendency to preserve its tradition and to protect it from any infringement or attack. This phenomenon, according to Mensching, is to be observed in all religions.[120] Every so often, religious believers follow the old traditions without a real understanding of their origins, meaning and purpose. All too often, they do not care about the origins, meaning and purpose of a tradition or a custom. At times, they even deliberately avoid inquiring about them, precisely because they perceive them as sacred. The consequences of this attitude are two-fold. First, religious traditions are sometimes observed in a superficial or mechanical way. Secondly, and more importantly, the religious observer is expected to be highly intolerant of any attempt to criticise or modify these traditions. If seeing traditions and customs as sacred is a reason for religious intolerance, then it may be the case that the more sacred traditions and customs a certain religion has, the more it is likely to be intolerant. Judaism and Islam immediately come to mind as two central examples of religions that not

---

[117] D Hume, *Dialogues Concerning Natural Religion* (The Hafner Library of Classics, Edited and Introduction by Henry D Aiken, 1963, first published 1779) 90–91.

[118] Hume (n 117 above) 90.

[119] For the idea that such competition may be desirable as it creates more religious groups, each of which has less capacity to influence the government, see: Iannaccone and Berman (n 116 above) 123. See also pp 123–24 for Adam Smith's arguments for the separation of Church and State.

[120] Mensching (n 88 above) 120.

only regulate numerous trivial and everyday acts but also perceive these acts, or the command to perform them, as sacred. These trivial acts then become part of the unified, seamless web of a religious way of life (eg dietary require-ments; dress codes; times of daily prayers; observing the day of rest by avoid-ing numerous trivial chores and actions; and so on).

Judaism and Islam underwent a process of transforming trivial acts to reli-gious and sacred ones by developing the original sacred scripts and by add-ing numerous commands and prohibitions to those found in those scripts. These and other religions have transformed what originally was merely cus-tom, social habit or practical answers to everyday problems, into a matter of divine law, thus transforming an ancient answer to an ancient, often now irrelevant, problem, into a divine and sacred command or prohibition. This process results in greater intolerance towards those who deviate from the old traditions, who do not enable religious believers to follow them, or even those who do not pay adequate respect to those who follow them.

Apart from the intolerance that results from perceiving traditions, symbols and customs as sacred, there is also a connection between religion being either public or institutional, the characteristic of sacredness—and intolerance. An institutionalised religion, like any other institution, has to have some sort of hierarchy. When a hierarchy is a religious one, it becomes sacred, along with the inequality that results from its very existence. A sacred institutional and personal hierarchy can only lead to greater intolerance towards those who deviate from the dominant religious doctrines, those who challenge the exist-ing hierarchy and, naturally, towards heretics. Hunsberger and Jackson con-cluded that

> religion provides meaning as an important way for people to participate in their societies and derive value from them. This participation can involve legitimization of social structures and traditions by means of explanations and justifications for the social status quo ... hence, religiosity may be associated with prejudice if religion justifies existing inequalities.[121]

It is in the nature of religion to have an intolerant attitude towards those who disregard its traditions and symbols and as long as these traditions and sym-bols are perceived as sacred. Surely this is the nature of Judaism, Christianity and Islam, and other similar religions. How does that intolerance differ from the attitude of the patriot who is willing to harm those who burn his country's flag; the attitude of the football fan who will do the same to anyone who des-ecrates his team's symbols; or the attitude of members of an exclusive English club who keep strictly to the old traditions?

---

[121] Hunsberger and Jackson (n 52 above) 817.

The answer is two-fold. First, the religious response towards those who disregard or desecrate religious symbols or traditions is more likely to be exceptionally harsh (assuming that the group possesses the power to execute its intolerance), mainly because non-religious practices, traditions and symbols are rarely perceived as sacred, even by those who care deeply about them. This is not to say that the religiosity of traditions and symbols always generates greater commitment to them, yet it does appear to be the usual case. It is important to appreciate that I do not discuss here commitments to views and ideologies (in this case the argument about the uniqueness of religious commitment does not apply in the same way) but commitments merely to traditions and symbols. Perhaps the combination of the notion of sacredness, the assumption that religious symbols and traditions are dictated or inspired by a higher being, the idea of salvation, and the fear of imminent punishment or worse—punishment in the after-life—leads to a special commitment to religious symbols and traditions, and to a greater willingness to harm those who offend what they represent. Secondly, the number of sacred symbols and traditions within religion is significantly higher than within any other cultural or social practice. A non-religious person (a patriot, a football fan or a member of an exclusive club) would normally have a very limited number of symbols and traditions that he regards as of great importance; or as essential to his lifestyle, personhood and identity; or simply as 'quasi-sacred'. A religious person, on the other hand, would normally have a greater number of such symbols and traditions, precisely because the idea of sacredness is central to religion and because of the absolute nature of religion (as will be discussed shortly), ie because of its tendency to regulate numerous aspects of human life.

Therefore, with respect to the links between religion and intolerance, it is both the kind and the extent of the religious commitment to the protection of traditions, customs and symbols that differentiate religion from non-religious groups, cultures and individuals.

D. The Fourth Reason: The Religious Perception of the 'Truth'

Mensching argued that 'whenever one's own religion is regarded as *the* truth in an intolerant manner, the many other religions appear as a source of annoyance and as something that must be overcome for the sake of one's own faith'.[122] The connection between the religious perception of the truth and intolerance is stronger than that described by Mensching. It can be understood from Mensching's description that one's religion can often be regarded

---

[122] Mensching (n 88 above) 155.

as *the* truth in a manner that is not necessarily intolerant. I suspect, however, that more often than not a person cannot regard his religion as *the* truth in any way that is not intolerant. Hall puts it well when he argues that

> the belief that one orthodoxy is the only true religion—is an operative factor in persecution … a belief in the absolute truth of religious doctrine and dogmas, a corollary of the claim of possession of the only true religion, is logically incompatible with genuine toleration.[123]

McClosky and Brill argue in a same manner that

> the tendency for the faithful of one religion to display intolerance towards the followers of another arises, in part, out of the nature of religion itself, which is usually based on some form of 'revealed' truth … the types of freedom of expression and exchange thought by civil libertarians to be essential to the discovery of truth are less valued by people of strong religious convictions than by the secular-minded.[124]

This characteristic of religion is rarely concealed. Religions openly declare themselves as the sole carriers of the only truth, at least concerning matters and questions they aspire to answer, or—in their view—do answer. This is true not only regarding the obvious examples (Judaism, Islam and Christianity) but also regarding less obvious examples such as Buddhism, where one of its commentaries states that 'there is no other way to gain salvation than through his (i.e. Buddha's) teaching'.[125] It seems that, as far as the religious perception of the truth is concerned, religions will go as far as acknowledging that there is some truth in some other religions, but surely not in non-religious beliefs. This is, of course, unsurprising, as the same thing can also be said about atheists. Surely they will not acknowledge that there is some truth in religious beliefs. Similarly, most scientists will not accept the theory of intelligent design as a credible theory that can challenge the theory of evolution. Are both atheists (or evolutionary scientists) and religious adherents intolerant in the same way, simply because they categorically deny the truth of incompatible views, and—let us assume—are willing to treat differently and negatively those who act upon these views? The answer to this question would have to be 'no', even if we ignore the exact content of the competing views, or simply assume that the content of these views are not intolerant as such. This is so because of the difference between reason and faith.

It is one thing for someone to claim that he knows the truth about X, that X exists or that X does not exist, if this claim is based on the existence (or lack) of evidence, and when that individual is willing to change his mind according

---

[123] Hall (n 102 above) 69, 78.
[124] McClosky and Brill (n 42 above) 103, 407.
[125] Mensching (n 88 above) 126. That led Mensching to the conclusion that, in Buddhism, much like in the Catholic Church, for example, error can never be tolerated.

to new evidence. It is another thing to base one's claim about the truth merely on faith and to be unwilling to change one's view regardless of the existence of opposing evidence or the lack of any supporting evidence. This is true, of course, when the claim regarding 'the truth' is such that it requires, by its nature, evidential support or evidential-based reasoning. All other things being equal, the less someone is willing to change his mind about X, or to consider the possibility that he may be wrong about X, and the more X is of importance to him, the more he will hold intolerant views towards those who hold contrary views about X. If this is true and if religion, as such, leads to such an attitude regarding more issues than most non-religious beliefs do, it becomes clear, yet again, how the link between religion and intolerance is unique.

The religious claim to exclusivity in holding the truth was also discussed by Brian Barry. Barry argued that 'there is no reason why adherents of different beliefs system cannot exist peacefully' and that religions 'will clash only if there is something specific to fight about. Difference as such is not a source of conflict. What causes conflict among adherents of different religious faiths is their leading to incompatible demands'.[126] Barry also mentions that, in the Roman world, religious tolerance was the result of the non-exclusiveness of religious faith. Many contemporary religions, however, and surely most of the popular and influential ones, do claim exclusivity, and it is not surprising to find that the same religions do make incompatible demands. This is not a coincidence but a result of the nature of some religions. It seems that Barry is aware of this, since, when he describes the 'conditions for conflict', he adds that 'given that these are the conditions of conflict, it is scarcely surprising that the two proselytising monotheistic religions, Christianity and Islam, have been implicated in so much of it'.[127]

The religious claim to exclusivity in holding the truth becomes more interesting and problematic when we examine Judaism, Islam and Christianity. Not only does each of these religions claim exclusivity in knowing the truth but they also have the religious idea of being the 'chosen one'. Moreover, these religions offer different and contradictory understandings or interpretations of the same historical events. When each religion sees itself as the chosen one and when their traditions and narratives cannot be reconciled in any reasonable way or, indeed, at all, intra-religious intolerance becomes almost inevitable.[128]

---

[126] Barry (n 107 above) 24.
[127] Barry (n 107 above) 24–25.
[128] See also: A Beit-Hallahmi and M Argyle, *The Psychology of Religious Behavior, Belief and Experience* (London, Routledge, 1997) 220; Beit-Hallahmi (n 5 above) 147.

Although the argument about the religious claim to exclusivity in holding the truth applies to almost all religions as such, it gains extra strength when we examine monotheistic religions. It can be argued that, in these religions, the absence of tolerance results from their very nature. However, perhaps the same can be said about polytheistic religions. In other words, the difference between monotheistic and polytheistic religions regarding the relation between them and intolerance may be a matter of quantity or degree rather than one of quality or principle. Unfortunately, there are no studies that examine the links between polytheistic religions and intolerance. Therefore, one can only speculate about the nature and extent of such links.

There is a connection between the claim to exclusivity in holding the truth and religion's will to gain political control or 'earthly powers'. Niebuhr mentioned this point in regard to Catholicism when he stated that 'its doctrinal position is that the true religion is known and validated and that it is the business of the state to support the true religion'.[129] There is no reason to believe that this connection exists only in Catholicism. On the contrary, it can be found in Judaism, Islam and in other Christian denominations as well.

Here, again, it can be claimed that what was said above also applies to non-religious beliefs and ideologies. To a certain extent, this is doubtless true. Every theory, whether moral, political, social, legal and so on, sees X as true or attractive and its opposite (or anything incompatible with X) as false or undesirable. More specifically, every person who seriously holds any meaningful theory on how people and institutions should behave, or how the behaviour (or nature) of people and institutions should be understood, must make adverse judgements about incompatible theories, and perhaps even about those who hold these theories. This fact does not undermine the argument that religion is, again, unique, and it is unique for various reasons. These reasons are the other characteristics of religion under discussion in this chapter. All of them have a slightly different meaning when read together with the argument about the religious perception of the truth.

Therefore, the argument that religion claims to hold the one and only truth should be read together with the above arguments about the sacred nature of religious prohibitions and commands, and about the religious aspiration to gain formal, earthly control in order for religion to be able to impose its perception of the truth on others. The argument that religion claims to hold the one and only truth should also be read together with the following arguments about religious absolutism and the intolerant content of religious values and beliefs. It may be true that almost every person who holds a certain theory

---

[129] Niebuhr (n 101 above) 126.

about morality and society has to make adverse judgements about competing theories (or their holders). Hence, almost every moral or social theory has at least the potential of being intolerant. Nevertheless, only a few aim to gain state power in order to impose their beliefs on society; perceive their utterances as sacred and, therefore, above rational criticism and evaluation; strictly regulate multiple aspects of people's public and private affairs, and do so in a way that places significant limits on people's free choice and autonomy, or in order to form such limits. If there are non-religious ideologies or theories that share these features, then we could say that the link between them and intolerance is similar to that between religion and intolerance.

E. The Fifth Reason: Religious Absolutism

Religious absolutism can simply mean that religion has views about almost every aspect of human life. A similar way to describe religious absolutism would be to apply Rawlsian terminology and describe religion as a conception which is 'fully comprehensive' in the sense that 'it covers all recognized values and virtues within one rather precisely articulated system'.[130] Moreover, religion is probably the most paradigmatic example of a fully comprehensive conception.

Not all religions aspire to regulate or influence most aspects of their followers' lives, yet it would not be far-fetched to argue that this is exactly what many religions do, albeit to varying extents. This is certainly a notable feature of Judaism, Christianity and Islam. Religious absolutism can take the form of public religion, ie taking part in the political sphere in order to extend the religious influence beyond personal relations to the relations between individuals and the state. It could also concentrate on the private sphere and regulate vast numbers of important and trivial private acts alike. It could also be a mixture of both, as in the case of Judaism and Islam.

Naturally, there is a close connection between religious absolutism and the religious claim to exclusivity in holding the truth. Mensching argued accurately that 'it can be observed everywhere in universal religions that the claim to absoluteness is founded, explicitly or implicitly, upon the conviction that one's own religious community is the sole possessor of truth'.[131] Indeed, the religious claim to absoluteness is usually accompanied by the religious claim to exclusivity. Those religions who wish to regulate or influence wide aspects of

---

[130] J Rawls, *Political Liberalism* (New York, Columbia University Press, 1993) 13.
[131] Mensching (n 88 above) 127.

their adherents' lives also wish to be the only authority to do so. Carter stresses this point, albeit in an essay that has completely different purposes to those of this chapter:

> a religion is, at its heart, a way of denying the authority of the rest of the world; it is a way of saying to fellow human beings and to the state those fellow humans have erected, 'No, I will not accede to your will'.[132]

John Stuart Mill also recognised religion's tendency to absolutism when he talked about

> religion, the most powerful of the elements which have entered into the formation of moral feeling, having almost always been governed either by the ambition of a hierarchy, seeking control over every department of human conduct, or by the spirit of Puritanism.[133]

He then went on to warn about an obvious danger that such absolutism can bring about, saying that separation between spiritual and temporal authority is a condition for preventing interference by law in the details of people's private lives.[134]

There is another way to explain the connection between religious absolutism and religious intolerance. Niebuhr noted that 'religious-cultural diversity may prove the most potent source of communal discord because varying answers to the final question about the meaning of life produce conflicting answers on all proximate issues of moral order and political organization'.[135] In other words, religion does not have to directly regulate various and specific aspects of human life in order for it to be considered as absolutist and thus intolerant, but it is the very fact that religion aims to answer the one question about the meaning of life, or other related questions, that necessarily extends its influence to personal and public morality.[136]

A final aspect of religious absolutism that strengthens the link between religion and intolerance is the tendency that religion has to provide absolute answers to central as well as to relatively insignificant issues, showing minimal or no willingness to compromise. Eisgruber and Sager mention that 'the

---

[132] SL Carter, *The Culture of Disbelief: How American Law and Politics Trivialize Religious Devotion* (New York, Anchor Books, 1994) 41.

[133] Mill (n 106 above) 16.

[134] Mill (n 106 above) 16.

[135] Niebuhr (n 101 above) 125.

[136] For a list of these questions see the: Pope Paul VI, 'Declaration on the Relation of the Church to Non-Christian Religions' (1965) *Documents of Vatican II*: 'What is man? What is the meaning, the aim of our life? What is moral good, what sin? Whence suffering and what purpose does it serves? Which is the road to true happiness? What are death, judgment and retribution after death? What, finally, is that ultimate inexpressible mystery which encompasses our existence: whence do we come, and where are we going?'

potential of religious belief to be arbitrarily demanding, to be greedy … is compounded by the possible all-or-nothing quality of religious dictates'.[137] Religious commands do not just tend to be absolute or categorical. They almost always are. Though this kind of absolutism does not have to result in unjustified intolerance, it does increase the tendency to such intolerance.

Lastly, the argument about religious absolutism does not stand alone. It should be read alongside the argument that religion (through its agents, ie religious leaders and institutions) aims to gain control over its believers, believers in other religions and heretics. The combination of these two arguments explains why the more absolute a religion is, the more it is likely to be an intolerant one.

F. The Sixth Reason: Religious Faith, Morality and the Law

In many religions (eg Judaism, Buddhism, Christianity and Islam), faith and morality are inseparable. Religious law and religious morality are also unified and both are eternal. Since they were not made by humans, they cannot be changed or modified by humans—at least not beyond a certain, limited extent. Naturally, religious reforms do occur and different interpretations of the divine law are adopted from time to time, but only within relatively narrow limits.

Identifying law and morality with the divine is a source of intolerance, as it allows less criticism and deviation than is possible with human law. It also does not require or even allow self-observation and scepticism, as opposed to secular law and, to a lesser extent, morality.[138] Religious commands are not just normative. They are taken categorically by their adherents.[139] They are 'exclusionary reasons' ie reasons that exclude other, 'non-religious reasons' from the balance of reasons.[140] When a religious command applies to a certain issue the religious believer will not act upon non-religious reasons, as they were excluded from the balance of reasons by the religious command.

Identifying law and morality with the divine, ie seeing the law as sacred, means that the false interpretation of sacred religious-legal texts is (or at least

---

[137] Eisgruber and Sager (n 88 above) 1257. See also P Roberts and E Lester, 'The Distinctive Paradox of Religious Tolerance: Active Tolerance as a Mean between Passive Tolerance and Recognition' (2006) 20 *Public Affairs Quarterly* 347, 351.

[138] Cohn mentioned this point with regard to Judaism, Christianity and Islam when he said that 'it is these monotheist religions which do not suffer dissents from within' and more generally that 'none of the monotheistic religions succeeded—or cared—to deal with dissidents from within in liberal and non-violent ways': Cohn (n 87 above) 40, 99.

[139] Leiter (n 4 above) 37.

[140] For more about the nature of exclusionary reasons see: J Raz, *Practical Reasons and Norms*, 2nd edn (Oxford, Oxford University Press, 1999) 35–36, 39–40.

can be) as misguided as disregarding religious law altogether. As human-made law is not sacred, it is easier, regarding such law, to draw a distinction between legitimate or reasonable interpretations of the law, unreasonable interpretations of the law, and complete disregard of the law. Even a Dworkinian interpreter would agree that the fact that there is one true answer to a legal question does not mean that we know what this answer is regarding each and every case; therefore a sense of scepticism remains. Within a religious legal system, the distinction mentioned above does not exist or at least does not carry with it any significant implications. If the religious command and the religious legal text are sacred, then their interpretation and application are also sacred. Any non-compliance with them should not be tolerated, regardless of whether the non-compliance is based on complete rejection of religious law as such or on disagreement about the proper way to interpret religious law. Moreover, at times, the religious intolerant response to challenges from within that religion would be harsher than that aimed at external challenges, whether religious or non-religious ones. This may be so because of pragmatic reasons, since, in most cases, religious institutions, communities or officials possess more power regarding members of their community than non-members (whether believers of other religions or non-believers), but this could also be the result of a doctrinal, principled approach.

McClosky and Brill concentrated on faith in divine revelations and received truth in their attempt to explain religious intolerance. In their view, and because of the above reasons, highly or truly religious persons 'are less likely to learn that a belief in freedom requires one to tolerate and legally protect an extraordinary variety of opinions, ideas, lifestyles, and practices, even including challenges to religion itself and the preaching of atheism'.[141]

Identifying law and morality with the divine is a source of intolerance also because, in the majority of religions, most religious-moral commands and prohibitions were enacted in earlier times when intolerance towards women, heretics, homosexuals, adherents to the 'wrong' religion, and so on, was the prevailing norm. When the core of the religious attitude towards the 'other' was created in an early and generally intolerant era, and when this core was believed to be determined by the divine and, therefore, on the whole, unchangeable, contemporary religious intolerance becomes almost inevitable. From the empirical point of view, it is helpful to refer to Spilka's observation that:

> It is not surprising that religion is related to people's attitudes on a host of morality related issues. Typically, people who are religious (as measured in many different ways) are 'more conservative' in their attitudes. In general, those who are more

---

[141] McClosky and Brill (n 42 above) 412.

religious show more opposition to abortion, AIDS education, divorce, pornography, contraception, premarital sexuality, homosexuality, feminism, nudity in advertising, suicide, euthanasia, amniocentesis … Highly religious individuals are also more likely to support marriage, capital punishment, vengeance, traditional sex roles, conservative political parties, more severe criminal sentences, and censorship of sex and violence in the mass media.[142]

These findings are meaningful in several ways. First, they demonstrate the extremely close connection between religion and morality. Secondly, they remind us how the identification of religion with morality is closely connected to religious absolutism, which was mentioned above as the fifth reason for religious intolerance. This identification implies that religion has a viewpoint regarding a vast number of issues (in this case—moral issues) relating to people's lives, and, while non-religious people may not feel strongly about each and every issue specified above, the highly devoted religious person does have or is more likely to have strong feelings about all of these issues, as a direct result or his religiosity. Thirdly, it should be noted that, while some of the attitudes concerning the issues mentioned above can be classified as merely 'conservative' and do not raise special problems regarding intolerance, other attitudes are clearly an expression of intolerance. It seems that the rationale or the inevitable outcome of the religious position regarding the above issues limits one's autonomy for moral reasons that have very little to do with either Mill's relatively narrow perception of the harm principle or Raz's broader perception of it. As noted above, the harm principle and the principle of autonomy help to identify intolerant attitudes and, in turn, justify, in principle, an intolerant response to them.

Yet, it should be borne in mind that it is one thing to hold intolerant views about a certain issue and quite another to act upon this view when one has the power to do so. As Spilka rightly noted, 'although associations between faith and moral attitudes are informative, they do not always accurately predict how religion will relate to moral *behavior*'.[143] The latter was the subject of the empirical research that was discussed above.

An interesting attempt was made by Jones to explain religious intolerance and actual violence by focusing not on the divinity of religious law and morals but on the very existence of a divine entity. Jones suggested that religious intolerance and violence may be rooted in factors that may be seen, at first, as unrelated to religion itself, such as shame and humiliation. Numerous studies have suggested that there is a close link between religiously driven terrorism

---

[142] Spilka, Hood Jnr, Hunsberger and Gorsuch (n 26 above) 418. These findings are the result of numerous studies that were mentioned by Spilka and were omitted from the quote above.

[143] Spilka, Hood Jnr, Hunsberger and Gorsuch (n 26 above) 419.

and experiences of shame and humiliation.[144] More generally, forensic psychologists often emphasise the connection between shame, humiliation and violence. Jones attempts to establish the link between religion and divinity on the one hand, and shame, humiliation and violence on the other, by arguing that:

> While often rooted in social and political circumstances, shame and humiliation are profoundly psychological, and often spiritual, conditions. By holding out an absolute and perfect ideal—whether it is a divine being or a perfect guru or master or sacred text—against which all mortals inevitably fall short and by insisting on the 'infinite qualitative difference' between human beings and the ideal, religions can easily exacerbate and play upon any natural human tendency toward feelings of shame and humiliation. I would suggest the more a religion exalts its ideal, or portrays the divine as an overpowering presence and emphasizes the gulf between finite human beings and that ideal ... the more it contributes to and reinforces experiences of shame and humiliation.[145]

These experiences of shame and humiliation may lead to violent acts towards others. Jones' description of the links between religion and violence is interesting, though perhaps he should have differentiated between three possible cases. In the first case, humiliation and shame are caused to X by Y's acts or omissions that are unrelated to X's religious belief. This may result in the violent acts of X towards Y. This may be the case when, for example, one's state or territory is occupied by another state that systematically infringes the human or political rights of the occupied. In the second case, humiliation and shame are caused to X by Y's acts or omissions that are related to X's religious beliefs. In the third case, humiliation and shame are created by X's own religious beliefs or practices that, in turn, lead to the violent acts of X towards groups that are condemned by his religion, either explicitly or implicitly, or simply towards those who, at least in his view, threaten the values of his religion. The link between religion, humiliation, shame and violence may take various forms, then, but, in any event, it should not be ignored.

G. The Seventh Reason: The Content of Religious Values and Beliefs

Here, I refer to religious values, beliefs, commands and prohibitions included in the formal scripts and authoritative interpretations of them. Although the argument about the intolerant content of religious values is a central argument,

---

[144] For a survey of some of the main studies and central examples, see: JW Jones, 'Why Does Religion Turn Violent? A Psychoanalytic Exploration of Religious Terrorism' (2006) 93 *Psychoanalytic Review* 167, 168–70.
[145] Jones (n 144 above) 169.

I will not explore it here in great detail as this is the only argument that cannot be easily generalised to cover all religions. There is nothing in religion, as such, that must entail intolerant commands and prohibitions regarding the 'other'. A religion can, in principle, preach only love, acceptance or tolerance. Even such a religion may still be intolerant but to a very limited extent and in an uninteresting way. It may be intolerant to the same extent as any ideology, belief or theory, which is intolerant towards those who are incompatible with it. Such a religion will not necessarily be linked to intolerance in any unique or meaningful way. Therefore, as far as the seventh argument goes, religions are to be regarded as intolerant whenever and insofar as intolerant values and beliefs are found at their core, or when these values and beliefs are an integral part of the religious adherents' holistic way of life. Having said that, it is a truism that most religions indeed hold an intolerant attitude towards the 'other', although the nature and extent of this attitude may vary. There is no doubt that some religious contexts reinforce open and blunt prejudice and intolerance. Other religious contexts, as argued by Hunsberger and Jackson, 'may reinforce implicit bias through nonproscription or encouragement of subtle prejudice (e.g., heterosexism) and/or exposure to social hierarchies in which power holders are consistently members of socially dominant groups'.[146]

If we limit our discussion to Judaism, Islam and Christianity, then the fact that their formal scripts and authoritative interpretations reveal significant intolerant attitudes towards the other is, I believe, well known and can be regarded as a matter of common knowledge.[147] It seems unnecessary to quote from the Bible, the Koran or the New Testament (nor from later additions to them) in order to establish this argument.

In a remarkable decision that dealt with the participation of an Islamic political party in a Turkish election, the European Court of Human Rights (ECtHR) made some extraordinary observations about the nature of the *Sharia*, the Islamic law:

> the Court considers that sharia, which faithfully reflects the dogmas and divine rules laid down by religion, is stable and invariable. Principles such as pluralism in the political sphere or the constant evolution of public freedoms have no place in it. The Court notes that, when read together, the offending statements, which contain explicit references to the introduction of sharia, are difficult to reconcile with the fundamental principles of democracy, as conceived in the Convention taken as a whole. It is difficult to declare one's respect for democracy and human rights while at the same time supporting a regime based on sharia, which clearly diverges from

---

[146] Hunsberger and Jackson (n 52 above) 820.

[147] For the complex relationship between Islam, the *Sharia* and the concept of Jihad (a holy or 'just' war), see: J Kelsay, *Arguing the Just War in Islam* (Cambridge MA, Harvard University Press, 2007).

Convention values, particularly with regard to its criminal law and criminal procedure, its rules on the legal status of women and the way it intervenes in all spheres of private and public life in accordance with religious precepts.[148]

Similar things can be said about Jewish religious law and about certain sects within Christianity and probably within other, similar religions as well.

I accept, of course, that the same religious texts that advocate intolerance may also reveal tolerant views or complex attitudes towards various types of sin or sinner in changeable circumstances, as well as attitudes such as 'hate the sin but love the sinner'.[149] Many accurate observations can be made about the Bible, the Koran and the New Testament. Perceiving these texts as coherent is not one of them. These texts suffer from major incoherencies and include numerous contradictory attitudes. These texts can inspire tolerant, kind and loving persons and at the same time prescribe hate, persecution and even genocide. This is why the Inquisition, the witch hunt and the Ku Klux Klan are not a distortion of Christianity; the Islamic State and the Taliban regimes are not a distortion of Islam; and the highly racist attitude of religious groups in Israel is not a distortion of Judaism. These phenomena result from reasonable interpretations of religious scripts—and at times rely on clear religious commands or permissions.

In these cases, where religious scripts contain both tolerant and intolerant contents, the question would be which attitude is dominant and, of course, how religious people actually behave and what they really think about the 'other'. These questions were answered above where the empirical links between religion and intolerance were described and explained.

H. Religion and Pragmatic Tolerance

One last argument remains before concluding the description of the theoretical links between religion and intolerance. According to this argument, religions tend to adopt a pragmatic, not to say a cynical approach, towards the principle of tolerance. Therefore, it is not the case that religions cannot ever tolerate the 'other' in any way. Yet, all too often religious tolerance will not be a principled tolerance, one that I call 'tolerance as a right', but merely

---

[148] *Case of Refah Partisi (The Welfare Party) and Others v Turkey* (Application nos 41340/98, 41342/98, 41343/98 and 41344/98), judgment of 31 July 2001 (ECtHR), paragraph 72. For an argument that this case exemplifies how the ECtHR uses the 'militant democracy' doctrine to curtail freedom of religion in order to protect 'substantive' conceptions of democracy, see: P Macklem, 'Guarding the Perimeter: Militant Democracy and Religious Freedom in Europe' (2012) 19 *Constellations* 575.

[149] For a possible positive yet complicated effect of the approach of 'hate the sin but love the sinner' on intrinsic religious people's attitude towards homosexuals see Hood (n 1 above) 416–17.

a pragmatic, temporary one that will be easily transformed into intolerance when circumstances change, eg when the religious institutions or community gain the power to persecute others. Mill addressed this point when he said that

> those who first broke the yoke of what called itself the Universal Church, were in general as little willing to permit difference of religious opinions as that church itself. But when the heat of the conflict was over … minorities, seeing that they had no chance of becoming majorities, were under the necessity of pleading to those whom they could not convert, for permission to differ.[150]

Niebuhr added, in the specific context of Catholic-pragmatic-tolerance, that 'Catholicism does not claim the right to suppress dissident faiths if it happens to have merely a majority in the nation. It must have an overwhelming majority so that the suppression of dissidence will not imperil the public peace'.[151] Cohn stressed this point from a more general perspective when he mentioned what he called 'the astonishing fact' that 'persecuted religious minorities would, as soon as they themselves become a majority and obtain the necessary power, start on their part to persecute other religious minorities'.[152] Lastly, McClosky and Brill also join this line of argument by saying that 'most advocates of religious freedom were not champions of democracy or advocates of civil liberties as such. Many, upon gaining a measure of security for themselves, were inclined to turn oppressor and persecute the disciples of other religions'.[153]

All the above suggests that religion has an inherent tendency to intolerance. At most, it is capable of exercising pragmatic tolerance which is, usually, not the kind of tolerance that can be perceived as a virtue (most scholars in fact do not perceive it as tolerance at all). This view is supported by the principled arguments and empirical findings discussed above concerning the link between religion and intolerance. This view explains why there is a positive correlation between religiosity and intolerance amongst Jews in Israel, whereas religious Jews in the United States are more tolerant than all Christian religious groups there (but not more than non-religious Americans). The most comprehensive survey about the links between religiosity and intolerance, which was conducted amongst nearly 150,000 respondents, also reinforces this view by finding that 'religions tend to increase intolerance only when they are dominant. Thus, Catholics are more intolerant in Catholic countries, but not in Protestant countries; Protestants are more intolerant in Protestant countries, but not in Catholic ones'.[154] Therefore, whenever we do encounter cases of religious

---

[150] Mill (n 106 above) 11. See also p 86.
[151] Niebuhr (n 101 above) 127.
[152] Cohn (n 87 above) 268.
[153] McClosky and Brill (n 42 above) 103.
[154] Guiso, Sapienza and Zingales (n 72 above) 264.

tolerance we should inquire whether these cases result from acknowledging the other's right to be tolerated or whether they result from a lack of power to carry out an efficient intolerant attitude (or from other pragmatic reasons).

I. Theoretical Links—Conclusions

Up to this point, I have suggested seven reasons or characteristics that explain why there are meaningful empirical links between religion and intolerance. This explanation is by no means exhaustive. There may be, of course, other ways of describing and explaining the links between religion and intolerance, prejudice and violence.[155] Apart from the seventh and last characteristic, not all of these characteristics must exist in order for the argument about the link between religion and intolerance to hold true. In that sense, the argument is a case-sensitive one, since some religions will be considered inherently intolerant, even when they share only some of these characteristics and to various degrees.

One way to interpret the links between religion and intolerance is to say that, whenever a specific religion meets the characteristics that have been presented so far, it should be regarded as an intolerant religion. A different way of understanding the main argument thus far is to acknowledge that many religions share all or most of these characteristics in a way that makes them intolerant by their nature. Some religions may lack some of these characteristics in a way that could lead to the conclusion that they are not intolerant by nature, but these cases are quite rare. John Stuart Mill generalised this point accurately when he said that

> in the minds of almost all religious persons, even in the most tolerant countries, the duty of toleration is admitted with tacit reserves. One person will bear with dissent in matters of church government, but not of dogma; another can tolerate everybody, short of a Papist or an Unitarian; another, everyone who believes in revealed religion; a few extend their charity a little further, but stop at the belief in a God and in a future state.[156]

This is a plausible interpretation of the above assertions, although it is quite difficult to support it by empirical findings.

A further argument is that religions that have the characteristics described above have them in a unique way that distinguishes them from other beliefs or ideologies. Indeed, the fact that some ideologies or political theories claim to be the sole holders of the only truth, or, more generally, the fact that other

---

[155] For a survey of a few relevant theories of religion that connect it with violence see: RA Segal, 'The Frazerian Roots of Contemporary Theories of Religion and Violence' (2007) 37 *Religion* 4.

[156] Mill (n 106 above) 11–12.

beliefs or ideologies also possess some of the seven characteristics, may result in them being regarded as intolerant by their nature, although this does not mean that there is nothing special about religion in the light of these seven reasons. The fact that only religion has all or most of these characteristics, and the fact that only religion—by definition—could have some of these characteristics make it a special case regarding the principle of tolerance.

IV. IS THE CO-EXISTENCE OF RELIGION AND PREJUDICE PARADOXICAL?

In his classic book, Allport made the following, much-quoted observation: 'The role of religion is paradoxical. It makes and unmakes prejudice. While the creeds of the great religions are universalistic, all stressing brotherhood; the practices of these creeds are frequently divisive and brutal'.[157] Hunsberger and Jackson suggested that the co-existence of religion and prejudice is indeed paradoxical. In their view 'religiosity no doubt is usually experienced as a vehicle through which one does good, and as such might be expected to mitigate against prejudice'.[158] They suggested three explanations for this paradox, or, more specifically, three explanations for how people are able to maintain a tolerant self-image while holding intolerant attitudes or engaging in discriminatory behaviour. Their first argument is that 'the coexistence of religious teaching related to tolerance and prejudice among religious individuals seems to be a contradiction only if prejudice is defined too narrowly, in terms of antipathy'.[159] They propose that even positive attitudes towards other groups can be construed as a form of prejudice in that they can legitimise the unequal treatment of, for example, women. Therefore, people can discriminate or treat other groups unfairly while maintaining a tolerant or egalitarian self-image.

Their second argument is that religious teaching that advocates tolerance or acceptance is insufficient to mitigate against intolerance and prejudice, because inter-group responses also involve implicit or unconscious attitudes. Hunsberger and Jackson submit that 'the evidence is clear that implicit biases are often strong ... that people are frequently unaware of the biased nature of their social responses ... and that discrimination can be rationalized in seemingly benign ways'.[160]

Their third argument, it seems, does not explain the paradox but instead implies that actually there is no such paradox in the co-existence of religion and prejudice. Here, they claim that 'some religious teachings themselves contain,

---

[157] Allport (n 25 above) 444.
[158] Hunsberger and Jackson (n 52 above) 819.
[159] Hunsberger and Jackson (n 52 above) 819–20.
[160] Hunsberger and Jackson (n 52 above) 820.

or are perceived to contain, justification for particular negative attitude'.[161] Hunsberger and Jackson conclude their arguments by saying that

> in brief, the content of one's religion (e.g., in proscribing or not proscribing specific prejudice), as well as one's connection to the religious meaning systems (e.g., I, E, Q, RF)—{intrinsic, extrinsic, quest, religious fundamentalism} and the social context may interact in influencing the meanings derived from religion and hence the levels and forms of prejudice.[162]

These observations are extremely helpful, although perhaps there is something more to be said about the general intolerant nature of some religions, ie monotheistic, communal, ethnic or political ones. I explored seven reasons for the link between some religions and intolerance. Only one of these reasons is related to the content of religion, and while social context may indeed matter, I suggest that the other six reasons apply in similar strength to most of the more popular and powerful religions nowadays. These reasons are also central explanations for why religious people are intolerant, regardless of their (or their religion's) tolerant self-presentation and self-image. Therefore, there is no paradox to be solved. Indeed, some religious writings and teachings uphold tolerance, acceptance, compassion and so on. They do that either in general terms or towards specific groups. At the same time, other writings and teachings either do not explicitly uphold tolerance towards specific groups, or implicitly or explicitly promote intolerance towards them. If we add to this the first six reasons mentioned above for the inherent intolerant nature of religion, it is clear why, on the whole and subject to the clarification already mentioned, being religious naturally leads to prejudice and intolerance, whereas any example to the contrary would be an exception to this natural link.

V. CONCLUSION

While the existence of a unique and meaningful link between religion and intolerance is undisputable in academic writing, little work has addressed the issue of why religion and intolerance are associated. In this chapter, I offered possible explanations for the clear relationship between religion and intolerance. Some of these explanations are merely assertions. Others are quite speculative. Presumably they are inevitably speculative. Regardless of how convincing these explanations may be to some people, the fact that there is a link between religious orientation and intolerance remains intact. Despite the fact that the vast majority of scholars agree that meaningful links between religious orientation and prejudice or intolerance do exist, I suspect that, of

---

[161] Hunsberger and Jackson (n 52 above) 821.
[162] Hunsberger and Jackson (n 52 above) 821.

all the variants that might affect attitudes towards tolerance, religion is still the most controversial. This is so for several reasons.

First, there is the difficulty in defining religion and, accordingly, the religious person. Secondly, religion matters. It is the 'master motive' in many people's lives, whether their private lives, their 'public-political' ones or both.[163] Therefore, any unflattering generalisation about it is likely to encounter great emotional, social and political opposition. Thirdly, any meaningful generalisation about religion, or even about specific types of religion, excludes meaningful counter-examples. More specifically, any argument about the intolerant nature of religion, however true, has to face clear and, at times, fundamental examples of religious tolerance both in religious writings and in practice. One can easily find tolerant commands and attitudes in religious writings. There is no need to specify them here as they are well known and on the whole undisputable.[164] At the very least, an argument about the intolerant nature of religion would have to face complex cases that do not fall fully within its scope.[165] Accordingly, any argument about the empirical link between religious orientation and intolerance needs complex clarifications and qualification.

Indeed, it would be silly to argue and impossible to prove that every religious person is intolerant or more intolerant than average in his society. Needless to say, that was not the purpose of this chapter. One clear and repetitive conclusion of numerous studies is that there are different types of religious believers and that their attitude towards tolerance varies significantly. Moreover, the percentages of these types of religious believer are unclear in contemporary,

---

[163] P Tillich, *The Shaking of the Foundation* (New York, Charles Scribner's Sons, 1948) 10–11; M Perry, *Love and Power: The Role of Religion and Morality in American Politics* (Oxford, Oxford University Press, 1991) 73.

[164] For a short description of the perception of tolerance in Judaism, Christianity and Islam, see: N Doe and A Jeremy, 'Justifications for Religious Autonomy' in R O'Dair and A Lewis (eds), *Law and Religion*, Current Legal Issues, vol 4 (Oxford, Oxford University Press, 2001) 421, 434–37. For a claim that the foundations of human rights, especially human dignity, equality and freedom, are to be found in Christianity, see: M de-Blois, 'The Foundation of Human Rights: A Christian Perspective' in P Beaumont (ed), *Christian Perspective on Human Rights and Legal Philosophy* (Milton Keynes, Paternoster Press, 1998) 14. For the principle of tolerance in Islam, see: M Abu-Nimmer, *Nonviolence and Peace Building in Islam: Theory and Practice* (Gainesville FL, University Press of Florida, 2003).

[165] To mention one example, there is a lively debate concerning the current view of the Catholic Church with regard to various issues of freedom of religion, religious tolerance and pluralism, and the Church and the State. Some claim that the Catholic doctrine changed since Vatican II and became less intolerant, whereas others see no doctrinal or practical change. See, for example: LL Christians, 'Religious Law and Secular Law in Democracy: The Evolutions of the Roman Catholic Doctrine After the Second Vatican Council' [2006] *Brigham Young University Law Review* 661; G D'Costa, 'Christian Orthodoxy and Religious Pluralism: A Response to Terrence W. Tilley' (2007) 23 *Modern Theology* 435; TW Tilley, 'Christian Orthodoxy and Religious Pluralism: A Rejoinder to Gavin D'costa' (2007) 23 *Modern Theology* 447.

popular and influential religions, and in different places worldwide. Also, it would be naïve to assume that religious believers can be rigidly divided into three, four or more types. Individuals turn to religion for different reasons and to fulfil different needs. Since every person's needs are unique, no two people seek religion for exactly the same reason or motive.[166]

Nevertheless, the cumulative effect of the principled arguments and the empirical findings lead to a few conclusions that, at the very least, can be seen as valid and accurate generalisations. First, monotheistic, communal, ethnic or public-political religions are intolerant by nature. Alternatively, Judaism, Islam and Christianity are intolerant religions by their nature, and so are other religions that have similar characteristics.

Secondly, the fact that some religions are intolerant by their nature does not mean that all their adherents are intolerant, either at all or to similar extents. A distinction should be made between various personal religious orientations.

Thirdly, on the whole, religious believers, that is, extrinsic, intrinsic and fundamentalist believers, are less tolerant and less committed to human rights and democracy than non-religious persons.

Fourthly, religiosity as such and, specifically, the kind and degree of religiosity, are presumably the clearest and strongest indications of holding intolerant and anti-democratic views.

Fifthly, a central explanation for the empirical findings may be the inherent nature of religion, specifically monotheistic, communal, ethnic or public-political ones. The inherently intolerant nature of these religions may also explain why religious persons are, on the whole, more intolerant than less religious or non-religious persons, despite the fact that some religious texts and teachings openly preach tolerance and acceptance. One speculation may be that these texts and teachings are too vague, general or abstract, and, as such, cannot overcome non-proscribed prejudice or the general inherently intolerant nature of religion.

In this chapter I have explored the empirical links between religion and intolerance and provided reasons for these links. This research does not reflect the whole picture, in the sense that, no doubt, religion is not the source of all evil nor is it purely evil.[167] I will not discuss here, however, the possible virtues

---

[166] S Reiss, 'Why People Turn to Religion: A Motivational Analysis' (2000) 39 *Journal for the Scientific Study of Religion* 47.

[167] If we take terrorism as an example, some scholars blame religious fundamentalism for almost all acts of terrorism that have occurred during the last few decades. A more accurate observation would be that 'Religious fundamentalism, however defined, is unlikely to be a single cause of terrorism, but it may often reflect other aspects of between-group, within-group and personal dynamics that may be causal factors in terrorism'. MB Rogers, 'The Role of Religious Fundamentalism in Terrorist Violence: A Social Psychological Analysis' (2007) 19 *International Review of Psychiatry* 253, 260.

of religion (and they may be psychological, social, and so on).[168] Suffice it to concur completely with Hunsberger and Jackson's conclusion that:

> Religious persons and groups do many helpful, cooperative and tolerant things in our world; there are surely many non-prejudiced religious persons as well as prejudiced nonreligious persons on this planet; and the frequently reported positive associations between religion and prejudice are often specific to certain definitions of religion or religious orientations, targets of prejudice and groups and cultural contexts. In spite of this we cannot ignore the religion-prejudice links found in research on this issue.[169]

Indeed, we cannot ignore the religion-prejudice links found in research on this issue nor can we ignore the reasons for these links. The next step is to explore the legal and political implications of these links.

---

[168] For a short and helpful survey of the consequences and correlates of religiosity, beyond the links between religion and intolerance or prejudice, see Beit-Hallahmi (n 5 above) chapter 6.
[169] Hunsberger and Jackson (n 52 above) 821.

6

Accommodating Religion by Granting Conscientious Exemptions: Is Religion Special?

I. ACCOMMODATING RELIGION BY GRANTING CONSCIENTIOUS EXEMPTIONS

NON-RELIGIOUS STATES CAN accommodate religion or religious demands in numerous ways. The questions of how religion should be accommodated—and to what extent—should be answered by taking into account the theoretical and empirical links between religion and intolerance that were described in Chapter five. These links should be borne in mind when the non-religious state formulates its policy on religious schooling, funding religious activities, presenting religious symbols in the public sphere and so on. In this chapter, however, the discussion will be limited to the issue of religious conscientious exemptions. Granting conscientious exemptions is only one possible way of accommodating religious conscientious objections. It is merely one way among many of protecting freedom of conscience and religion.[1] We shall ask whether religion is special within this context; which possible approaches can be applied when answering this question—and which approach is preferable. Even though the arguments will be presented within the context of religious conscientious exemptions their rationales can be applied also to related issues.

A conscientious exemption is called for when a deeply held belief based on the deeply held moral values of a group or an individual runs into the demands or determinations of the law. In other words, the conscientious objector seeks an exemption from the law not because of his status (as is sometimes the case with constitutional, non-conscientious exemptions) but because he holds an alternative set of basic values or an alternative way of balancing basic values—which are all part of his conscience, or the result of it—that conflicts

---

[1] For other techniques for protecting freedom of conscience within the criminal process, see: K Greenawalt, *Conflicts of Law and Morality* (Oxford, Oxford University Press, 1989) ch 15 (eg non-prosecution, nullification, sentencing and pardon).

with the ends, the means or the values of a specific law and, ultimately, contra-dicts the demands or the determinations of that law. The best-known example of granting conscientious exemption is the common exemption from compul-sory military service, usually granted to religious or secular pacifists. However, conscientious exemptions are given or at least demanded in relation to many other laws dealing with, for example, equal treatment; drug use; dress codes in schools, prisons and the armed forces; animal slaughter; the official day of rest ('Sunday laws'); taxes; and healthcare.

We should expect a growing demand, both from groups and individuals, to be granted conscientious exemptions. There are various reasons for this. First, the modern state regulates the public and the private sphere more than ever; secondly, there is an increasing sensitivity to the discourse of human rights and increasing use of it amongst individuals, organisations and communities; and, thirdly, there is significant movement in Western democracies away from the cultural model of a relatively homogeneous nation state to a far more hetero-geneous, multicultural one. This being so, the need to understand the nature of conscientious exemptions, the common practice surrounding them, and the difference between religious and non-religious conscientious objections, becomes even more important, both from the theoretical and the practical points of view.

There are views according to which conscientious exemptions can hardly be justified and normally should not be granted. Brian Barry suggests a gen-eral argument against the 'rule-and-exemption' approach. Barry argues that it is hard to steer a path between the conclusion that doing X or the avoid-ance of X is so important that all should do it, and the alternative of saying that this is a matter that people should be left free to decide for themselves.[2] Despite Barry's scepticism, such a path can be found and at times must be found. There is no general theoretical difficulty in proposing that there are cases where X is so important that all should do it, cases where X is less impor-tant so people should be left free to decide for themselves, and cases where X is sufficiently important that all should do it apart from those who object to X for conscientious reasons. The question, therefore, is not whether the state should grant conscientious exemptions but rather concerns the nature of such exemptions and the main guidelines to be considered when the state needs to decide whether to grant them. In the following section it is argued that grant-ing conscientious exemptions is better perceived as an expression of tolerance. This means that when deciding whether to grant conscientious exemptions

---

[2] B Barry, *Culture and Equality* (Cambridge, Polity Press, 2001) 46. See also p 50: 'there is a pos-sible case for letting everybody do what they please and a possible case for constraining everyone alike, but ... a great deal of finagling is needed in order to support a general rule with exemp-tions based on religious beliefs'.

we in fact decide the limits of tolerance towards conscientious objections and conscientious objectors. Therefore, a detailed discussion about conscientious exemptions—and about whether religion is special within this context—is the best way to clarify and exemplify the arguments made thus far about the limits of liberal tolerance and about the intolerant nature of religion.

II. CONSCIENTIOUS EXEMPTIONS AS AN EXPRESSION OF TOLERANCE

Different scholars perceive the practice of granting conscientious exemptions (religious and non-religious) and their underlying justifications in varying ways. Some of these ways may be contradictory, while others may be compatible or cumulative. Arguments have been made for justifying the right to be granted conscientious exemptions as a communal right,[3] as a minority right[4] or as a way of implementing affirmative action.[5] Such explanations fail, as they exclude the conscience of the secular individual who is not part of a distinct group or community. They also fail because they ignore the individual religious conscience or individual interpretations of religious values or demands. Other scholars perceive the right to be granted conscientious exemptions as an individual right; yet this explanation—much like the former—also fails, since in some cases no moral or legal, communal or individual right to be granted an exemption exists.[6] Put differently, an accurate way of understanding the practice of granting conscientious exemptions and the nature of these exemptions should not be dependent on having a right to be granted exemptions, as at times there is no such right. In these cases, conscientious exemptions are granted as a matter of grace or for pragmatic reasons.

Here I argue that granting conscientious exemptions is usually the outcome of tolerance and that the principle of tolerance better explains both

---

[3] LM Hammer, *The International Human Right to Freedom of Conscience* (Farnham, Ashgate, 2001) 243–44.

[4] W Kymlicka, *Multicultural Citizenship: A Liberal Theory of Minority Rights* (Oxford, Oxford University Press, 1995) 37–38; DE Steinberg, 'Religious Exemption as Affirmative Action' (1991) 40 *Emory Law Journal* 77; Hammer (n 3 above) 246.

[5] Steinberg (n 4 above); and in the context of the First Amendment: M McConnell, 'The Problem of Singling Out Religion' (2000) 50 *DePaul Law Review* 1, 9–10.

[6] For a description of the judicial practice in the USA of granting religious exemptions while relying on individual or on classic liberal rights rather than on religious-communitarian ones, see: S Carter, 'Evolution, Creationism, and Treating Religion as a Hobby' (1987) *Duke Law Journal* 977, 985; M McConnell, 'Accommodation of Religion' [1985] *Supreme Court Review* 1, 19; M Tushnet, 'The Constitution of Religion' (1986) 18 *Conneticut Law Review* 701, 734; CL Eisgruber and LG Sager, 'Mediating Institutions: Beyond the Public/Private Distinction: The Vulnerability of Conscience: The Constitutional Basis for Protecting Religious Conduct' (1994) 61 *University of Chicago Law Review* 1245, 1248, 1268, 1291–96.

the practice of granting conscientious exemptions and the attitude of those who grant the exemptions. Typically, granting conscientious exemptions from a legal rule presupposes that the state does not share the conscientious objector's values or his way of balancing between values, or believes it would be unbearable and indeed intolerable if everyone shared the objector's kind of conscience and reasoning. Otherwise, the exemption would have been the general rule rather than the exception to it. In other words, the state usually makes an adverse judgement about the conscientious objector's values or his way of balancing between values. This judgement gives the state reasons not to grant the conscientious objector an exemption from the legal rule (thereby harming him). If the state decides to grant conscientious exemptions after all, it can be seen as tolerant.

The argument that granting conscientious exemptions is usually the outcome of tolerance needs a few clarifications. Most of them merely explain the argument in more detail. Two of them, however, describe the only two cases (albeit quite marginal ones) where the argument does not apply. First, it is necessary to clarify the distinction made above between the case in which the state makes adverse judgements about the conscientious objector's values and the case in which the state makes adverse judgements about the conscientious objector's balance of values or balance of reasons. This distinction stresses that conscientious exemptions are the outcome of tolerance even when the state and the conscientious objector share the same values and differ only in the weight they give to these values (or reasons). Moreover, the state and the objector may differ only in evaluating factual circumstances that affect the weight that is or should be given to certain values (or reasons). Either way, as long as adverse judgements exist and as long as they constitute reasons not to grant the exemptions, the right discourse is still that of tolerance. Secondly, the argument that granting conscientious exemptions is normally the outcome of tolerance might be seen as too broad and too ambitious to be true. Aren't there too many important cases, one may ask, in which granting conscientious exemptions has nothing to do with tolerance? I suspect that there are not, subject to two marginal exceptions that will be discussed shortly. In the following paragraphs I will analyse some specific cases of granting conscientious exemptions that may appear to have nothing to do with tolerance. Nevertheless, I shall argue that tolerance can be found in these cases as well.

Granting conscientious exemptions is an act of tolerance even in cases where the legislature has not foreseen the harm caused to a person's conscience. This could happen in at least three instances: (1) when the legislature fails to anticipate the impact of a specific law on a person's conscience; (2) when the harm is caused because of a change in circumstances; or (3) when the harm is a result of an unanticipated demand created by various laws operating together. In all these cases, the law now demands what the conscientious objector does not want to do, and in a way cannot do. The legislature now has three options: (1) to change the general demands of the law in a way that granting a conscientious exemption would not be necessary; (2) to leave the general demands intact but to add a statutory conscientious exemption from it, or (3) to do nothing. By choosing the second option over the first, the legislature implies that whatever the reason for the clash between the demand of the law and the conscientious objector's conscience, now that the clash is clear the general rule should not reflect the objector's conscience. Usually, choosing the second option shows that—at least to some degree—the attitude of the legislature is that of tolerance. Otherwise, the legislature would have chosen to change the general demands of the law in such a way that granting a conscientious exemption would not be necessary, ie in a way that reflects the objector's conscience and incorporates it into the general rule itself.

Granting a conscientious exemption is an expression of tolerance also in cases where an exemption is granted to anyone who claims it, ie to anyone who declares himself as a sincere conscientious objector. Take, for example, the duty to take a religious or a religiously-oriented oath whenever one testifies in court. Even when an exemption is granted from that duty to anyone who claims it, the fact remains that the general rule demands a religious oath and not simply any oath or affirmation. It would be wrong to argue that such an exemption reflects a pluralistic approach or mere indifference. This is in fact a case of what can be called 'symbolic intolerance' on the one hand and 'de facto tolerance' on the other hand; symbolic intolerance—because the law reflects symbolic preference for religious values and by definition rejects non-religious values; de facto tolerance—because no harm (other than symbolic, if any) is caused to the conscientious objector.

When the law sets a rule, such as a duty to vaccinate one's child, and explicitly exempts from the rule any sincere conscientious objector, it is plausible to assume that this model of granting exemptions will be applied only as long as the anticipated number of objectors does not jeopardise the rationale of the rule itself. In other words, since the objectors will be granted exemptions only up to a certain point—ie since the state would not want to face too many people who hold an 'anti-vaccination conscience'—there is at least an implicit notion of tolerance as the basis of this kind of exemption as well, albeit in a weaker sense than the one we can find in typical cases of conscientious exemption.

Finally, granting conscientious exemptions can be understood as an expression of tolerance even when it may be perceived at first sight as favouritism, such as in cases where the exemption is granted only to one kind of conscientious objector, eg to religious objectors. Take, for example, the Israeli case (which is now under re-evaluation) in which all Jewish orthodox students ('Yeshiva students') are exempt from compulsory enlistment in the army whereas secular students, and secular conscientious objectors, are not (with the exception of pacifists, who are sometimes granted conscientious exemption as well). One can argue that limiting the scope of the exemption to religious reasons has nothing to do with tolerance, but rather with favouritism or perhaps with 'substantive equality'. Nevertheless, this exemption is granted in part because the state believes it does not result in significant compromise for important state interests (eg national security). The state may sympathise and even identify with the religious values and culture that are the reasons for granting the exemption, and may even see them as more valuable than non-religious ones; but as long as compulsory enlistment into the army is the general rule, it is clear that this religious exemption will be granted only up to the point at which the purpose of the law is diminished. In other words, assuming the government believes in the necessity of compulsory enlistment in the army, it hopes that not too many citizens will hold the religious values and culture that dictate absolute objection to obey the general rule. Regardless of how valuable the government thinks these religious values are, it would not want them to be held by the state itself. Thus, the willingness to grant the exemption may reflect (and presumably usually does reflect) an attitude of tolerance, although it is a much weaker notion of tolerance than the one that can be found in other cases of granting conscientious exemptions and although it is indeed mixed up with what may be called pluralism or even favouritism.

The same line of argument can be taken in regard to other cases such as exempting the Amish (a group of traditionalist Christian communities) from mandatory educational requirements in the US and exempting religious minorities from Sunday laws. In the well-known *Yoder* case,[7] where an exemption was granted to members of the Amish community from a compulsory education law, the court clearly favoured a religious way of life over non-religious ones, at least in the constitutional context of granting conscientious exemptions, when it stated that 'a way of life, however virtuous and admirable, may not be interposed as a barrier to reasonable state regulation of education if it is based on purely secular considerations'.[8] Moreover, the Supreme Court praised the Amish way of life, was clearly sympathetic towards its unique culture and even referred to the Amish way of educating their youth as equally valuable.[9] Nevertheless, the Amish community presents a very special case and it would be misguided to perceive it as the paradigm case of granting conscientious exemptions. The Amish are a powerless minority, very small in numbers, have no aspiration to gain political power or to influence the public sphere, and are quite unlikely to gain sufficient power to threaten the majority

---

[7] *Wisconsin v Yoder* 406 US 205 (1972).
[8] *Wisconsin v Yoder* (n 7 above) 215.
[9] *Wisconsin v Yoder* (n 7 above) 222–23.

in any way. Thus, one may conclude that in fact the majority does not bear any burden by granting the exemption; that there was no need to exercise restraint from harming the Amish in this case; and, as such, that it is wrong to describe the court's attitude as 'tolerant'. However, there may be an element of tolerance in the state's attitude, which is expressed in its consideration of these unique characteristics of the Amish. Unless the state would not mind if the Amish culture became dominant in the United States, and provided the state is willing to grant the exemption precisely because there is no chance of the Amish culture becoming dominant, there is a small element of tolerance in its attitude, alongside the Court's sympathy and respect. This would not be the case if the state thought that the Amish way of life was preferable; that everyone who lives according to the Amish way of life should be granted the exemption and that it would be fabulous if everyone in the United States adopted the Amish way of life. The argument here is that a distinction should be made between the case in which the state honestly thinks that the way of life of the minority is indeed preferable and should be adopted by everyone, and the case where the state thinks that the way of life of the minority is indeed valuable but at the same time would not want it to be adopted by the majority. In the latter case, there is or may be an element of tolerance in the state's attitude after all.

Thus far, I have described how and why the principle of tolerance explains the practice of granting conscientious exemptions. I also mentioned that this argument has two exceptions. According to the first exception, granting a conscientious exemption does not have to be the outcome of tolerance when the exemption is granted from compliance with a law whose ends have nothing or very little to do with the values the legislature holds or wishes to promote, or when it is highly unlikely that these values would be disputable. Perhaps the clearest example of such a law is one the sole purpose of which is to coordinate behaviour. I do not refer here to a law that coordinates behaviour as a means to an end that may itself be disputable as a matter of conscience or values (eg income tax laws). Rather, I mean a law that coordinates people's behaviour for purposes that have nothing or very little to do with morality or deeply held beliefs (and here I wish to set aside the argument that coordinating behaviour is itself a moral virtue of the law). Such laws typically protect personal or public safety—for example, laws that provide that there should be traffic lights, or stipulate the traffic-light colours that signal cars and pedestrians to go or stop, or determine the side of the road on which to drive and so forth.

It is quite clear why granting conscientious exemptions from such laws does not have to be, and presumably will almost never be, an act of tolerance. Although these laws might contradict the conscience of some, the fact that these laws merely coordinate behaviour and do not reflect any significant moral decision made by the legislature means that granting a conscientious

exemption from them can—but does not have to—entail a negative judgement about the objector's conscience. This exception to the general argument
does not affect its strength, since examples of conscientious objections to laws
that merely coordinate behaviour are quite rare. As noted, these kinds of laws
are unlikely to be disputed as a matter of conscience.[10] Indeed, this exception
presents no more than a peripheral case that should not affect the general way
of understanding the practice of granting conscientious exemptions.[11]

The same can be said about the second exception to tolerance as a basis for
granting conscientious exemptions. Up until now I have assumed that conscientious exemptions can be given and are given from legal demands, duties
or prohibitions. Whereas this is indeed the usual case, one can think of other
cases in which conscientious exemptions are or can be given from a law that
does not impose duties or prohibitions but rather grants what the state perceives as a right or a benefit. Take, for example, a law stating that a person
who, as a result of injury or illness, lacks the ability to consent to medical treatment is deemed to consent to life-saving or simply beneficial medical treatment administered by state authorities. Some may object to this presumption
of consent on religious grounds. Jehovah's Witnesses, for example, may object
to blood transfusions. Exempting Jehovah's Witnesses from the application of
the presumption may reflect an attitude of tolerance (in cases involving minors
or if the state itself has an interest in granting medical treatment to its injured
or ill residents), but equally may not. However, as in the former case, claiming
conscientious exemptions from laws that do not impose duties or prohibitions
is rare and is no more than a marginal exception to the general argument that
granting conscientious exemptions is first and foremost the result of tolerance.

To sum up, accommodating conscientious objections by granting conscientious exemptions is a paradigm example of tolerance for two main reasons.
First, in the most frequent and typical cases, it describes the attitude of the
state in the most accurate way. Secondly, the principle of tolerance—however
narrow in some aspects—is wide enough to describe the practice of granting
conscientious exemptions in most cases. Furthermore, it can accommodate
various other, even non-compatible, ways of understanding the matter.

---

[10] But see, for example, in *State v Hershberger* 462 NW 2d 393 (Minn 1990), where the law in
Minnesota required an orange and red 'triangular slow moving vehicle sign' to be displayed on
buggies and wagons. Some Amish residents believed the bright colours of the sign and the symbol itself would put their faith in 'worldly symbols' rather than in God. As a result, some of them
preferred to display a black triangle whereas others refused to use any sign and instead outlined
their buggies with silver reflective tape.

[11] For the general approach in jurisprudence to identifying the central meaning of a concept
while putting aside the reasoning of peripheral cases that do not affect the focal meaning of that
concept, see: HLA Hart, *The Concept of Law*, 2nd edn (Oxford, Oxford University Press, 1994)
3–17.

A further possible claim is that granting conscientious exemptions is all about equality.[12] One can argue that a justifiable conscientious exemption is one that is granted only to those who are different from non-objectors or from non-conscientious objectors in some relevant way. The idea of equality can indeed justify a decision to grant or to refuse to grant conscientious exemptions.[13] However, things are more complicated than that. There are some deficiencies and ambiguities in the concept of equality that make it a less suitable candidate than the principle of tolerance for explaining the nature of the practice of granting conscientious exemptions. It is not my purpose here to discuss in great length equality as a possible justification for granting exemptions. Rather, I discuss whether this principle can explain what we are doing when we grant an exemption. First, there is the well-known view about the 'emptiness' of the idea of equality. If this view is true, then there is little sense in describing a concept or explaining a practice by turning to an 'empty idea'. The emptiness of equality can be described in two different ways. The first is to argue that the entitlements people attribute to the idea of equality derive from external substantive rights that are valuable for independent reasons.[14] The second is to argue that the proposition that 'people who are alike should be treated alike' is tautological. If these arguments are sound, equality will provide no meaningful and independent foundation for rights and will not be a good candidate for explaining the practice of granting conscientious exemptions.

Bernard Williams argues that 'for every difference in the way men are treated, a reason should be given' and that that reason should be 'relevant'.[15] Even though this may be true, all too often there is no neutral way to decide when one is relevantly different from another. Frequently, it is merely a question of unshared values or balance of reasons. Therefore, these values or reasons should be our main concern and not the idea of equality. In other words, when two sides disagree about what exactly equality requires, their disagreement is not about the concept of equality but rather about other substantive values. Therefore, the main question—who is equal and who is not—remains open, as in many important cases no meaningful guidelines can be given to answer it.[16]

---

[12] Robert Wintemute, 'Accommodating Religious Beliefs: Harm, Clothing or Symbols, and Refusals to Serve Others' (2014) 77 *The Modern Law Review* 223, 226.

[13] Barry (n 2 above) 319–20.

[14] J Raz, *The Morality of Freedom* (Oxford, Oxford University Press, 1986) 240.

[15] B Williams, *Problems of the Self* (Cambridge, Cambridge University Press, 1973) 241.

[16] See also HLA Hart, 'Are There Any Natural Rights' in A Quinton (ed), *Political Philosophy* (Oxford, Oxford University Press, 1967) 53, 65: '*any* differences between men could … be treated as a moral justification for interference and so constitute a right, so that the equal right of all men to be free would be compatible with gross inequality'.

The idea of tolerance fills this emptiness with some content. In short, while tolerating someone and treating him equally (ie granting him equal treatment) can involve identical behaviour or lead to the same result, there are important differences between these concepts that are sometimes overlooked. Although the result of tolerance is usually identical to the result of an equal treatment approach, the tolerant person, while comparing himself to the other, either thinks of himself as superior, or thinks that his values are superior, or that his manners are more appropriate, and so on. Nevertheless, he treats the other equally because the other has a right to be tolerated (in the name of autonomy) or for pragmatic reasons or because of mercy. Thus one can say that the tolerant person treats equally things he regards as unequal. Equality of persons or their values cannot be a sufficient basis for tolerance for the simple reason that tolerance entails a negative judgement of the other or his values. If I, as a man, treat women equally because I do not see any relevant differences between men and women, I cannot be regarded as tolerant. If I, as an agnostic, treat religious beliefs and practices in the same way as I treat non-religious ones because I see them as equally worthy, I again cannot be regarded as tolerant. The tolerant person does not grant equal treatment to others or avoid harming others because they are equal but rather *despite* his belief that they are *not* equal. It is one thing to think 'I will treat you equally because there are no relevant differences between us, our values and so on' and another to think

> I will treat you equally although you (or your values and so on) are different and inferior in relevant aspects, because if I don't, your personal autonomy or human dignity will be harmed or because you have a right not be harmed despite your inferiority.

The latter reflects tolerance more accurately than the former.

If we follow Raz's argument about equality, then the very fact that we are discussing tolerance as a right implies that equality is of little importance for us. When a person has a right to X (to be tolerated), his right to X is an independent right that has nothing to do with equality. One has a right to be tolerated regardless of others being tolerated. Only when one sees tolerance as grace can one argue that equality matters, since now he has a right to be tolerated only if others are being tolerated under relevantly similar circumstances.[17]

Thus, whether there is a right to be granted conscientious exemptions or whether it is a matter of the state's discretion (because the state may decide to grant it for pragmatic reasons or as a matter of grace), tolerance is, again, a wide enough and the most accurate way to explain the nature of the practice of granting exemptions and the attitude of the one who grants them. Although

---

[17] It is also quite clear that tolerance as for pragmatic reasons, as well as tolerance as grace, has nothing to do with respecting the other or thinking of him as an equal.

equality may be important for understanding the practice of granting conscientious exemptions, it does not capture its essence and cannot explain it in all circumstances.

If, as I suggest, granting conscientious exemptions is in most cases the outcome of tolerance, then the practice of granting conscientious exemptions is closely related to the complex question of the limits of tolerance. Within this context we now ask whether religion is special: whether there is something special about religion that justifies a greater or lesser amount of tolerance towards claims to be accommodated or to be granted religious conscientious exemptions.

III. IS RELIGION SPECIAL?: FIVE POSSIBLE ANSWERS

There are several possible views about the proper way in which the state should treat religious conscientious objections and how that treatment should compare to the response to non-religious conscientious objections. The guiding question is often: 'is religion special?'; in other words, 'should religious conscientious objections be treated any differently from non-religious ones?'

Any view regarding the general question about the uniqueness of religion and about the implications of the answer to this question must be derived from a more comprehensive political theory. Classes of theories, such as neutral liberalism, perfectionist liberalism, religiously-oriented natural law theories, communitarianism, multiculturalism, and so on, may lead to different answers to the question 'is religion special?' Answering this question within the context of granting conscientious exemptions must also take into consideration general theories about the relationship between religion and the state; the proper place that religion should have in the public sphere; the link between religion and public reason; and that between religion and public choice theory. These important issues are outside the scope of this chapter.[18]

---

[18] Suffice it to say that, in my view, religion should be separated from the state in a clear and radical way; religion should generally be excluded from the public sphere; and religious reasoning should not be part of public reasoning and public choice. Although these views will not be discussed further here, the following discussion should be read in the light of these general statements.

For the view that political acts and even views should not be based on religious reasons or for the view that religion should be excluded from politics (and for the more specific view that religious symbols and speech should be excluded from the public sphere), see: R Dworkin, *Is Democracy Possible Here?* (Princeton NJ, Princeton University Press, 2006) 74–77; B Ackerman, *Social Justice in the Liberal State* (New Haven CT, Yale University Press, 1980) 10–11; T Nagel, 'Moral Conflict and Political Legitimacy' (1987) 16 *Philosophy and Public Affairs* 215, 223–34; R Audi, 'The Place of Religious Argument in a Free and Democratic Society' (1993) 30 *San Diego Law Review* 677, 690; R Audi, 'Religion and the Ethics of Political Participation' (1990) 100 *Ethics* 386, 392–97; S Gey, 'Why is Religion Special? Reconsidering the Accommodation of Religion Under

Aspects of the academic discussion of this area should be read in the light of specific constitutional provisions. I will try, however, to ignore arguments that are clearly related to specific constitutional or statutory backgrounds. The arguments discussed in this chapter are those that can be applied to a very general model of liberal democracy, ie to almost any liberal democracy. References to specific legal texts will be made, but only to exemplify possible ways of applying the more general, principled arguments.

I will divide the main views that address the issue of granting conscientious exemptions into five main categories: (1) neutral approaches; (2) 'equal regard' approaches; (3) liberal value-based approaches; (4) 'pro-religion' approaches; and (5) 'anti-religion' approaches. An approach to the issue of conscientious exemptions can be regarded as 'neutral' if the decision whether to grant an exemption is not affected, at least not directly, by the content of a person's conscience. Such an approach takes into account 'neutral' considerations, such as the expected harm to the objector, the public interest, administrative difficulties, the harm caused to the interests and rights of others and so on. Few neutral approaches put the emphasis on the argument that religious conscientious objections and non-religious ones should be treated in the same way. This is the equal regard approach. An equal regard approach suggests that, when an exemption is granted to a non-religious conscientious objector, an exemption should also be granted to his equivalent religious objector, and vice versa. As will be explained below, an equal regard approach can, but does not have to be, a neutral approach. 'Liberal value-based approaches' do take into account the content of a person's conscience but not its religiosity as such. According to this approach, some conscientious objections should not be tolerated at all—or not beyond a certain extent—because of the content of the conscience that grounds the objection. When the content of the objector's conscience is morally repugnant (and, sometimes, utterly irrational), it generates a reason not to grant exemptions regardless of whether the objector's conscience is religious or non-religious. The two other value-based approaches consider the religiosity of the objector's conscience as a relevant reason for granting exemptions (the pro-religion approach) or refusing to grant them (the anti-religion approach).

It is important to appreciate that this is not an exhaustive list of possible approaches. One can think of other views that combine elements of some of the views described above. One can hold a pro-religion approach that also

the Religion clauses of the First Amendment' (1990) 52 *University of Pittsburgh Law Review* 75; S Gey, 'When is Religious Speech not "Free Speech"' [2000] *University of Illinois Law Review* 379.

   For an argument that people can base their political views on religious grounds but cannot justify publicly their political views on these grounds, see: K Greenawalt, *Religious Convictions and Political Choice* (New York, Oxford University Press, 1987) 228, 238–39; K Greenawalt, 'Religious Convictions and Political Choice: Some Further Thoughts' (1990) 39 *DePaul Law Review* 1019, 1035–36, 1045.

has neutral characteristics. Such an approach would give priority to religious claims to be granted conscientious exemptions but, at the same time, would apply neutral tests to decide exactly when to grant religious conscientious exemptions. The value of such 'mixed approaches' depends on the value of each particular approach as described below.

IV. NEUTRAL APPROACHES

A. About the Neutral Approaches

Neutral approaches to the issue of conscientious exemptions do not take into account the religiosity of the conscience when a decision is made whether or not to grant an exemption to a conscientious objector. This approach is neutral in a strong sense if it is merely a specific implementation of a more general approach according to which the attitude of the state towards conscientious objections should not be affected by the state's moral evaluation of the content of the objector's conscience.[19] I will first demonstrate how the neutral approach to granting conscientious exemptions perceives the connection between such an approach, liberalism and autonomy. I will then describe a few possible versions of the neutral approach, explain how some of them work in practice and will finish by evaluating the soundness of the neutral approach. I will not discuss here the debate between neutral liberalism and non-neutral liberalism (or perfectionist-liberalism, value-based liberalism, substantive liberalism and so on). I already noted that this book is based on a form of perfectionist liberalism. It is enough to mention the core of the debate to the extent to which it is relevant to this chapter. Gedicks, who argues against giving priority to religious claims to be granted conscientious exemptions, based his objection on a neutral perception of autonomy, commenting that 'in the end, the contemporary liberal commitment to individual autonomy makes it unlikely

For the view that political acts and views can or should be based on religious reasons or for the view that religion should not be excluded from politics and the public sphere, see: M Perry, *Morality, Politics, and Law: A Bicentennial Essay* (New York, Oxford University Press, 1988); M Perry, *Love and Power: The Role of Religion and Morality in American Politics* (New York, Oxford University Press, 1991) 112; M Perry, 'Religious Morality and Political Choice: Further Thoughts—And Second Thoughts—On Love and Power' (1993) 30 *San Diego Law Review* 703, 713–16; S Carter, *The Culture of Disbelief: How American Law and Politics Trivialize Religious Devotion* (New York, Basic Books, 1994); S Smith, *Foreordained Failure: The Quest for a Constitutional Principle of Religion Freedom* (New York, Oxford University Press, 1995) 123; S Fish, 'Mission Impossible: Settling the Just Bounds Between Church and State' (1997) 97 *Columbia Law Review* 2255, 2264; PJ Weitman, *Religion and the Obligations of Citizenship* (Cambridge, Cambridge University Press, 2002) 65.

[19] A good example of such a neutral approach can be found in Dworkin's views about conscientious objections: R Dworkin, *Taking Rights Seriously* (Cambridge MA, Harvard University Press, 1977) 197–222.

that government interference with religious conscience will be understood as a serious harm distinct from interference with secular conscience'.[20]

This is one way to understand the liberal commitment to autonomy. This understanding of what liberalism requires suggests that one should always have the opportunity to choose one's belief or to act upon it regardless of the content of that belief. Alternatively, if the opportunity to choose is always limited to some extent, the pertinent question according to this version of neutral liberalism is whether one has an adequate range of choices (rather than an adequate range of *valuable* choices). A better way to describe what autonomy requires is to say that denying the individual the opportunity to choose does not necessarily diminish his autonomy, as long as he still has an adequate range of valuable options. Here, the content of one's options is relevant for deciding whether an adequate range of valuable opinions exists or remains. Accordingly, the religiosity of one's choices (or options) may well be a consideration that could be taken into account. More specifically, and in contrast to Gedicks' view, this perception of autonomy does enable the liberal theory and the liberal state to distinguish between religious practices and any secular lifestyle choice.

Whatever the case may be, emphasising autonomy as a central concept within the issue of conscientious exemptions implies that one should have a choice or that one does have a choice. I will return later to the relationship between autonomy, choice and belief.[21] For now, suffice it to say that one cannot choose one's deepest beliefs. One also does not always have a meaningful choice about whether to act upon one's beliefs. Therefore, with regard to granting conscientious exemptions, we should use the concept of autonomy with caution, as granting conscientious exemptions—and tolerating conscientious objectors—so often does not reflect respect for the conscientious objector's right to choose but rather acknowledges his lack of real ability to refrain from acting upon his conscience, ie his lack of real choice.

A further appealing argument concerning autonomy, insofar as autonomy is important in the issue of conscientious exemptions, is that governments should help to make morally valuable options available to people and discourage them from pursuing empty, non-valuable or immoral ones. Accordingly, there are some options that one is better off not having.[22] Raz argues

---

[20] FM Gedicks, 'An Unfirm Foundation: The Regrettable Indefensibility of Religious Exemptions' (1998) 20 *University of Arkansas at Little Rock Law Journal* 555, 563: 'The constitutional harm that results when government interferes with autonomy is less the substantive harm that follows from the choice imposed upon the individual than the procedural harm of denying the individual the opportunity to choose. This leaves the liberal theory unable to distinguish between religious practices and any secular lifestyle choice including a choice motivated by personal commitment to a secular morality'.

[21] See below, text to n 146 onwards.

[22] Raz (n 14 above) 410, and see also p 133: 'it is the goal of all political action to enable individuals to pursue valid conceptions of the good and to discourage evil or empty ones'.

that the 'pursuit of the morally repugnant cannot be defended from coercive interference on the ground that being an autonomous choice endows it with any value'.[23] Raz also argues that governments may use means short of coercion to eliminate the availability of bad options without violating the principle of autonomy. If this view is to be applied here, we can then say that a refusal to grant conscientious exemptions will not always be equivalent to legal coercion. In many cases, failing to grant the exemption will only mean that the conscientious objector loses benefits or opportunities if he chooses to follow his conscience rather than to comply with a legal demand, which is the condition for being entitled to the benefit or for gaining access to certain opportunities.[24]

There is more to be said on this issue. However, the purpose of the above discussion is merely to illustrate how the neutral approach to granting conscientious exemptions differs from non-neutral yet still liberal approaches.

There are a few typical neutral approaches to the issue of granting conscientious exemptions. One typical way of formulating a neutral approach to this issue is to suggest that conscientious exemptions should be granted if they do not result in harm to others,[25] or when no burden-shifting is involved.[26] Another way is to engage with a balancing process and to decide whether the harm caused to the public interest, private interests or private rights, should an exemption be granted, exceeds the harm that would be caused to the conscientious objector, should an exemption not be granted. This is a simplistic, utilitarian balancing test that does not require us to apply the principle of proportionality. This test merely aims to minimise the amount of harm caused. A different balancing process can require weighing the importance of the public interest, private interest or private rights against freedom of conscience on a case-by-case basis. Within all of these approaches, there is no need to make any moral evaluation of the content of the conscience in order to decide whether an exemption should be granted or not; hence their neutral nature.

---

[23] Raz (n 14 above) 418.

[24] Brian Barry makes this point when he argues that: 'The claim that exemptions for ritual slaughter are about religious freedom ... is just as bogus as in the crash helmet case, and for exactly the same reason ... nobody is bound to eat meat ... we must insist on the crucial difference between a denial of equal opportunities to some group (for example, a law forbidding Sikhs to ride motorcycles) and a choice some people make out of that from a set of equal opportunities (for example, a choice not to ride a motorcycle) as a result of certain beliefs. Those who believe that, even with a crash helmet, riding a motorcycle is too dangerous to be a rational undertaking are (in exactly the same, misleading, sense) "precluded" from riding one': Barry (n 2 above) 45.

[25] For a detailed account of this view, see JC Lipson, 'On Balance: Religious Liberty and Third Party Harms' (2000) 84 *Minnesota Law Review* 589; Wintemute (n 12 above). See also Kugler, who argues for a general defence in criminal law that would exempt conscientious objectors from criminal liability unless the exemption caused 'real harm' or 'actual harm' to the public interest or simply greater harm to rights of others: Y Kugler, 'On the Possibility of a Criminal Law Defence for Conscientious Objection' (1997) 10 *Canadian Journal of Law and Jurisprudence* 387.

[26] Brian Leiter, *Why Tolerate Religion* (Princeton NJ, Princeton University Press, 2013) 101.

B. Neutral Approaches in Practice

In order to appreciate the ways in which neutral approaches are applied, two main examples will be briefly presented: the first is taken from European juris-prudence and the second from American jurisprudence.

Neutral-liberal approaches can be found in the vast majority of international and European treaties and conventions that do not take a stand regarding the a priori weight that should be accorded to religiously based claims to be granted conscientious exemptions. In these documents, the type of balancing test that should be applied is described in general, vague terms. A good example is Article 18(3) of the International Covenant on Civil and Political Rights (ICCPR), which states that 'Freedom to manifest one's religion or beliefs may be subject only to such limitations as are prescribed by law and are necessary to protect public safety, order, health, or morals, or the fundamental rights and freedoms of others'.[27] It has been argued that this is the dominant view of international and European law and that it does not provide direct and meaningful guidelines for deciding the desirable approach concerning claims to be granted religious conscientious exemptions.[28] The international and European approach to the issue of religious conscientious exemptions is complex and will not be discussed here. Suffice it to say that this approach, insofar as it finds expression in Article 18(3) of the ICCPR and similar articles, can be regarded as mostly neutral, since it does not grant any priority to the religious conscience and also because freedom of religion or the freedom to manifest one's religion (if it includes the right to be granted conscientious exemptions) can be limited for various reasons, all of which are neutral, apart from the vague exception of 'morals'.

Some scholars, alongside the American courts, sometimes refer to section 3(b) of the Religious Freedom Restoration Act (RFRA) of 1993 as a clear statutory example for an adoption of a neutral approach. Section 3(b) states that

> Government may substantially burden a person's exercise of religion only if it demonstrates that application of the burden to the person:
>
> (1)   is in furtherance of a compelling governmental interest; and
> (2)   is the least restrictive means of furthering that compelling governmental interest.

[27] Similar terms can be found in Art 9(2) of the European Convention on Human Rights (ECHR).
[28] MD Evans, 'Human Rights, Religious Liberty, and the Universality Debate' in R O'Dair and A Lewis (eds), *Law and Religion—Current Legal Issues*, vol 4 (Oxford, Oxford University Press, 2001) 205, 219. I will not discuss here how this observation coincides with the application of the principle of proportionality in the European Court of Human Rights jurisprudence.

Therefore, if a claimant proves that not granting him a religious conscientious exemption substantively burdens the exercise of his religion, then, in the absence of a compelling governmental interest or if restricting his freedom of religion is not the least restrictive means to achieve that interest, the government and the courts are under a duty to grant a religious conscientious exemption.[29] The RFRA adopts a neutral approach to granting conscientious exemptions in a very limited way. The Act is neutral in the sense that it ignores the content of the religious belief. It merely balances the harm caused to the religious person by not granting him a conscientious exemption and the harm caused to the public interest should an exemption be granted. This balance of harms cannot be detached from the according of a certain weight to certain public interests vis-à-vis religious conscience, yet the existence of harm and the amount of harm caused to the religious conscientious objector are the dominant considerations rather than the content of the religious belief. The RFRA rejects the neutral approach in a clear, meaningful way by imposing a duty to grant only religious conscientious exemptions rather than any conscientious exemption.[30] The 'compelling interest' test is a central component of the RFRA. This test has been long established in US jurisprudence regarding religious conscientious exemptions. It was first applied in the *Sherbert* case in 1963[31] and was the governing test in American jurisprudence until 1990.[32] In 1990, in the *Smith* decision, the 'compelling interest' test was replaced by a different, and this time mainly neutral test.[33] According to *Smith*, a religious conscientious exemption will not be granted if the law is neutral by its nature; that is, if its purpose was not to impose burdens on one's religious freedom. There are two exceptions to this rule. First, cases in which the law also harms another constitutional right, apart from freedom of religion and when granting an exemption to the law is an adequate remedy, and secondly, cases where the harm caused to the religious conscientious objector is not a direct result of the neutral law but rather a result of applying the neutral law

---

[29] See also: RF Drinan, 'Reflections of the Demise of the Religious Freedom Restoration Act' (1997) 86 *Georgetown Law Journal* 101.

[30] This has led some scholars to argue that the RFRA is 'not constitutional': Eisgruber and Sager (n 6 above), 1306–11.

[31] *Sherbert v Verner* 374 US 398 (1963).

[32] For decisions to grant religious conscientious exemptions while applying this test, see: *Wisconsin v Yoder* (n 7 above) 215; *Thomas v Review Board of the Indiana Employment Security Division* 450 US 707 (1981); *Hobbie v Unemployment Appeals Commission* 480 US 136 (1987); *Frazee v Illinois* 489 US 829 (1989). For decisions not to grant religious conscientious exemptions while applying the same test, see: *Braunfeld v Brown* 366 US 599 (1961); *United States v Lee* 455 US 252 (1982); *Goldman v Weinberger* 475 US 503 (1986).

[33] *Employment Division, Department of Human Resources v Smith* 494 US 872 (1990).

on a case-by-case basis, ie when the neutral law does not contain a relatively specific rule but a general principle that leaves meaningful discretion to the executive.[34]

It can be argued, of course, that, in fact, most laws that infringe freedom of religion also infringe at least one more constitutional right and that, all too often, the harm to freedom of religion is a result of the executive exercising its discretion according to a statutory principle and not a direct result of a relatively specific statutory rule.[35] Nevertheless, the test in the *Smith* case is, for the most part, a neutral test in the sense that it prescribes that religious conscientious exemptions should not be granted from neutral laws, regardless of the content of the religious belief (and, apparently, regardless of the harm caused to the conscientious objector). This test does not provide an answer to the question of when non-religious conscientious exemptions should or can be granted; nor does the test answer directly the question of 'whether religion is special', or, to be exact, whether religious reasons, as such, are uniquely weighty reasons or weak ones for granting conscientious exemptions. Nevertheless, both the rule that religious exemptions will not be granted from neutral laws—and its exception (that they may be granted when another constitutional right is violated)—imply that, at the very least, religious reasons are not especially weighty ones for granting conscientious exemptions.

C. Evaluating the Neutral Approaches

The neutral approaches to the issue of granting conscientious exemptions are unsatisfactory and should be rejected inter alia for all the reasons that were mentioned in Chapter three in relation to intolerance as the limit to tolerance. In short, if intolerance should not be tolerated, then, when the conscience that grounds the objection reflects intolerant values or relies on them, the state has a strong reason, which may also be a prevailing reason, not to grant the exemption. Despite the fact that the general claim in Chapter three (that intolerance should not be tolerated) is sufficient for rejecting the neutral approach for granting conscientious exemptions, there are more specific issues within the relatively narrow topic of granting conscientious exemptions that should be addressed. In the following I will critically discuss three popular types of

---

[34] The *Smith* case (n 33 above) 881–84. The same approach is applied by the European Court of Human Rights concerning Art 9 of the ECHR: J Martinez-Torron, 'The European Court of Human Rights and Religion' in *Law and Religion—Current Legal Issues*, vol 4 (Oxford, Oxford University Press, 2001) 185, 199. For a recent defence of the 'neutral law' approach see Leiter (n 26 above) 101.

[35] McConnell (n 5 above) 3.

neutral tests: tests that focus on the existence of harm; the 'compelling state interest' test as an example of a constitutional balancing test; and the 'neutral law' test.

(i) The 'Harm Principle'

Applying neutral approaches within the context of granting conscientious exemptions raises a clear difficulty, to the extent that the crucial criterion for granting exemptions is the amount of harm that may be caused to the conscientious objector should an exemption not be granted. The difficulty is that applying such approaches will result in granting unjustifiable exemptions to religious, intolerant and irrational conscientious objectors. At times, this may result also in the granting of unjustifiable priority to religious, intolerant and irrational conscientious objections over non-conscientious objections that rely on sound reasons. Here, I assume a state that is more willing to grant exemptions to the law when the objection is conscience-based rather than interest-based.

The more the beliefs that form a person's conscience are absolute in the sense that they relate to almost every aspect of human life, the more they are likely to contradict the demands of neutral laws (ie laws that do not aim to diminish religious values). In Chapter five it was argued that absolutism is one feature that differentiates religious beliefs from non-religious ones. The links between absolutism, religion and intolerance and—to a lesser extent—religion and irrationality, were also pointed out. It seems that the conscience of persons who hold absolute, intolerant or irrational beliefs is more likely to be affected by laws of liberal democracies than that of relatively tolerant, rational persons. Therefore, applying a neutral test to the issue of granting conscientious exemptions, a test that simply measures the harm caused to a person should a conscientious exemption not be granted, might give priority to the religious, intolerant, or irrational conscience over the conscience or important interests of non-religious, tolerant, rational people.

A response to this argument may be: isn't that the point of granting conscientious exemptions? Shouldn't we grant them only to conscientious objectors and only to those who will be more severely harmed should they not be granted the exemption? If this is true, and if those who have a conscience that is based on religious, intolerant or irrational values or beliefs are more affected by neutral laws and are more severely harmed by them, then they are the ones who should be granted exemptions. But this is exactly the problem with most versions of this neutral approach. Their only concern is with the amount of harm caused to the conscientious objector. They do not consider the content of that conscience. While it is true that conscientious exemptions are normally granted to those who, in the ruler's opinion, are mistaken, it does not follow that the content of one's conscience should not be taken into consideration at all times. The rationale of the general principle according to which intolerance should not be tolerated applies here as well.

When the state decides whether or not to grant conscientious exemptions, the state should not conduct a contest by asking 'who will be more severely harmed if he did not get the exemption' or by asking 'who needs the exemption more?' The existence of harm is important but there are other considerations that should be taken into account. One of these is the content of the conscience (or the interest) that grounds the objection. Those who object to the law for conscientious reasons and whose conscience does not rely on intolerant—and to a lesser extent—irrational values or beliefs, have a strong case (other things being equal) to be granted conscientious exemptions. Those who base their conscientious claim on values that are intolerant or on utterly irrational beliefs have a much weaker case. They may be granted an exemption but, often, their case will be weaker than that of those who are not conscientious objectors yet they may still have good reasons, interest-based reasons, to be exempt from the law. Whether the demand for an exemption is based on conscience or on strong interests and preferences, the content of the conscience or the personal interest should be taken into account, along with other relevant considerations, if the state is allowed, as I suggest it should be, to eliminate the availability of bad options, to discourage people from making bad choices and not to tolerate intolerance. Two examples can clarify this point. The first deals with a racist employer. The second deals with the common case of Sunday laws.

Assume that the law prohibits discrimination in the workplace on the ground of race. Also assume that there are just one or two employers in a major city who refuse to employ non-whites because of religious conscientious reasons. Finally, we shall assume that, normally, there is no serious problem of racism in the workplace in that city (as opposed to many other cities in the same state). Applying a neutral test merely compares the harm that may be caused to the objectors should an exemption not be granted and the harm that may be caused to potential employees or to the public interest should an exemption be granted. The result will have to be the granting of an exemption. This would also be the case if we do not compare the harm that may be caused to both sides but merely try to avoid inflicting harm on the employee.[36] In our case, if the job-seeker who was discriminated against found or is likely to find another job, easily and quickly, then apart from being offended by the racist employer, no meaningful harm was caused here. This means that yet

---

[36] Compare to Wintemute (n 12 above) 228–29, who argues that religious objections should be accommodated if no direct or indirect harm is likely to be caused to others.

again an exemption from the equality law should be granted. Thus, if we wish to avoid granting exemptions to objectors who rely on a racist conscience, we need to consider the content of the conscience as a reason for not granting the exemption.

The example of granting exemptions from Sunday laws also illustrates the need to examine the content of the objection to the law, whether it is a conscientious objection or an interest-based one. I will assume that there is a compelling social reason to impose a duty not to work for one day a week and that there is also a compelling social or administrative reason to impose a duty on everyone not to work on the same day of the week. I will also assume that, for cultural and historical reasons, the state allocates Sunday as the official day of rest. This means that Sabbatarians and orthodox Jews, who cannot work on Saturday for religious reasons, would be unable to work for two days a week instead of only one. Alternatively, they would have to work on Saturday, even though their religion prohibits it. They would prefer to work on Sunday, ie to be exempt from the provisions of the Sunday law, and to be allowed not to work on Saturday without suffering any disadvantages as a result. Failing to exempt them from the law would either cause them substantive financial harm or force them to work on Saturday in order to provide for their families. I will also assume that John, a non-religious person, prefers not to work on Saturday instead of Sunday, because Saturday is the only day he can spend with his child, who normally lives with John's ex-wife at a distance elsewhere.

Applying a neutral test in this case will probably give priority to the religious conscientious demand to be exempt from the Sunday law over the non-religious demand, even though the non-religious demand is grounded in reason, whereas the religious one is not. Even if the rationale of the religious (Sabbatarian or Jewish) duty not to work for one day a week is grounded in reason, the requirement for that day to be Saturday and not Sunday, or any other day, is purely irrational.[37] Still, when the religious conscience is compared to John's wish to spend more time with his child, it seems that applying a balancing test that only measures amounts of harm, may result in granting exemptions only to religious objectors. This might be the case if we adopt the common view that the state is (and perhaps should be) more willing to grant exemptions from the law to those who object to the law because of conscientious reasons than to those who object to the law because of 'comfort-related reasons'.[38] A different,

---

[37] This assertion is accurate if the obligation not to work on a certain day relies on a person's interpretation of God's will and under the assumption that religious belief is, by its nature, irrational.

[38] This view is based on the assumption that the harm caused to a person who is prevented from acting upon his conscience is greater than the harm caused to a person who suffers (any degree of) discomfort when he obeys the law. This view can be disputed but I will not elaborate on this point here.

non-neutral and therefore preferable approach would also examine the reason for the objection, evaluate its merits, and decide that, even though John's objection is not grounded in conscience but merely in comfort or preference, it provides a stronger (though not necessarily compelling) reason to exempt him from the law than the irrational religious conscience.

This anti-neutral approach does not contradict the insight that, normally, the state grants conscientious exemptions to those who are mistaken, in the state's view. I argued that, more often than not, granting conscientious exemptions reflects an attitude of tolerance. However, the fact that the ruler normally grants conscientious exemptions to those who do not share the ruler's values or method of balancing different values does not mean that the ruler should not take into account the content of the conscience that grounds the objection. Various kinds of moral disagreement (or other types of disagreement) should be tolerated by the ruler, whereas other kinds of disagreement should not. In order to distinguish the two, a value-based examination of the conscience in question must be made.

Neutral liberals may respond by arguing that the content-based approach to the issue of conscientious exemption reflects 'monoculturalism', which denies the right to hold moral positions on certain issues that differ from the majority acceptance of them. Parkinson, for example, uses this argument in order to support the granting of an exemption from equality laws to those who refuse to take part in the registration of same-sex marriage or partnership— or in conducting these ceremonies.[39] Parkinson accuses perfectionist-liberals of 'monoculturalism' within the context of equality laws. However, it seems a bit odd to criticise equality laws for denying the right to hold and act upon certain moral positions—as this is the exact purpose of most equality laws. When equality laws include protected characteristics, and in our case—sexual orientation—they take a moral view on this issue which almost always contradicts other moral views that some people may hold. The prohibition on discriminating against others on the basis of their sexual orientation is not aimed at enlightened people who would never consider discriminating against LGTBs nor is it mainly aimed at those who discriminate against LGTBs because of mere preferences or interests. It is aimed at homophobes and those who have moral reasons for discriminating against LGTBs. From the tolerant-liberal state's point of view, it makes no sense to exempt from equality laws the same people who are the reason for enacting such laws. It appears that the argument against 'monoculturalism' is in fact an argument against core liberal values and, perhaps not deliberately, against certain aspects of equality laws as such.

---

[39] P Parkinson, 'Accommodating Religious Beliefs in a Secular Age: The Issue of Conscientious Objection in the Workplace' (2011) 34 *University of New South Wales Law Journal* 281, 294.

Parkinson applies pure neutral reasoning when he argues that those who refuse to obey equality laws within the context of providing services should be exempt from the law when their refusal to perform a service 'forms a very small part of the workload of the organisation and where those services could readily have been performed by many others'.[40] This reasoning, if taken seriously, can easily justify granting an exemption to those who refuse to register marriages or partnerships—or to provide any service of any kind (educational, medical, financial etc) on the basis of race, religion, sexual orientation etc, as long as the discriminated group is a very small minority (generally—or within the group of potential customers) and as long as the service can be provided by others. It may mean that a customer who is interested in a certain service may be answered by a very polite and 'multicultural' person that

> 'I am sorry, but according to my religion I must not serve Muslims, Jews, Christians or LGTBs, but if you can please take a seat for me, I will be happy to find someone who is willing to provide you with the service'.

More seriously, the point made here is that the liberal state should not hurry to compromise its liberal values—when they are expressed in value-based legislation—by applying neutral tests and granting exemptions to those who do not share these values. Such compromises will make the law redundant. It should be easier for the liberal state to apply neutral tests when it considers granting exemptions to those who, for conscientious reasons, object to laws that do not reflect liberal values (eg safety laws that impose a duty to wear helmets) or to those who object to laws that contradict their conscience, yet their conscience does not reflect intolerant and anti-liberal values (eg an objection to performing abortions—and here I assume that perceiving the foetus as a person is not necessarily intolerant or illiberal). The liberal state does not have to grant exemptions in cases that fall within these categories, as further considerations should also be taken into account, but the fact that granting exemptions in these cases does not run against core liberal values is a reason not to refuse granting exemptions. Equality laws, however, do not fall in either of these categories.

(ii) The 'Compelling State Interest' Test

Up to now I have discussed neutral tests that focus on the existence of harm. A different kind of criticism of the neutral test for granting conscientious exemptions focuses on the American 'compelling state interest' test, one of the central examples of applying a neutral balancing test within the context of conscientious exemption. This is not an exclusively American test. On the

---

[40] Parkinson (n 39 above) 294.

contrary, its rationale can be found in European human rights law and other jurisdictions as well. It should be noted that even though the 'compelling state interest' is often perceived as a neutral test, it is only neutral in the sense that it does not, in and of itself, give priority to either religious or non-religious claims to be granted exemptions. However, it is far from being a truly neutral test, since a 'compelling interest' has to be compelling in relation to another interest, and both should be accorded some weight according to their content. Therefore, value-based evaluation of those interests is inevitable.

Other aspects of the criticism of this test focus on the principled deficiencies of constitutional balancing tests as such[41] and especially on the tendency of the 'compelling state interest' test to lead to an 'all or nothing' conclusion.[42] Other criticisms focus on the inadequacy of this test in settling disputes regarding the practice of granting conscientious exemptions, or merely on the misapplication of the test. The 'compelling state interest' test is actually a specific implementation of the general 'strict scrutiny' test that, in the United States, settles contradictions between the public interest and more central and weighty constitutional rights. The strict scrutiny test aims to allow violations of these rights only in the most exceptional cases. However, it has been argued that, since 1963, where the 'compelling state interest' test came into force, the American courts have granted religious exemptions in only a few cases and refused to grant them in many other cases, even though a critical examination failed to find genuine 'compelling state interest' that could justify these decisions.[43] In other words, the 'compelling state interest' test was simply a rhetorical statement, lacking any practical implication. Eisgruber and Sager, therefore, concluded that 'while in other constitutional areas the compelling state interest test is fairly characterized as "strict in theory and fatal in fact", in the religion cases the test is strict in theory but feeble in fact'.[44] The gap between the rhetoric of the 'compelling state interest' test and the actual implementation of that test is unsurprising, since this test, which is a type of 'strict scrutiny' test, is clearly too strict to answer the complexity of the issue. It also fails to reflect the rationale for granting conscientious exemptions or the typical cases in which such exemptions should or may be granted. Eisgruber and Sager put it well when they say that

> the compelling state interest test is normally applied in constitutional contexts where practically all instances of collective behavior with the triggering feature are

[41] Eisgruber and Sager (n 6 above) 1260: 'the compelling state interest test becomes just another balancing test, obscuring rather than clarifying analysis'.

[42] Eisgruber and Sager (n 6 above) 1259.

[43] WP Marshall, 'The Case Against the Constitutionally Compelled Free Exercise Exemption' (1990) 40 *Case Western Reserve Law Review* 357, 369 (and the text to fn 59).

[44] Eisgruber and Sager (n 6 above) 1247. See also pp 1306–7: 'To mandate the compelling state interest test … is to invite confusion, duplicity, and dilution'.

expected to be unconstitutional ... but in many religious exemptions cases, the presumptive invalidity implicit in the compelling state interest test is misplaced. There is a substantial range of religiously motivated conduct ... that quite clearly must yield to conflicting secular laws.[45]

They rightly add that 'conscientious governments, acting for sound, unbiased reasons, will nevertheless promulgate general rules that interfere with some religious beliefs'.[46] Thus, the 'compelling state interest' test, which is perhaps the most common example of applying a neutral test to cases of conscientious exemptions, gives too much weight to freedom of conscience at the expense of other rights or interests. The opposite can be said about another common neutral test, which can be called the 'neutral law' test.

(iii) The 'Neutral Law' Test

The 'neutral law' test, which can be found in the United States after 1990 and also in the jurisprudence of the European Court of Human Rights,[47] provides that religious conscientious exemptions will not be granted from neutral laws; that is, from laws that do not intend to harm religious values or frustrate religious practices. This test presents state 'neutrality' at its worst.

First, the 'neutral law' test ignores the principle of proportionality and does not require the state to justify the infringement of freedom of (religious) conscience. All the state needs to prove is that there was no intention to violate freedom of conscience and that the harm caused to the conscientious objectors is incidental to other purposes that the law aims to achieve. The 'neutral law' test is neutral in the sense that it does not take into consideration the content of the conscience when deciding whether or not to grant an exemption. Its clear drawback is that it makes no effort to weigh the importance of the legitimate aim that the law is trying to achieve against the amount of harm caused to the conscientious objector. According to the 'neutral law' test, the fact that the harm is incidental is a decisive reason to completely ignore the harm caused to the conscientious objector whereas, in fact, it should be a marginal, often even an irrelevant reason for deciding cases of conscientious exemptions. In short, the relevant considerations should be the amount of harm caused to the conscientious objector, the content of the conscience and the harm that might be caused to the rights or interests of others should a

---

[45] Eisgruber and Sager (n 6 above) 1259–60.
[46] Eisgruber and Sager (n 6 above) 1306.
[47] Evans (n 28 above); Martinez-Torron (n 34 above).

conscientious exemption be granted. The intention of the legislature when it enacted the law should be of little importance.

Secondly, the 'neutral law' test assumes that the genuine intention of the law is either clear, or can be discovered by applying some methods of interpretation, and that there is a 'legislative intention' initially. It ignores the fact that, sometimes, there is no genuine, consistent legislative intention, apart from the intention to enact a law. When the legislative intention is unknown or vague, it is common for the court to apply purposive methods of interpretation, which actually determine what the intention of a reasonable legislature should have been. It can then be assumed that a reasonable legislature did not intend to harm potential conscientious objectors and that the harm that may be caused to them is incidental to the law's legitimate aim. However, it can also be assumed that a reasonable legislature did not intend not to grant exemptions from such a law. In other words, purposive interpretation may well lead to the conclusion that the law is indeed neutral and, at the same time, to a conclusion that the legislature intended to exempt conscientious objectors from the law in appropriate cases.

Thirdly, the 'neutral law' test also ignores the possibility that the legislature did not have in mind and did not expect the harm that may be caused to conscientious objectors by enacting the law. More accurately, the 'neutral law' test is indifferent to the question of whether the legislature had in mind or expected the harm that may be caused to conscientious objectors, as long as it did not intend to cause them harm. This attitude eliminates judicial discretion not only in cases where the severe harm caused to conscientious objectors was not intended, but also in cases where the harm was not expected at all. In cases where the legislature did not take a stand on this issue when it enacted the law, there is no convincing reason to completely deny judicial discretion in deciding whether or not to grant an exemption.

Fourthly, the 'neutral law' test places too much power in the hands of the legislature at the expense of the judiciary. The 'neutral law' test provides that a religious conscientious exemption *as a judicial remedy* will not be granted from neutral laws. The legislature, however, is free to decide whether to create statutory exemptions to its neutral laws. It is not surprising to find out, 20 years after the 'neutral law test' was introduced by the US Supreme Court, that State legislatures in the United States are overly responsive to majoritarian interests at the expense of minority religious liberty, and that expected constituent voting support heavily affects legislative decisions as to whether to create statutory exemption from neutral laws.[48] The 'neutral law' test thus gives rise to complex questions relating to the separation of powers and judicial review,

---

[48] Z Robinson, 'Rationalizing Religious Exemptions: A Legislative Process Theory of Statutory Exemptions for Religion' (2011) 20 *William & Mary Bill of Rights Journal* 133.

which will not be discussed here. Suffice it to say that when one completely trusts the legislature to protect minority rights—and in fact excludes judicial review in these cases—a failure to protect these rights in the right cases is quite predictable.

Fifthly, the 'neutral law' test also ignores the more troubling possibility that the legislature actually did intend to harm a certain group of conscientious objectors but disguised its intention by enacting an allegedly neutral law. To take one example: a school that wishes to prohibit its pupils from wearing religious symbols decides to create a dress code, which includes no exceptions. While the real intention behind the dress code is to exclude religious symbols from the school, the overt intention is to promote unity and discipline. For the judge who examines this case and knows nothing about the covert intention to exclude religious symbols from the school, the decision to create a dress code and the dress code itself are clearly neutral. Should the judge inquire into the hidden intention? Should he reach a conclusion based only on direct evidence or on the circumstances? And why does it matter? If, for whatever reason, religious pupils should be allowed to wear religious symbols to school, they are entitled to an exemption, even when there was no intention to exclude religious symbols by forming a dress code. Accordingly, if, for whatever reason, religious pupils should not be allowed to wear religious symbols to school, they are not entitled to an exemption, even when there was an intention to exclude religious symbols by forming a dress code.

Lastly, the neutral law test creates a temptation to perceive non-neutral laws as neutral in order to get to the desirable result (not granting religious exemptions) without having to make adverse judgements against those who claim such exemptions. Legislatures, judges and scholars may have various reasons to conceal their true views about minorities or about religion by applying a neutral discourse. At times, this temptation may lead to unintentional mistakes. Wintemute, for example, is right when he suggests that it is justified not to grant exemptions from the rule requiring all employees to serve all customers, without regard to sex, race, religion, disability, age or sexual orientation, but he is wrong in classifying this rule as neutral.[49] The rule is indeed neutral in a narrow sense: it does not aim to impose burdens on religious people as such. The rule, however, is not neutral in a more meaningful way—as it is not 'value-neutral'. It protects core liberal values. The rule maker knew very well that these values run against the values of most religions, which do prescribe discriminating against others on the basis of sex, race, religion, or sexual orientation. In other words, it is right not to grant exemptions in these cases, but not because the law is 'neutral' but because the state should not tolerate those who reject the liberal values that are reflected in equality laws.

---

[49] Wintemute (n 12 above) 240.

It is difficult to see why the real or alleged neutrality of the law should be a decisive criterion for deciding what rights people have. The neutrality of the law does not indicate its importance, the harm that it may cause to conscientious objectors and the harm that may be caused by granting exemptions. In this section I have discussed a few of the deficiencies of some common neutral tests. Other important drawbacks of such tests will be discussed when particular kinds of neutral tests are presented in the next section.

V. 'EQUAL REGARD' APPROACHES[50]

A. The 'Equal Regard' Approach—A Description

Equal regard approaches to the issue of conscientious exemptions suggest that, when an exemption is granted to a non-religious conscientious objector, an exemption should also be given to the equivalent religious objector, and vice versa. An equal regard approach does not have to be a neutral one. The main argument of the equal regard approach is that, if X is granted an exemption, anyone who is similar to X in relevant aspects should also be granted an exemption. The question of when an exemption should be granted in the first place can be decided either by applying neutral tests as described above or by applying liberal value-based tests, as will be described shortly. As a result, various equal regard approaches do not have to provide the same answers to questions such as when conscientious exemptions should be granted or whether they should be granted at all. Equal regard approaches can express a principled, general reluctance to grant conscientious exemptions.[51] They can also be supportive of a more willing regime. They are equal regard approaches because, whatever their approach to granting conscientious exemptions may be, it is applied to religious and non-religious claims equally.

Some of the scholars who hold an equal regard approach perceive it as a remedy for the current state of affairs, where religious claims to conscientious exemptions have priority over non-religious ones,[52] whereas others view an equal regard approach as a remedy for what they regard as a practice

---

[50] The term 'equal regard' in this context is borrowed from Eisgruber and Sager (n 6 above).

[51] See, for example: I Lupo, 'Where Rights Begin: The Problem of Burdens on the Free Exercise of Religion' (1989) 102 *Harvard Law Review* 933, 970–72; I Lupo, 'The Case Against Legislative Codification of Religious Liberty' (1999) 21 *Cardozo Law Review* 565; I Lupo, 'The Trouble with Accommodation' (1992) 60 *George Washington Law Review* 743, 778–79; I Lupo, 'To Control Faction and Protect Liberty: A General Theory of the Religion Clauses' (1996) 7 *Journal of Contemporary Legal Studies* 357, 384. For an argument that in the United States 'the current free exercise jurisprudence disfavours exemptions', see Marshall (n 43 above) 372.

[52] A Bradney, *Religions, Rights and Laws* (Leicester, Leicester University Press, 1993) 97, 115.

of discriminating against religious claims to conscientious exemptions.[53] In the American context, those who hold an equal regard approach may do so because they believe that giving priority to claims for the granting of religious conscientious exemptions contradicts the non-establishment clause of the First Amendment.[54]

One way to argue for an equal regard approach is to assert that, whenever the law mentions freedom of religion (or free exercise of religion) or simply grants religious exemptions, 'religion' should be interpreted as incorporating non-religious and even anti-religious or atheistic beliefs.[55] A similar way is to abandon the legal distinction between a religious conscience and a non-religious one, and to argue for a general legal principle that will protect freedom of conscience by allowing or imposing a duty to grant conscientious exemptions regardless of the religiosity of the conscience that grounds the objection to the law.[56] A different way to apply an equal regard approach is to argue that equality requires the state to accord the same weight to religious values, beliefs and conventions, and to any other legitimate interests—even those that have nothing to do with conscience or deeply-held beliefs. Kramnick and Moore argue along these lines and suggest, quite provocatively, that religion should have 'the same rights in the public sphere as General Motors, no more no less'.[57]

A further type of equal regard approach, proposed within the First Amendment context but also applicable to other constitutions, is suggested by William Marshall, who argues that 'free exercise claims advanced by those seeking relief from laws of general applicability should be resolved under the speech clause'.[58] This is an equal regard approach because, as Marshall himself writes, 'if free exercise is treated as expression, the result will obviously be that the religious and non-religious groups will be accorded the same level of

---

[53] McConnell (n 5 above) 47.

[54] FM Gedicks, *The Rhetoric of Church and State* (Durham NC, Duke University Press, 1995) ch 6; FM Gedicks, 'The Improbability of Religion Clause Theory' (1997) 27 *Seton Hall Law Review* 1233.

[55] D Laycock, 'Religious Liberty as Liberty' (1996) 7 *Journal of Contemporary Legal Studies* 313, 326–27, 338–39; EP Abbott, 'Atheism and the Religious Liberty Protection Act: A Place for Everyone or Everyone in their Place' (2000/2001) 2 *Rutgers Journal of Law and Religion* 4. See also J Finnis, *Natural Law and Natural Rights* (Oxford, Oxford University Press, 1980) 89, where religion is defined as thinking reasonably and, when possible, correctly about questions of the origins of cosmic order and of human freedom and reason.

[56] Marshall (n 43 above) 360–62; RK Smith, 'Converting the Religious Equality Amendment into a Statute with a Little Conscience' [1996] *Brigham Young University Law Review* 645, 662–75; Gedicks (n 20 above) 571–72.

[57] I Kramnick and L Moore, *The Godless Constitution: The Case Against Religious Correctness* (New York, WW Norton, 1996) 15. See also Barry (n 2 above) 50: 'there is a possible case for letting everybody do what they please and a possible case for constraining everyone alike, but ... a great deal of finagling is needed in order to support a general rule with exemptions based on religious beliefs'.

[58] Marshall (n 43 above) 360.

protection … the presence of a free exercise interest notwithstanding'.[59] This approach, which is often called 'the reduction principle', has one major flaw, of which Marshall is well aware. Many religious and non-religious claims to be granted conscientious exemptions do not fit easily within an analysis of free expression (eg claims to be exempted from compulsory enlistment into the army, performing abortions, vaccinating one's child, receiving blood transfusions, and so on).[60] It is difficult to see why they should be constitutionally ignored for that reason alone.[61]

Kent Greenawalt holds the view that 'the connection of a belief to religion does not in and of itself confer any special claim to be accommodated'.[62] He then mentions other possible, neutral reasons for making religious belief or practice a criterion for granting exemptions: first, some laws are likely to be objected to on conscientious grounds only by religious believers; secondly, in some cases, religious believers have stronger reasons, in a psychological sense, not to perform an act than non-religious believers; thirdly, on occasion, it is easier to decide the sincerity of religious conscientious objectors (because of the communal, formal structure of religious commands), so that non-religious objectors might be excluded to minimise problems relating to accurate administration and perceived unfairness.[63] Although these reasons for preferring the religious conscience are related directly to the religiosity of that conscience, and, in that sense, are not completely neutral, they remain generally neutral reasons given that the specific content of the conscience is, after all, irrelevant.

Eisgruber and Sager offer one of the clearest, most comprehensive approaches to cases of claiming conscientious exemptions and to freedom of religion in general.[64] The exact meaning of their view, which they indeed

---

[59]   Marshall (n 43 above) 360–61.

[60]   But compare Marshall's view, according to which 'the breadth of religious activity covered under the speech clause is already expansive and to a large degree includes the core of religious exercise': (n 43 above) 396.

[61]   Moreover, the claim that 'if free exercise is treated as expression, the result will obviously be that the religious and non-religious groups will be accorded the same level of protection' may be true when free expression jurisprudence is generally neutral, as in the United States. However, a theory of free expression does not have to ignore the content of the speech or the content of the values that find expression within the speech.

[62]   Greenawalt (n 1 above) 321.

[63]   These reasons led Greenawalt (n 1 above) to say that, with regard to military service, 'if an exemption continues to be given to pacifist conscientious objectors, no religious restriction should be adopted' (p 326), whereas, regarding Saturday employment, the exemption should be limited 'to those who combine membership in a Sabbatarian group with a strong conviction against Saturday work' (p 335). Compare these conclusions with Greenawalt's view (p 324) that 'some administrative difficulty is not a weighty basis for narrowing the exemption (from military service)'.

[64]   CL Eisgruber and LG Sager, *Religious Freedom and the Constitution* (Cambridge MA, Harvard University Press, 2007). Chapter 3 of this book reworks their religious exemption theory, parts of which I will refer to later.

call 'the equal regard approach', is relatively straightforward: 'Equal Regard requires simply that government treat the deep, religiously inspired concerns of minority religious believers with the same regard as that enjoyed by the deep concerns of citizens generally'.[65] The 'equal regard' approach focuses on equality rather than the value of the religious belief. It is equality that should be protected or promoted rather than the religious value as such. The state should not discriminate against religious practices, as part of the general prohibition of discrimination rather than because religious practices are uniquely valuable.

A central part of the 'equal regard' approach is the distinction between privilege and protection. Eisgruber and Sager submit that

> privilege and protection refer not to the fact of constitutional (or judicial) priority, but to the grounds for such priority. A claim for constitutional privilege requires a showing of virtue or precedence, while a claim for constitutional protection requires a showing of vulnerability or victimization.[66]

According to Eisgruber and Sager, 'what transforms religious accommodation from a mere policy concern to a constitutional issue is the vulnerability of religion to prejudice and persecution'.[67] Eisgruber and Sager develop their argument even further when they compare holding a religious belief to having a physical disability.[68] Both may prevent or make it harder for a person to obey neutral laws, ie laws that do not intend to harm or impose an exceptional burden on either religious adherents or disabled people. An exemption from the law may be required in both cases and for the same reason—the vulnerability of religious believers and disabled people with regard to neutral laws. More generally, Eisgruber and Sager write that 'as a judicially enforced constitutional principle, equal regard must be justified by vulnerability to discrimination'.[69]

How does the equal regard approach work in practice? A religious person seeking an exemption from the demands of the law needs to prove the following: first, that the requirements of the law prevent him from exercising his

---

[65] Eisgruber and Sager (n 6 above) 1283. For an updated version of this theory, which is now called 'equal liberty', see CL Eisgruber and LG Sager, 'Chips Off Our Block? A Reply to Berg, Greenawalt, Lupo and Tuttle' (2007) 85 *Texas Law Review* 1273: 'Equal Liberty consists of two basic principles, one focused on equality and the other focused on liberty. First, no members of our political community ought to be devalued on the basis of the spiritual foundations of their important commitments and projects. Second, all members of our political community ought to enjoy rights of free speech, personal autonomy, and private property that, while neither uniquely relevant to religion nor defined in terms of religion, will allow a broad range of religious beliefs and practices to flourish'.

[66] Eisgruber and Sager (n 6 above) 1251. See also pp 1248–54.

[67] Eisgruber and Sager (n 6 above) 1278.

[68] Eisgruber and Sager (n 6 above) 1267.

[69] Eisgruber and Sager (n 6 above) 1291.

religious belief or impose a substantial burden should he choose to do so; and secondly, that if his religious values were accorded the same weight accorded to non-religious values in the case in issue, he would have been granted the exemption. The last point can be proven in two ways. The religious believer can show that the state failed to evaluate properly his religious commitment to act (or to refrain from acting) in a certain way. He can also show that non-religious exemptions are granted from the same law, so that he is discriminated against because of his religious beliefs.[70]

This description of how the equal regard approach actually works demonstrates its neutrality and draws attention to another central consideration: the centrality of the value or the belief to the life of the person seeking the exemption. Eisgruber and Sager clearly say that 'we have to separate the general appeal of people being motivated by conscience from the content of their conscientious motivations'.[71] The content of the value or the belief is unimportant. What is important is that values and beliefs that are central to the life of persons in a similar way will be treated equally by the state. Thus, religious and non-religious consciences should be treated with equal regard as reasons for granting conscientious exemptions. Both types of conscience should take priority over other reasons for seeking exemptions from neutral laws, such as 'love, passionately demanding life projects, and the infinitely creative demands of strong psychological compulsion'.[72]

Eisgruber and Sager's equal regard approach is indeed neutral, but with one important exception. Two interrelated questions that are often raised with regard to the issue of granting conscientious exemptions are whether the state should decide the sincerity of the conscientious objector and whether it should decide the reasonableness of his claim that the relevant value or belief is central to his conscience and life. Regarding religious conscience, Eisgruber and Sager claim that the liberal, non-religious state should not, and, moreover, cannot question the objector's sincerity or the reasonableness of his claim that the value or the belief at issue is central to his conscience and life. This is not the case regarding non-religious consciences. In more detail, their argument is that:

> The protection of religious conscience requires that the state treat religious belief as a 'black box'; for purposes of assessing the impact of a sincerely held scheme

[70] Eisgruber and Sager (n 6 above) 1285.
[71] Eisgruber and Sager (n 6 above) 1269.
[72] Eisgruber and Sager (n 6 above) 1269. This view raises the difficulty of defining 'conscience'. I will not discuss this issue here. For Eisgruber and Sager's view, see (n 6 above) 1291: 'a person is in the grip of conscience when an ethical tug toward doing the right thing becomes a central, dominating feature of her motivation and self-identity'. See also pp 1268–69.

For a different view, see Greenawalt (n 1 above) 313: 'although a conscientious objector need not feel certain of the moral rightness of his view, he must believe that performing the required act would probably involve him in grave moral wrong'.

of religious belief upon the believer, the ultimate truth or the reasonability of the scheme is beyond the constitutional competence of the state. This is implicit in the requirement of equal regard that the state defer to the perspective of a religious believer as to the existence of an interest of great weight within her life; it is a function of the epistemically distinct, closed logic of religious belief.

With secular claims of conscience, however, the believer and the state in principle share a common epistemic foundation. For that reason, the state may legitimately reflect upon and respond to the reasonability of the secular claimant's conscientious commitments. Reasonability here speaks not so much to the plausibility of a given belief, as to the elevation of that belief to a dominant position with regard to motivation and self-identity.[73]

This view clearly gives priority to religious claims to be granted conscientious exemptions. Eisgruber and Sager apply this approach to the case of 'selective objection' to military service, arguing that

we might think it unreasonable for secular objectors to build moral identities around distinctions that they themselves recognize as matters inviting political resolution. This argument carries less weight with respect to religious objectors, since the state may no more pass upon the reasonableness of religious distinctions among just and unjust wars than it may pass upon the reasonableness of religious beliefs about wearing yarmulkes or eating beef on Friday.[74]

It is interesting to note that Michael McConnell, one of the prominent advocates of the pro-religion approach, argues, at different times and even simultaneously, for a type of equal regard approach as well. In one place, he argues for an equal regard approach within the specific context of the First Amendment, stating that

rather than insisting that religious concern receive no more protection than is accorded nonreligious analogues, it may be more helpful to think of ways in which the twin protections of free exercise and nonestablishment could be extended to nonreligious spheres of life.[75]

This view does not coincide with McConnell's general view, according to which 'religion is a special phenomenon'.[76] If religion is indeed special, then it is unclear why certain principles, such as the free exercise of one's conscience and the non-establishment of ideologies, should be applied in the same way with regard to religious and non-religious beliefs. If religion is indeed special, it should be treated differently to other sets of beliefs. The nature of the different treatment is, of course, a separate question. Elsewhere, McConnell

---

[73] Eisgruber and Sager (n 6 above) 1292–93.
[74] Eisgruber and Sager (n 6 above) 1296–97.
[75] McConnell (n 5 above) 47.
[76] McConnell (n 5 above) 42.

argues for a more specific view, in a fashion similar to one of Eisgruber and Sager's arguments, that religious conscientious exemptions should be granted whenever non-religious exemptions (not necessarily conscientious ones) are granted by law on a case-by-case basis, ie according to the discretion of the executive.[77]

Another way to apply an equal regard approach is by addressing the issue of conscientious exemptions, and indeed freedom of religion, from an economic point of view. Michael McConnell and Richard Posner suggest that 'churches can receive benefits from government, and be exposed to burdens, as long as the benefits and burdens have approximately neutral consequences for comparable institutions. Exemptions from burdens and inclusion in benefits are indistinguishable in their economic effects'.[78] But McConnell and Posner's approach entails more than this. On the one hand, they acknowledge, in principle, the authority of government to impose burdens on the freedom of religion if this is being done by neutral legislation, ie by legislation that does not intend to harm the freedom of religion.[79] On the other hand, neutral legislation, in their view, is only a necessary condition for imposing burdens on the freedom of religion. It is not a sufficient condition. The need to question the importance or the weight of the interest that justifies the neutral legislation still exists. The result is a complex test that contains both neutral and value-based components. The law that imposes burdens on the freedom of religion should be neutral (this is the only requirement in American jurisprudence after 1990). The interest that grounds the law or the reason for enacting the law should be compelling (and that was the only requirement in American jurisprudence until 1990). Finally, the weight given to the compelling reason for enacting the law should be proportionate to the amount of harm caused to freedom of religion.[80]

It turns out that this economic-neutral test is not neutral at all. At the beginning of their article, McConnell and Posner state that 'we propose using an economic definition of "neutrality" to determine when government action impinges impermissibly on religious choice'[81] (the term 'impermissibly' is ambiguous here). However, later, they state more clearly that 'the critical

---

[77] M McConnell, 'Neutrality under the Religious Clauses' (1986) 81 *Northwestern University Law Review* 146, 156.

[78] M McConnell and RA Posner, 'An Economic Approach to Issues of Religious Freedom' (1989) 56 *University of Chicago Law Review* 1, 12. According to McConnell and Posner, granting religious exemptions is always a way of 'subsidizing' religion, even when the subject-matter of the exemption is the freedom to exercise one's belief in a non-economic context.

[79] McConnell and Posner (n 78 above) 34.

[80] McConnell and Posner (n 78 above) 54: 'A stronger governmental interest should be required in order to overcome an onerous burden on religious freedom than in order to overcome a trivial one, and vice versa'.

[81] McConnell and Posner (n 78 above) 1.

question from an economic standpoint is not whether the government policy uses neutral terminology but whether it imposes unjustifiable costs on the exercise of religion'.[82] Although neutral-economic criteria may be helpful in deciding this question, no answer can be provided without recourse to a value-based judgement about the virtue of religion and its appropriate place in society and public life. If the main question is whether the government policy imposes unjustifiable costs on the exercise of religion, and if we should ask whether the weight accorded to the reason for imposing burdens on religion is proportionate to the amount of harm caused to freedom of religion, it is difficult to see how we can answer these questions without evaluating the weight and importance of religious values. In other words, the answers to these questions cannot rely solely on neutral or economic considerations.

B. Evaluating the 'Equal Regard' Approach

In the present section, I will focus on Eisgruber and Sager's equal regard approach and attempt to evaluate its coherence and strength. As previously noted, this approach 'requires simply that government treat the deep, religiously inspired concerns of minority religious believers with the same regard as that enjoyed by the deep concerns of citizens generally'.[83]

As with any other equality-based theory, the equal regard theory is exposed to the 'levelling down' problem. There is nothing in the equal regard approach that prevents governments from suppressing religious and non-religious conscientious objectors alike, provided it does so even-handedly. Eisgruber and Sager's response to this difficulty is to say that their theory is actually a theory of equal liberty, which means that it is not merely an anti-discrimination theory but also a liberty-based one.[84] This shift is supposed to solve the 'levelling down' or 'equal oppression' problem. In other words, we should understand their theory as one that requires governments to treat the deep, religiously inspired concerns of minority religious believers with the same regard as that enjoyed or which should be enjoyed by the deep concerns of citizens generally. The question is whether this shift demands the surrender of many of their objections to what I call the 'pro-religious' approach. In addition, the shift from equal regard to equal liberty does not solve many other difficulties regarding Eisgruber and Sager's theory. I will return to this point shortly, after evaluating the drawbacks of a 'pure' equal regard approach.

A pure equal regard approach, which is one that does not contain elements of equal liberty, suffers from several deficiencies. First, this approach is partly

---

[82] McConnell and Posner (n 78 above) 40.
[83] Eisgruber and Sager (n 6 above) 1283.
[84] Eisgruber and Sager (n 64 above) 93–94.

empty, and, at times, meaningless. The approach is empty because equality itself is an empty idea, at least in part. When we apply the equal regard approach, we are required to accord some weight to religious considerations. The weight we are required to accord to religious considerations depends on the weight we actually accord to non-religious considerations, or would have accorded to non-religious considerations in similar circumstances. But how are we to decide which non-religious considerations are the right bases for comparison? Can these decisions be neutral? If the law imposes a duty to wear crash helmets when riding a motorcycle, and a religious Sikh requests an exemption from the law because his religion requires him to wear a turban at all times, should we compare this demand to a non-religious demand to be exempt from the law because of a medical condition that prevents someone from wearing a helmet, or perhaps to a non-religious demand to be exempt from the law because wearing a helmet ruins a fashion-model's hairstyle for the rest of the day? Moreover, it is plausible that, in some cases, we shall find no secular analogues to religious claims for conscientious exemptions. Eisgruber and Sager agree, for example, that secular moral commitments will rarely be comparable to religious duties regarding dress codes. Still, they argue that the principle of equal regard (and equal liberty) calls for religious exemptions in most dress code cases, because the 'burdens imposed in such cases are especially likely to result from neglect'.[85] This has nothing to do with the existence of similar exemptions or with the expected legislative response to similar demands for exemptions, as there are no such comparable demands. The only argument is that the legislature did not consider fairly the imposition on religious believers of a uniform dress code.

Greenawalt uses this example to highlight yet another difficulty with the theory of equal regard. According to Greenawalt,

> it might be that the reason *not* to make a particular exception—say for girls in schools wearing head scarves—is that usage reflects and conveys (for some people) a prescribed role for women that does not correspond to liberal democratic values. Does that constitute a failure of equal regard?[86]

With the absence of secular analogues to the above religious claim for a conscientious exemption, the questions whether a refusal to grant an exemption constitutes a failure of equal regard and whether the refusal is justified, must be answered, inter alia, by assessing the strength of the state's interest in protecting liberal democratic values and presumably also the rights of at least

---

[85]   Eisgruber and Sager (n 64 above) 97.
[86]   K Greenawalt, 'How Does "Equal Liberty" Fare in Relation to Other Approaches to the Religious Clauses?' (2007) 85 *Texas Law Review* 1217, 1243. Greenawalt also argues that Eisgruber and Sager fail to distinguish forms of dress that are motivated by one's religion and those that are required by it.

some religious women not to wear head scarves, compared with the importance of the religious requirement to wear head scarves. However, Eisgruber
and Sager reject this type of balancing test.

Even if we do find the right basis for comparison, we will probably find
numerous other comparable personal commitments and interests, some of
which are accommodated by exemptions (not necessarily conscientious ones)
and others which are not. How can the equal regard approach operate in
this case?[87] There is nothing in the equal regard approach that answers such
questions. Presumably, there is no point in trying to answer at least some of
them. McConnell rightly points out that: 'since the various nonreligious commitments of our society are themselves treated with unequal regard, it is not
logically possible to achieve equality of regard between each secular concept
and religion'.[88]

Two different aspects of the emptiness of equality affect the creditability
of the 'equal regard' approach.[89] First, it has been suggested that the proposition that 'cases that are alike should be treated alike' is tautological. I submitted earlier that, all too often, there is no neutral way of deciding when one
case is relevantly different from another. All too often, it is merely a question
of unshared values or balance of reasons. Therefore, these values or reasons
should be our main concern and not equality, 'equal regard' or the like. This
aspect of the emptiness of equality corresponds with the arguments outlined
in the previous paragraphs. Secondly, if there is a right to be granted religious
conscientious exemptions, it results from independent reasons that are unrelated to the fact that a conscientious exemption is granted, or would have been
granted, to non-religious objections on similar or 'equal' grounds. This is why
the equal regard approach is empty, at least in part. Yet, this is not its only
flaw, as the 'equal regard' is also incoherent. This flaw, as well as others that
will be elaborated on shortly, are not remedied by the shift from equal regard
to equal liberty.

The fact is that the 'equal regard' approach does not pay equal regard
at all to religious and non-religious objections. According to this approach,
the sincerity of the non-religious objection and the centrality of the value
that grounds the objection to the objector's personality or identity, are to be
examined and evaluated by the state. However, the sincerity of the religious

---

[87] See also TC Berg, 'Can Religious Liberty Be Protected as Equality?' (2007) 85 *Texas
Law Review* 1185, 1194. For a different argument regarding the problem of comparison, see
Greenawalt (n 86 above) 1241: 'what are we to make, from the standpoint of Equal Liberty, of
failures to forbid firmly entrenched practices that are dangerous?'

[88] McConnell (n 5 above) 46. For McConnell's criticism, see also pp 15–38.

[89] I described the partial emptiness of the idea of equality in the text to n 12 above, where
I discussed the practice surrounding conscientious exemptions. Therefore, the following
discussion should be read in the light of that discussion.

objection and the centrality of the value that grounds the objection to the objector's personality or identity are immune from any evaluation. It is difficult to see how this view can be part of what is called an equal regard or equal liberty approach.[90]

The 'equal regard' approach consists of three main ideas: first, religious conscientious objections should always be perceived as sincere. In addition, the centrality of the value that grounds the objection to the objector's life and personal morality is unquestionable; secondly, the government should treat the deep, religiously inspired concerns of religious believers with the same regard as that enjoyed by the deep concerns of citizens generally; and, thirdly, only with respect to non-religious objections can the state question the sincerity of the objector, and the centrality of the value that grounds the objection to the objector's life and personal morality. Here, I share McConnell's categorical conclusion that 'the three parts of the "equal regard" principle are mutually inconsistent'.[91] McConnell also points out a further, related flaw in the equal regard principle as applied by Eisgruber and Sager, by arguing that their approach

> assumes that all religious commitments are as powerful and worthy of protection as the most powerful and worthy of secular commitments. No secular commitment receives such automatic deference ... Thus, it seems that Eisgruber and Sager's theory 'privileges' religion no less than, and in the same way as, the RFRA [that Eisgruber and Sager are criticising].[92]

If this is an accurate interpretation of the 'equal regard' principle, then it is indeed inconsistent for the reason pointed out by McConnell. However, I am unconvinced that this is indeed an accurate interpretation of the 'equal regard' principle. Eisgruber and Sager submit that 'to appreciate the gravity of the religious believer's interest in complying with the commands of her faith, the state must adopt the perspective of the believer; it is not at liberty to judge that interest',[93] but add that 'the state is not obliged, however, to accept a religious believer's judgment about the importance of her religious interests

---

[90] In his review of Eisgruber and Sager's recently published book (n 64 above), Thomas Berg makes a similar claim, according to which 'Eisgruber and Sager cannot give religious liberty the robust protection they claim without giving it more protection than some deeply felt nonreligious reasons for acting, and without showing some special concern for religious autonomy': Berg (n 87 above) 1188.

[91] McConnell (n 5 above) 35.

[92] McConnell (n 5 above) 37. See also Berg (n 87 above) 1204: 'Eisgruber and Sager offer a potentially powerful method for protecting religious liberty by comparing it with other interests. But they can only do so by comparing it with the most weighty secular interest, and thus by treating freedom in religious matters as more important than freedom for many other deeply felt secular commitments'.

[93] Eisgruber and Sager (n 6 above) 1285.

as compared to the legitimate secular interest of the state'.[94] On the one hand, this means that Eisgruber and Sager do not assume that all religious commitments are as powerful and worthy of protection as the most powerful, worthy, secular commitments, as McConnell argues. On the other hand, this raises a different kind of incoherence, since it remains unclear how the state can (and must) adopt the perspective of the believer with regard to the gravity of his interest in complying with the commands of his faith and, at the same time, not be obliged to accept the religious believer's judgement about the importance of his religious interests, compared to the legitimate secular interest of the state.

Apart from the incoherence of the equal regard approach, the priority that Eisgruber and Sager give to religious conscientious objections by placing them beyond any evaluation of their sincerity and centrality (if this is indeed what they are doing) is wrong for a few independent reasons. First, it is always a challenge for the majority or the state's organs to evaluate correctly how central a certain value is to individuals. This task becomes trickier the more unfamiliar or individualistic these values are. This is true with regard to religious and non-religious minorities and individuals alike. Eisgruber and Sager's epistemological argument fails to explain adequately why the secular state is more competent to decide the issues of sincerity and centrality regarding non-religious objectors than regarding religious objectors. The fact that the state and the non-religious objectors are secular does not mean anything more than that. All that it may mean is that secular conscientious objectors and the state do not share a common epistemic foundation with religious objectors. It does not mean that secular conscientious objectors and the state share a common epistemic foundation, at least not necessarily. Non-religious objections can be exercised regarding various issues, such as vegetarianism, environmental naturalism, naturism, animal rights, drugs, nuclear energy and taxes. It would be naïve to assume that the state is more competent to decide about the sincerity and centrality of these reasons for objections than about all religious reasons for objection, simply because the state itself is politically non-religious.

Secondly, religious belief is indeed—and by definition—irrational,[95] or at least based on faith, not reason.[96] This does not mean, however, that non-religious

---

[94] Eisgruber and Sager (n 6 above) 1286.

[95] For a different view about the rationality of religious commitment (rather than religious faith) see R Audi, *Rationality and Religious Commitment* (Oxford, Oxford University Press, 2011). It seems, however, that Audi's understanding of what rationality means is too permissive. This, in turn, weakens the strength of some of his arguments. For the possibility that believing in something that cannot be proved may still be reasonable see D Richards, *Toleration and the Constitution* (New York, Oxford University Press, 1986) 75–77.

[96] For a view that what distinguishes religious belief is that it is based on faith, not reason, see: T Macklem, 'Faith as a Secular Value' (2000) 45 *McGill Law Journal* 1, 133. I am aware that this view is controversial and that some scholars suggest that religious belief or simply religion is

beliefs are necessarily rational. Non-religious conscientious objections can be based, in principle, on sincerely held, yet irrational or esoteric beliefs that are central to the personhood of the objector. There can be a secular society in which individuals, minorities, or even great parts of the population hold utterly irrational beliefs about major aspects of their lives. They may also seek conscientious exemptions based on these irrational beliefs. In such cases, it cannot be argued that the secular state which bases, or should base, its political discourse on reason and rational grounds shares what Eisgruber and Sager call 'a common epistemic foundation' with the non-religious objector who holds irrational or esoteric beliefs, values and, indeed, conscience.

Thirdly, the fact that a state or its political organs are politically non-religious does not necessarily mean that the state is also culturally non-religious or that most state officials are non-religious.[97] There is no reason to assume that a politically secular but culturally religious state and its officials will be less competent to evaluate the sincerity and centrality of religious claims to be granted conscientious exemptions, in comparison to similar non-religious claims.

Fourthly, Eisgruber and Sager argue for the incompetence of the state in evaluating correctly the sincerity of religious objections and the reasonableness of the claim that the values that ground the objection are central to the objector's personhood. Even if we agree that the state might encounter some difficulties in that respect, it would be mistaken to suggest that these difficulties cannot be solved, at least in part. The state can turn to experts for an opinion concerning these issues. Religious leaders or even non-religious, authoritative experts on a certain religion can assist the state in evaluating the sincerity and centrality of the religious objection. Precisely because most popular religions have communitarian characteristics; because within a certain religion its adherents will take part in common practices; and because, every so often, religions have authoritative texts and an institutional hierarchy, it may be easier to discover the one true answer about issues of sincerity, reasonableness and centrality than in cases of non-religious, individual conscientious objections.

The difficulty that Eisgruber and Sager mention concerning the issues of sincerity, reasonableness and centrality poses a genuine problem. Eisgruber and Sager's solution—to make a distinction between religious and non-religious objections—is unsatisfactory. The distinction, if there is one, should be drawn between minority, relatively unknown or esoteric beliefs, and popular ones.

---

grounded in reason. See, for example, Finnis (n 55 above) 378–88. For describing Aquinas' 'five proofs of God' see: J Cottingham (ed), *Western Philosophy: An Anthology* (New York, Wiley, 2008) 348–51. I do not wish to establish any argument in this matter since Eisgruber and Sager themselves agree that, normally, religion is not grounded in reason.

[97] It is ironic that Eisgruber and Sager offer the equal regard approach within the American context, as the United States is an excellent example of a secular state from the political aspect, but, at the same time, deeply culturally religious.

The religiosity of the belief as such should not be a relevant factor. A genuine equal regard approach requires one of two courses of action: either to treat all conscientious objections as sincere, and as such to treat them as based on values that are central to the objector's personhood; or to evaluate the sincerity of all objections on a case-by-case basis. Since the first option may compromise important public interests and the rights of third parties more than is necessary, there is no escape but to adopt a case-by-case approach. In their later writings, it appears that Eisgruber and Sager abandon the attempt to exclude secular moral claims from constitutional entitlement on the ground that they can be deemed unreasonable.[98] The result is, of course, and as Thomas Berg rightly says, that 'without limits on the kind of strongly felt secular moral claims that must receive equal regard, the regime of accommodation will be so radical as to undermine itself'.[99]

Thus, the equal regard approach is inconsistent and partly empty. In some cases (eg when there are no secular analogues to religious claims for conscientious exemptions) it cannot be applied at all. In other cases, it cannot be applied without compromising important public interests. Lastly, its aspiration to neutrality exposes it to the criticisms of the neutral approaches as described in the previous section.

VI. LIBERAL VALUE-BASED APPROACHES

Liberal value-based approaches take into account the content of the conscience that grounds the objection, yet the religiosity of that conscience remains irrelevant. Therefore, these approaches prescribe that some conscientious objections should not be tolerated at all—or only to a certain extent—because of the content of the conscience that grounds the objection. The exact reason may be that the conscience is based on irrational belief or morally repugnant values, regardless of whether it is religious or non-religious.

A liberal value-based approach can argue for a hierarchy of values, rights and interests or, similarly, can argue that, if granting a conscientious exemption would result in a certain amount of harm to rights (or certain rights) of third parties, then it should not be granted, regardless of the harm that may then be caused to the conscientious objector. Martha Nussbaum argues for a general, universal balancing test between the freedom of religion and other human rights. Nussbaum submits that 'the state and its agents may impose a substantial burden on religion only when it can show a compelling interest … protection of the central capabilities of citizens should always be understood

---

[98] Berg (n 87 above) 1201.
[99] Berg (n 87 above) 1201.

to ground a compelling state interest'.[100] These 'central capabilities of citizens' are, in fact, according to Nussbaum, many of the central human rights protected by international treaties and conventions (eg equality in the workplace, political equality, the right to property, freedom of movement, autonomy, and so on). Therefore, we should not mistake Nussbaum's use of the 'compelling interest' test for an application of the general strict scrutiny test, because, according to Nussbaum, imposing substantial burdens on the freedom of religion is always justified by protecting 'the central capabilities of citizens', which are actually the core of the human rights of others. More specifically, refusing to grant religious conscientious exemptions is always justified if it protects the core of the human rights of others.

Nussbaum has also made a slightly different argument, according to which 'to apply penalties for conforming to the dictates of one's conscience, in matters where peace and safety are not at stake, is an affront to the person and the person's equality'.[101] It is not quite clear whether the absence of a threat to peace and safety is a sufficient condition for granting conscientious exemptions. In other words, it is not clear whether Nussbaum thinks that conscientious exemptions should be granted every time when peace and safety are not at stake. If the argument is indeed that the absence of a threat to peace and safety is a sufficient condition for granting conscientious exemptions, it has two main deficiencies: first, violating human rights does not always result in jeopardising peace and safety. Therefore, this argument is utterly different from Nussbaum's early and more appealing argument that refusing to grant religious conscientious exemptions is always justified if it protects the core of the human rights of others. Secondly, this is an overly narrow and simplistic condition for granting conscientious exemptions, as it excludes many other relevant, central considerations.

Nussbaum emphasises how egalitarian and value-based views are both part of her theory of conscientious exemption. Nussbaum argues for equal respect or equal liberty of conscience as a principle that requires

> giving citizens ample space to pursue their conscientious commitments, even when this involves giving them exemptions from some laws that apply to all citizens. Only what is called in the law a 'compelling state interest' should ever be able to justify any diminution of that space.[102]

---

[100]   MC Nussbaum, *Sex and Social Change* (New York, Oxford University Press, 1999) 201.

[101]   MC Nussbaum, 'Liberty of Conscience: The Attack on Equal Respect' (2007) 8 *Journal of Human Development* 337, 347. See also MC Nussbaum, *The New Religious Intolerance: Overcoming the Politics of Fear in an Anxious Age* (Cambridge, The Belknap Press, 2012) 65.

[102]   Nussbaum (2007) (n 101 above) 339. She immediately adds that 'liberty of conscience is incompatible with any type of religious establishment, even one that is so gentle and benign as to escape most people's notice'.

The 'compelling state interest' test is, in a way, a value-based test for granting conscientious exemptions. Therefore, it coincides with Nussbaum's general view about conscientious exemptions. Even so, the attempt to identify compelling state interests solely with the need to protect peace and safety is misguided for the reasons mentioned above.

Another liberal value-based approach is suggested by Frances Raday, who argues generally that 'constitutional democracy cannot tolerate enclaves of illiberalism whose inhabitants are deprived of access to human rights guarantees'.[103] Raday argues that equality and freedom are the basis of all other human rights, so that the limit or the scope of these rights, and especially freedom of religion, is defined inter alia by equality and freedom. More specifically, freedom of religion ends when it unjustly harms the freedom of others or when it unjustly discriminates against others. The rationale of Raday's approach is appealing. Raday discusses the equality of women within illiberal religious or cultural communities. She suggests three main methods of protecting equality at the expense of freedom of religion: first, by outlawing any discriminatory treatment towards women within the community; secondly, by withdrawing any governmental support of acts or omissions that discriminate against women within the community; and, thirdly, by creating a real option to leave the community. I will not discuss these suggestions here. Suffice it to say that refusing to grant religious conscientious exemptions can be involved in all three of these methods, which protect women from discrimination at the expense of freedom of religion. One thing could be said though about the demand to create a real option to leave the community ('a right to exit'). This demand is often presented as a substitute to not tolerating intolerant religions and communities. Some liberals claim that as long as a genuine option to leave exists, the liberal state should not interfere with illiberal or intolerant practices of communities, or that instead of interfering with illiberal or intolerant practices of communities, the state should assure a genuine option to leave. However, it may be the case that the right to exit could only be established by invalidating central religious practices and conventions, eg the practice of excluding women from educational institutions or the practice of refusing to teach non-religious subjects in religious educational institutions. In the Israeli context, for example, a meaningful right to exit from the ultra-orthodox Jewish community cannot be maintained unless some central features of this community are eradicated. This is a vicious circle: 'communitarian autonomy' can be tolerated if a right to exit exists, yet a right to exit may only be secured by not tolerating, at times quite significantly, communitarian autonomy.

[103] F Raday, 'Culture, Religion and Gender' (2003) 1 *International Journal of Constitutional Law* 663, 701.

Chaim Gans offers a slightly more complex value-based approach, which is still very similar to that of Nussbaum and Raday. His approach combines neutral and value-based considerations, according to which

> the value of freedom of conscience must be balanced against the intensity of the value protected by the specific law that is a candidate for violation, and against systemic damages liable to be caused by granting an exception on the basis of conscience[,] such as damage to the sense of equality and of stability. The balance must also take into account the severity of the expected damages and the chances of them occurring.[104]

Gans adds that he is sceptical

> as to whether those with a theocratic or romantic-nationalist ideology would have the philosophical and moral resources that would enable them to recognize a universal rule sanctioning a right to conscientious objection, even of a limited scope, for their ideological opponents. This privilege is reserved for certain types of humanists. It is not available to those whose core values are rooted in divine commands or in the nation as an entity enjoying moral precedence over its individual members.[105]

However, Gans does not discuss the question of whether it can be justified to grant conscientious exemptions to those who, should they have the power, would refuse to grant such exemptions to others in similar circumstances. For Gans, 'the intensity of the value protected by the specific law' is determined by liberal, humanist criteria. Therefore, we can expect that if the law protects imperative or highly important liberal, humanist values, conscientious exemptions should not be granted to those who, by definition, oppose these values, regardless of the harm that may be caused to them as a result.

From the examples given thus far, it can be appreciated how the liberal value-based approaches give priority to liberal principles and to the liberal perception of rights over any possible conscientious objection to them. The following approach takes this trait a little further. Cass Sunstein makes an interesting case for the priority of the principle of equality in cases where an exemption is sought because the objector holds discriminatory values. Sunstein sets the principled question: 'is government permitted to control discriminatory behavior by or within religious institutions?'[106] This is indeed an interesting, troubling question, since the common practice in most democracies is that religious institutions are usually permitted to discriminate, typically on the basis of religion, sex and sexual orientation in cases where other, non-religious

---

[104] C Gans, 'Right and Left: Ideological Disobedience in Israel' (2002) 36 *Israel Law Review* 19, 35.

[105] Gans (n 104 above) 38.

[106] CR Sunstein, *Designing Democracy: What Constitutions Do* (New York, Oxford University Press, 2001) 210. For an analysis of this issue in English law, see: R Sandberg and N Doe, 'Religious Exemptions in Discrimination Law' (2007) 66 *Cambridge Law Journal* 302.

motives for the discriminatory practice are unacceptable. Sunstein, however, argues that 'if sex discrimination is troublesome because it offends the anti-caste principle, then discrimination by religious institutions might be particularly troublesome, especially because such institutions sometimes inculcate the values and norms that create a caste system in the first instance'.[107] Sunstein attacks what he calls 'the asymmetry thesis', which states that, whereas it is unproblematic to apply civil and criminal law to religious institutions, it is problematic to apply anti-discrimination law to them.[108] I am unconvinced that this is an accurate way to describe the common practice in contemporary democracies. The fact is that religious individuals and institutions are exempt from some civil and criminal laws as well, so there is no clear asymmetry that poses a problem. The more important problem does remain, however, and that is the question of whether exempting religious institutions from anti-discrimination laws can be justified. If we accept the *Smith* test, according to which judicial exemptions should not be granted from neutral laws, then the question is answered quite easily, as most, if not all, prohibitions on sex and sexual orientation discrimination are neutral, in the sense that they do not intend to offend against religious values. However, the *Smith* test, as has already been argued, is not satisfactory in principle. Moreover, in practice, most of the religious conscientious exemptions in these cases are statutory ones, so the *Smith* test does not apply. The more attractive option, which is indeed endorsed by Sunstein, is that the decision whether or not to grant an exemption should be dependent on both the strength of the state's interest (which is usually a value-based question) and on the extent of the adverse effect on religion (which is a neutral consideration).[109] This view, like many others, leaves us with almost no specific guidelines for solving specific cases. Moreover, taking into consideration the extent of the adverse effect on religion should an exemption from equality laws not be granted can lead to unsatisfactory results. If a certain religion or religious institution may be adversely and severely affected by not being exempted from equality laws, and if that religion or religious institution is not capable or willing to change, it in fact means that that religion or religious institution is heavily based on discriminatory practices. Such religions or religious institutions do not form or promote a valuable way of life according to liberal standards. As such they should not be tolerated by the liberal state and should not be exempted from equality laws that reflect desirable liberal values.[110]

---

[107] Sunstein (n 106 above) 210.

[108] Sunstein (n 106 above) 210.

[109] Sunstein's more specific conclusion is that there is no general barrier to applying anti-discrimination laws to religious institutions and that, in certain specific cases, reasonable people can reach different conclusions: (n 106 above) 219.

[110] See also the text to nn 39–40.

A more subtle, perhaps even borderline, liberal value-based approach is suggested by Alon Harel and Aharon Shenrach, who argue that conscientious exemptions should also be granted to those who disobey the law because they hold intolerant or morally questionable values, if the following conditions are met: first, that the intolerant values are an integral part of a holistic way of life, ie they are inseparable from a set of social-cultural conventions; secondly, that this holistic way of life is valuable; and, thirdly, that the acts based on the intolerant values are neither cruel nor humiliating.[111] This is a liberal value-based approach because it assumes that (some) anti-liberal values are questionable, repugnant, intolerant or simply 'wrong'; because the question whether a way of life is, on the whole, valuable is decided by liberal standards; and because the question whether a certain act or behaviour is cruel or humiliating is also decided according to liberal standards.

However, this is a very narrow, liberal value-based approach. The examples chosen by the authors to demonstrate their argument prove this point. According to Harel and Shenrach, being a member of the Ku Klux Klan cannot form a valuable way of life. Also, murdering women for indecent behaviour, and the practice of female genital mutilation, are cruel or humiliating practices. To make these statements, one must first undertake a moral evaluation of relevant practices according to liberal standards. However, these are all extreme examples of what can be seen as extremely easy cases.[112] A more meaningful or simply broader liberal value-based approach would uphold liberal values towards more controversial cases. Such a case might be the practice of segregating men and women in public transport, which is exercised in Israel mainly or solely by orthodox Jews. Harel and Shenrach argue that this practice is not humiliating.[113] I will use this practice as a test case in the following discussion. There is much to be said regarding Harel and Shenrach's guide to granting conscientious exemptions. I will refer only to some of the main possible criticisms of them and only to those that are more relevant to this chapter's topic.

There is ambiguity in Harel and Shenrach's attitude towards the question of how we decide whether a certain practice is cruel or humiliating. At some point, they clearly state that we should decide this question according

---

[111] A Harel and A Shenrach, 'Segregation of Men and Women in Public Transportation' (2003) 3 *Allay Mishpat* 71, 92 (in Hebrew).

[112] It can be understood from Harel and Shenrach's arguments and examples that other illiberal practices, especially discriminatory practices, are not cruel or humiliating in and of themselves.

[113] The segregation of men and women is a common practice on public transport in Israel, where a bus route serves only or mainly Jewish Orthodox neighbourhoods. On these routes, men force women to sit at the back of the bus, and to get on and off the bus only by using the back door.

to liberal standards. However, when they argue that the segregation of men and women on public transport is not a humiliating practice, they base their argument on the 'internal point of view'—that of the religious women or the Jewish religion. At times, they argue that if religious women do not perceive this practice as discriminatory and humiliating, there is no prevailing reason for liberal interference. At other times, they argue that, if the purpose of the segregation is not to humiliate women but, for example, to regulate modesty and decency and to prevent what the Jewish religion perceives as improper social contact between unmarried men and women, then again, there is no prevailing reason for liberal interference. The general problem is that adopting an 'internal point of view' often fails to reflect the more complex reality. In our case, even if we adopt the 'internal point of view' and consider the motives and the wills of the members of the illiberal community, we find that many women do object to this practice and do perceive it as humiliating.[114] The clash is not between liberal principles and illiberal groups, but between individuals in the illiberal group who object to a certain illiberal practice and other individuals within that group who support it. This argument is not limited to the specific case of segregation as discussed here, but applies to many similar cases as well.[115]

Moreover, it is naïve to take the 'internal point of view' and to argue that the religious motive in this case (and in similar cases) is defending modesty or proper relations between unmarried men and women, when the facts prove otherwise. In fact, women who sit at the front of the bus are treated violently, whereas men who sit at the back are not.[116] The requirement that women should sit at the back of the bus is not neutral: it symbolises inferiority. Lastly, the implied assumption is that women are to be blamed if they inspire indecent or sinful thoughts among men; therefore, they should hide their presence and remain unseen on public transport (or indeed, cover their faces in public).[117]

---

[114] In 2007, a group of Ultra-Orthodox Jewish religious women filed a petition to the Israeli High Court of Justice against the 'kosher' (gender segregated) bus lines. According to the court's preliminary ruling, which was delivered on 21 January 2008, the segregation is constitutional, in principle, but in order for it to be constitutional in practice it has to be incorporated in a specific law or by-laws: HCJ 746/07 *Ragen v Ministry of Transport* Tak-el 2008(1) 666. In its final ruling, which was delivered on 5 January 2011, the court decided that coerced segregation was in fact illegal.

[115] See for example: R Higgins, *Problem and Process: International Law and How We Use It* (Oxford, Oxford University Press, 1994) 96: 'It is sometimes suggested that there can be no fully universal concept of human rights, for it is necessary to take into account the diverse cultures and political systems of the world. In my view this is a point advanced mostly by states, and by liberal scholars anxious not to impose the Western view on others. It is rarely advanced by the oppressed, who are only too anxious to benefit from perceived universal standards'.

[116] The *Ragen* case (n 114 above).

[117] There are, of course, many similarities that will not be discussed here, between forcing women to sit at the back of a bus and forcing them to cover their face, hair or body. For the

This problem with Harel and Shenrach's approach (ie adopting the internal point of view) is significant, as it is typical of many other liberal value-based approaches. It gives too much credit to illiberal practices at the expense of liberal values, such as equality and autonomy. It ignores implied and unacceptable motives for certain illiberal practices and attempts to isolate possible legitimate explanations for these practices in order to legitimise them. Finally, it assumes free will on the part of those subjected to the relevant practices (sitting at the back of the bus, wearing a veil), even though it is clear that some are forced into these practices, that others have no real option to protest or to object in any meaningful way, and that many were brought up in an educational, cultural and religious environment that puts in question their ability actually to exercise free will or to appreciate the need to have free will.

A further problem with Harel and Shenrach's approach is that they set a high benchmark for deciding whether or not a practice is cruel or humiliating. If we accept this standard, we may find that such practices are hard to find, even within highly illiberal and intolerant groups. Moreover, it would be a mistake to examine each practice when it is isolated from many other similar practices within the same community. Each and every practice, when it stands on its own, may not be considered as cruel or humiliating according to Harel and Shenrach's standards, but, when combined, they may create a critical mass that may lead to the conclusion that the relevant set of practices is indeed cruel or humiliating to its subjects.

Harel and Shenrach do not ask whether an illiberal, intolerant practice is central to what they call a 'holistic way of life' and accordingly do not ask what harm may be caused to this holistic way of life should the illiberal, intolerant practice be prohibited. Harel and Shenrach submit that the religious person appeals to a comprehensive belief system that dictates many components of his life. Being forced not to comply with one religious requirement has implications for other aspects of the believer's life. If one practice is undone, all may collapse or be put in jeopardy. The view that any integral part of a generally valuable way of life should be protected, even if this part consists of intolerant practices, is questionable. The further argument that any religious command, prohibition or practice is, in fact, integral to a religion and forms an inseparable part of it is indefensible. Even if we assume that Judaism, Islam and Christianity can form the basis for an overall valuable life, this does not mean that each and every Jewish, Islamic or Christian command or custom which is not cruel or humiliating should be tolerated because it is inseparable from this

---

link between the modesty discourse and applying discriminatory practices against women see: F Raday, 'Modesty Disrobed—Gendered Modesty Rules under the Monotheistic Religions' in Marie Failinger, Elizabeth Schiltz and Susan Stabile (eds), *Feminism, Law and Religion* (Farnham, Ashgate, 2013) 283.

valuable way of life. Religion has central commands and less important ones. Not every religious command is so vital that forcing it out of a certain religion will render the religion meaningless or significantly weakened. Many religions, including Judaism, Christianity and Islam, formally acknowledge that their sacred scripts, and later interpretations of them, contain a hierarchy of commands and prohibitions, and that there is a difference between commands and prohibitions that form the core of a religion and those that do not.[118] The fact is that religions have undergone many changes, some of them quite significant. Nowadays, some religions, or denominations within religions, allow practices and behaviour that were banned a few decades ago. Even if a voluntary change or a forced change from within is not equal to forced changes imposed by secular authorities, such a distinction would not affect the argument that religion is not a set of inseparable, equally important commands and practices. The liberal state should be more willing to eradicate religious intolerant practices if they are separable from the generally valuable religious way of life and if these practices are not at the core of a religious belief or way of life. Whereas Harel and Shenrach's approach accords absolute immunity to any intolerant, immoral or anti-liberal religious practice, provided that it is not cruel or humiliating, I suggest a more flexible, pro-liberal approach that allows not tolerating intolerant, immoral or anti-liberal religious practices even if they are not cruel or humiliating.

Lastly, Harel and Shenrach fail to provide detailed or even general guidelines for deciding which ways of life can be seen as valuable. We know that they think that being a member of the Ku Klux Klan cannot form a valuable way of life and that the most extreme, anti-liberal, intolerant, religious-Jewish Orthodox culture can ground a valuable way of life. It would have been easier to criticise their view if they had presented further examples of what they

---

[118] Within Judaism, there have been fierce disagreements about what constitutes the core of the religious Jewish belief and practice. Since Judaism does not have a centralised authority dictating religious dogma, there are many different formulations as to the specific theological beliefs inherent in the sacred scripts. One can find within present denominations in Christianity important differences of interpretation and opinion. There is a diversity of doctrines and practices among groups calling themselves Christian. Some claim that Christians share a rather narrow set of beliefs that they hold as essential to their faith: RE Olson, *The Mosaic of Christian Belief* (Downers Grove, InterVarsity Press, 2002). Within Islam, there are the five pillars of Islam (five practices essential to Sunni Islam; and eight for Shi'a Muslims), which include a testament that there is none worthy of worship except God and that Muhammad is the Messenger of God; a ritual prayer, which must be performed five times a day; a practice of giving based on accumulated wealth; fasting during the month of Ramadan; and pilgrimage to the city of Mecca. In addition, there is the Islamic concept of *Hudud*, which is used to describe the bounds of acceptable behaviour and the punishments for serious crimes, which are crimes against God, such as unlawful intercourse, false accusation of unlawful intercourse, consumption of alcohol, theft, and highway robbery: M Momen, *An Introduction to Shi'i Islam: The History and Doctrines of Twelver Shi'ism* (New Haven CT, Yale University Press, 1987) 178.

perceive to be non-valuable ways of life, apart from the esoteric example of the Ku Klux Klan. It seems that Harel and Shenrach are willing to tolerate, also by granting conscientious exemptions, highly illiberal and intolerant practices and behaviour that are part of a highly illiberal and intolerant culture and way of life, as long as none of them are cruel or humiliating. This is indeed a very narrow value-based approach, closer to the neutral ones than to the meaningful, value-based liberal approaches. Any approach to the question of religious conscientious exemptions applies various neutral considerations that disregard the content of the values of a person's conscience. Some approaches also consider value-based considerations that refer to the content of the values that ground a person's conscience. Since Harel and Shenrach's value-based approach is exceptionally narrow and since it allows not tolerating intolerant practices only in the most extreme and rare cases, the focus of their approach shifts from value-based or perfectionist liberalism to neutral liberalism, and, accordingly, from taking into account value-based considerations to applying mostly neutral considerations.

I refer to the liberal value-based approaches as ones that take into account the content of the conscience that grounds the objection, without making any a priori judgement regarding the religious conscience as such. These approaches can accord various weights to substantive liberal values vis-à-vis illiberal and intolerant practices. Still, they all adopt, at least in most cases, a liberal standpoint, rather than the point of view of the intolerant, illiberal group, or a neutral point of view. Value-based liberal approaches hold a perception of the 'good' that relies on a liberal understanding of autonomy, freedom and equality. These are the goods or the values that should be protected or promoted by the state. They are also the criteria for evaluating the legitimacy of beliefs, practices and ways of life, or for evaluating the weight that should be accorded to the values that ground practices and ways of life.

Kent Greenawalt argues that, even when we adopt the standpoint of the liberal state, it does not take us much further. On the subject of the legislative dilemma of whether to allow or tolerate discriminatory religious practices, he submits that since 'protection of religious freedom and autonomy and promotion of equal opportunity against socially unwarranted discrimination are both legitimate governmental objectives in a liberal society, the model of liberal democracy yields no easy resolution to this legislative dilemma'.[119] One can agree with Greenawalt but add that, although the protection of religious freedom and the promotion of equal opportunity are both legitimate governmental objectives in a liberal society, they are not necessarily equally weighty or equally important. No principle prevents a liberal democratic state from setting a hierarchy of values or rights or giving a priori priority to certain

---

[119]   Greenawalt (n 18 above) 93–94.

rights over others or over specified rights in typical cases. More specifically, liberal democracies could decide that, in principle, freedom of religion should defer to contradictory rights, such as equality or the autonomy of others, when freedom of religion is used to exercise intolerant or anti-liberal values and when the harm caused to the equality or autonomy of others (whether non-religious persons or persons within the religious community) is meaningful.[120]

VII. PRO-RELIGION APPROACHES

A. About the Pro-Religion Approaches

I will not discuss here all the unique or distinctive features of religion, nor will I discuss all of the possible reasons for protecting and promoting freedom of religion by granting religious exemptions or by any other alternative means. I will propose only a few pro-religion arguments with regard to the practice of granting conscientious exemptions, and evaluate them in turn. There is, I think, little doubt that religion is special in some aspects. Michael McConnell describes it nicely when he says that

> religion is a special phenomenon ... it is an institution, but it is more than that; it is an ideology or worldview, but it is more than that; it is a set of personal loyalties and locus of community, akin to family ties, but it is more than that; it is an aspect of identity, but it is more than that; it provides answers to questions of ultimate reality, and offers a connection to the transcendent, but it is more than that ... there is no other human phenomenon that combines all of these aspects.[121]

The question is whether the fact that religion is special justifies according it a special weight as a reason for either granting conscientious exemptions or

---

[120] It is hard to find in domestic and international law provisions that give a priori priority to some liberal values and rights over others, especially when the conflict is between freedom of religion and the rights of others. There are two notable exceptions, however. The first is the Convention on the Elimination of All Forms of Discrimination against Women (CEDAW), which states in Art 5(a) that: 'The parties shall take all appropriate measures ... to modify the social and cultural patterns of conduct of men and women, with a view to achieving the elimination of prejudices and customary and all other practices which are based on the idea of the inferiority of either of the sexes or on stereotyped roles for men and women'.

The second is Art 2(f) of the same convention, which provides that the states have to: 'pursue by all appropriate means and without delay a policy of eliminating discrimination against women and, to this end, undertake: To take all appropriate measures, including legislation to modify or abolish existing laws, regulations, customs and practices which constitute discrimination against women'.

This text, of course, does not indicate that this is the dominant position of international law with regard to these issues. For a discussion of the implications of these articles of the convention, see Raday (n 103 above).

[121] McConnell (n 5 above) 42.

for refusing to do so. I have already discussed the possibility of giving a certain priority to religious reasons, not because of their content but because of largely neutral reasons. Eisgruber and Sager argue along these lines when they suggest that religion is distinctive rather than unique. They believe that

> religion deserves constitutional solicitude because religious convictions are important constituents of how people view themselves and others and that these convictions have historically been targets of hostility, discrimination, and neglect. This does not render religion constitutionally *unique:* race and gender attract constitutional attention in the name of equality for very similar reasons. But it does render religion constitutionally *distinctive* in the sense that it justifies subjecting the government's treatment of religion to greater scrutiny than many other topics or policies receive.[122]

Pro-religion approaches, however, give priority to religious reasons as reasons for granting conscientious exemptions, because of the religiosity of those reasons. The priority may be given to religious reasons for granting the exemptions over general reasons for not granting them, and to religious reasons for granting exemptions as opposed to non-religious ones. This priority is often a specific implementation of a more general view, according to which religion is special in the sense that it has unique virtues as a religion. Quite often, the approach adopted is a functionalist approach, which focuses on the positive social, cultural and psychological functions of religion.[123]

Michael McConnell argues that there may be cases where the religious value is so important and the harm that may be caused to it if an exemption is not granted is so severe that the state is under a *duty* to grant the exemption.[124] Undoubtedly there are such cases, but McConnell's actual intention is not to argue that sometimes there is a duty to grant religious exemptions. He means to say that there are cases where conscientious exemptions should be granted only to religious objectors, since some religious values are so important that only the need not to harm them severely can override contradictory rights and interests, whereas there is nothing special in non-religious values that leads to such results in similar cases. McConnell argues that 'singling out' religion for special constitutional protection is fully consistent with the American constitutional tradition.[125] Note that this argument is not limited to the scope of the

---

[122] Eisgruber and Sager (n 6 above) 1274.

[123] See, for example: WSF Pickering, *Durkheim's Sociology of Religion—Themes and Theories* (Cambridge, Lutterworth Press, 1984) 300–320; M Weber, *The Sociology of Religion* (E Fischoff trans) (London, Methuen, 1965); TF O'Dea and J O'Dea, *The Sociology of Religion* (Upper Saddle River, Prentice-Hal, 1983) 1–20; P Horwitz, 'The Sources and Limits of Freedom of Religion in a Liberal Democracy: Section 2(a) and Beyond' (1996) 54 *University of Toronto Faculty of Law Review* 1, 48–57; TL Hall, 'Religion and Civic Virtue: A Justification of Free Exercise' (1992) 67 *Tulane Law Review* 87; McConnell and Posner (n 78 above) 4–5; Eisgruber and Sager (n 6 above) 1259.

[124] McConnell (n 77 above) 157.

[125] McConnell (n 5 above) 3.

First Amendment's jurisprudence.[126] McConnell's argument is that there is nothing in the First Amendment that prevents applying what he thinks is the generally right approach—according to which religion is entitled to special constitutional protection—also by granting exemptions only to religious conscientious objectors.

It is not always easy to understand what McConnell's view is regarding giving priority to religion. At times, he describes his view as neutral, in the sense that religion should not be singled out for any reason. For example, he states that 'the only constitutional regime that would not "single out" religion would be one that deconstitutionalized the issue of religion, leaving (this) issue ... to the discretion of political branches',[127] and that 'the question of singling out religion is not one of "privilege", but rather one of balance'.[128] But then, and from a more analytical point of view, McConnell also argues that 'there is no way to distinguish between government action that treats a religious belief as worthy of protection, and government action that treats a religious belief as intrinsically valuable'.[129] This view ignores the fact that the state may tolerate religious beliefs, ie may protect them not because the state acknowledges that religious beliefs are intrinsically valuable but because the state acknowledges the right of religious believers to be wrong. As argued above, protecting the beliefs of others by granting them conscientious exemptions is usually the result of tolerance rather than acknowledging the intrinsic value of those beliefs.

A further argument for the uniqueness of religion is that the belief in a transcendent authority has significant and unique ramifications for religious adherents. It can either be said that 'religious claims—if true—are prior to and of greater dignity than the claims of the state',[130] or that the fear of

---

[126] For an argument regarding the First Amendment, see McConnell (n 5 above) 43: 'the free exercise principle "singles out" religion for special protection against governmental hostility or interference. The disestablishment principle prevents the government from using its power to promote, advocate, or endorse any particular religious position'. For arguments that the text of the First Amendment and its historical background support giving priority to the religious conscience, see: M McConnell, 'The Origins and Historical Understanding of Free Exercise of Religion' (1990) 103 *Harvard Law Review* 1409; Laycock (n 55 above) 314. For an argument that the non-establishment clause compels governments to assist religion and religious institutions in the same way in which it assists non-religious ones, and that, at the same time, the free exercise clause compels governments to grant special protection to religious practices, see: JH Garvey, 'All Things Being Equal...' [1996] *Brigham Young University Law Review* 587, 604–9.

[127] McConnell (n 5 above) 11.

[128] McConnell (n 5 above) 11.

[129] M McConnell, 'Religious Freedom at a Crossroads' (1992) 59 *University of Chicago Law Review* 115, 151.

[130] M McConnell, 'Accommodation of Religion' [1985] *Supreme Court Review* 1, 15.

extra-temporal consequences as a cause of suffering provides an explanation of the uniqueness of religious liberty.[131]

An interesting, almost provocative view is that held by Garvey, according to which what separates religion from non-religion is that the former 'is a lot like insanity'.[132] Therefore, the religious believer is truly compelled by his belief to do something or to avoid doing something because he lacks the will—in the same way as an insane person lacks the will—to choose to do otherwise, at least not without completely diminishing his personhood. In Garvey's words, we should protect religious believers' freedom precisely because they are not free.[133]

B. Evaluating the Pro-Religion Approach

In the following sections I will evaluate a few unconvincing arguments that support the pro-religion approach. I will also evaluate a few unconvincing arguments rejecting that approach, ie arguments that reject the pro-religion approach for the wrong reasons. The discussion will be made by putting forward a list of pressure points. Even though much more can be said about these pressure points, I will avoid discussing them in great detail here.

(i) Should any Type of Belief not be Privileged?

Eisgruber and Sager point out that 'in a liberal democracy, the claim that one particular set of practices or one particular set of commitments ought to be privileged bears a substantial burden of justification'.[134] This is true, of course, in a neutral liberal democracy. A perfectionist liberal democracy or a tolerant-liberal democracy may indeed prefer one particular set of commitments—the liberal one. Therefore, in a liberal democracy, the claim that bears a substantial burden of justification is the claim that one particular, or any, set of illiberal practices or set of illiberal commitments ought to be privileged. This is indeed what the liberal state usually faces when a claim is brought to privilege religious conscientious objectors. Eisgruber and Sager mark the target of their criticism by saying that

> the underlying logic of the privileging view of religious exemptions is this: It is a matter of constitutional regret whenever government prevents or discourages persons from honouring their religious commitments; accordingly, government should

---

[131] JH Garvey, 'Free Exercise and the Values of Religious Liberty' (1986) 18 *Connecticut Law Review* 779, 793; McConnell (n 129 above) 125.

[132] Garvey (n 131 above) 798.

[133] Garvey (n 131 above) 801.

[134] Eisgruber and Sager (n 6 above) 1260.

act so as to avoid placing religious believers at a substantial disadvantage by virtue of their efforts to conform their conduct to their beliefs. This is the principle of unimpaired flourishing.[135]

Eisgruber and Sager reject the principle of unimpaired flourishing as a reason for privileging religious exemptions. As neutral liberals, they dispose with ease of religious sectarian arguments such as 'our God's commands are the highest commands therefore we must answer to them in priority to the mundane commands of the state'.[136] Another way to reject the principle of unimpaired flourishing is to argue for an anti-religion approach. This approach will be discussed in section VIII below.

(ii) The 'Special Harm' Argument

A common argument is that there is something special about the anguished state of the religious believer who is forced to act against his beliefs and therefore takes the risk of eternal suffering in the afterlife. Eisgruber and Sager reject this argument because

> it asks us to assume—in a way that seems especially inappropriate when it comes to matters spiritual—that self-interest rather than conscience is the stronger human drive. It expects us to treat the religious believer's very long-term self-interested reason for obedience as motivationally more powerful than other persons' immediate self-interest and driving passions ... it also asks us to accept as true for the believer that heaven and hell are at stake, while holding to the contrary as a matter of our belief.[137]

The first part of this response is quite convincing, as the mere wish to avoid suffering in the next world is not necessarily a matter of conscience any more than it is a matter of self-interest. The second part is quite interesting, as here Eisgruber and Sager dismiss a central religious belief, and refuse to see it as a possible reason for granting conscientious exemptions simply because they believe that the belief that there is heaven and hell is false. This is interesting because, according to Eisgruber and Sager's 'equal regard' principle, the liberal, non-religious state should not, and moreover cannot, question the objector's sincerity or the reasonableness of his claim that the value or the belief in question is central to his conscience and life. Eisgruber and Sager specifically state that 'equal regard bars the state from disparaging religious interests that seem unreasonable from a secular perspective'.[138] It is unclear whether dismissing

---

[135] Eisgruber and Sager (n 6 above) 1254.
[136] Eisgruber and Sager (n 6 above) 1260–62.
[137] Eisgruber and Sager (n 6 above) 1263.
[138] Eisgruber and Sager (n 6 above) 1285–86.

the belief in heaven and hell as a reason for giving priority to religious objections coincides with Eisgruber and Sager's own equal regard approach.

If we ignore this inconsistency, the argument itself is convincing, as it requires the state to evaluate the content of the belief that grounds the objection from a liberal and rational point of view. When I argue for a liberal value-based approach to granting conscientious exemptions, I do not limit the evaluation of the content of the conscience or the belief to cases where this content is morally repugnant or highly intolerant. Examining the content of the belief from a liberal point of view also requires an examination of the rationality of the belief. This is not the most important consideration, as in some cases irrational beliefs should be tolerated also by granting conscientious exemptions.[139] Neither am I trying to deny that a great deal of irrational beliefs and activities have been and should be protected in liberal democracies. Yet, when the belief is utterly irrational, such as the belief in heaven and hell, it does provide the state with a legitimate reason for not granting conscientious exemptions. It has been said that reason is the hallmark of a liberal government.[140] It has also been said that the process of understanding reality through religious belief is dissimilar from developing that understanding through practical reasoning.[141] Therefore, a liberal, rational political regime that should aspire to be based on reason should not hurry to compromise the public interest, or the rights and interests of individuals, in order to satisfy the utterly irrational demands of religious (and non-religious) conscientious objectors. It should be noted that the argument here is not that there is no principled reason to single out utterly irrational beliefs for more protection.[142] The argument is that there is a reason to single out utterly irrational beliefs for less protection.

Gedicks adds that the 'special harm' argument is both under-inclusive and over-inclusive.[143] It is under-inclusive because not all religious believers believe

---

[139] These cases cannot be fully predicted, but I tend to the view that whereas the immorality of a person's conscience or its intolerant nature may be a sufficient reason to refuse to grant him a conscientious exemption, this is not the case regarding the irrational conscience.

[140] J Rawls, *Political Liberalism* (New York, Columbia University Press, 1993) 216–20.

[141] Garvey (n 131 above) 798; Marshall (n 43 above) 384; Leiter (n 26 above) 34–35, but compare to Finnis (n 55 above).

[142] And see Brian Leiter's argument that 'there may be compelling principled reasons for the state to respect liberty of conscience, but there is no apparent moral reason why states should carve out special protections that encourage individuals to structure their lives around categorical demands that are insulated from the standards of evidence and reasoning we everywhere else expect to constitute constraints on judgment and action. Singling out religion for toleration is tantamount to thinking we ought to encourage precisely this conjunction of categorical fervor based on epistemic indifference. And it is hard to see what utilitarian rationale there could be for that': B Leiter, 'Why Tolerate Religion?' (2008) 25 *Constitutional Commentary* 1. See also Leiter (n 26 above) 63–64.

[143] Gedicks (n 20 above) 562. For a similar argument, see also Marshall (n 43 above) 383–84; and Greenawalt (n 1 above) 324.

in heaven and hell or in the more general idea of life after death. The argument is also over-inclusive because, according to Gedicks, there is no reason
to assume that a speculative guess about what may happen in the afterlife as a
result of obeying a legal demand today may cause more harm or anguish to
the religious believer than that caused to non-religious persons who may suffer
severe, visible harm as a result of obeying the legal norm. Greenawalt adds
a further difficulty in taking the 'special harm' (or the 'extratemporal consequences') argument seriously, when he states that it would put the administrative bodies and courts in the impossible position of trying to settle just how
close the perceived connection between moral wrongs and extratemporal consequences is with regard to the immense variety of beliefs that can be found
in different religions.[144]

A more subtle way of applying the 'special harm' approach is to exempt
only those whose conscience is connected to any belief in a transcendental
being. The assumption is, of course, that persons who think that they are
violating moral principles laid down by a transcendental being will feel more
severely disturbed than those who think that they are violating other moral
principles. Greenawalt's convincing response to this argument is that 'belief
in a transcendent being probably does not correlate sharply with intensity of
feeling that one should not violate one's convictions'.[145] Thus, all variations
of the 'special harm' argument fail to justify singling out religion for special
protection.

(iii) The 'Lack of Choice' Argument

A predictable response to Garvey's argument about 'religion as insanity' is
stating that there is a presumption of free will and voluntarism that underlies the principle of individual freedom and freedom of religion.[146] This
presumption may be valid with regard to certain aspects of the principle of
individual freedom. I doubt, however, if it is normally valid regarding freedom of conscience, belief and religion. Benjamin Beit-Hallahmi put it well
when he submitted that 'religious identity has nothing to do with choice or
deliberation and everything to do with the accidents of birth and history'.[147]

---

[144] Greenawalt (n 1 above) 325.

[145] Greenawalt (n 1 above) 325.

[146] Marshall (n 43 above) 385. Marshall makes this argument with regard to the American
Constitution, but it undoubtedly applies to all democratic constitutions. As to the American
Constitution, Michael Sandel argues to the contrary, ie that Madison and Jefferson's argument
for religious liberty 'relies heavily on the assumption that beliefs are not a matter of choice':
M Sandel, 'Religious Liberty—Freedom of Conscience or Freedom of Choice?' [1989] *Utah
Law Review* 597, 610.

[147] B Beit-Hallahmi, *Psychological Perspectives on Religion and Religiosity* (New York, Routledge,
2015) 234.

This observation is true with regard to non-religious beliefs as well. Freedom of conscience (any conscience) does not protect the right to *choose* to do X (or not to do X), as much as it protects the right to do X (or not to do X). Generally, the 'will theory' or the 'choice theory' of rights has its appeal, in the sense that, when one has a right (or liberty), one has a choice whether or not to exercise it. However, when one is compelled by one's conscience to do X or to avoid doing X, one is simply seeking a legal right to act upon one's conscience, which may mean having a legal right to do what one would do anyway, because one does not have a real choice in this matter. Therefore, having a legal right in these cases does not have to entail a choice whether to exercise it.

Brian Leiter asks why it promotes human well-being to protect liberty of conscience. His answer is that

> many of the arguments trade, at bottom, on a simple idea: namely, that *being able to choose what to believe and how to live* ... makes for a better life. Being told *what you must believe* and *how you must live*, conversely, make lives worse.[148]

I suggest, however, that being able to choose what to believe and how to live is not the only alternative to being told what to believe and how to behave. There is a third option according to which protecting a person's right to have a certain conscience and act upon it promotes his well-being because in relation to a person's conscience one cannot really choose what to believe and, at times, how to live.

The argument about 'lack of choice' will not be discussed in depth here. It does, however, require some further clarification. Within the context of the 'lack of choice' argument, a distinction should be drawn between having a certain conscience and acting upon it. With regard to having a certain type of conscience, the 'lack of choice' argument applies strongly. A person cannot choose his conscience. It is hard, perhaps even impossible, to comprehend why and how a person ends up having a certain conscience and not another. A person also cannot simply choose to change his conscience, beliefs and views. One may be convinced of the rightness or wrongness of certain arguments and, accordingly, may change his conscience, beliefs or views, but he cannot choose to make such a change, as the ability to be convinced by some arguments and not by others depends on personal traits and other factors (eg education, childhood experiences, cultural variants, etc) over which we have little or no control.

However, with regard to acting upon one's conscience, the 'lack of choice' argument applies in a weaker, yet still meaningful way. One does have a choice whether or not to act upon one's conscience. Even when the only options are either to act against one's conscience and to live, or to act upon one's

---

[148] Leiter (n 26 above) 9.

conscience and consequently suffer a horrible death, the choice still exists. This is, of course, an overly narrow and, therefore, unsatisfactory perception of what having a choice means. According to a broader, more desirable perception of what having a choice actually means, it can be said that, normally, a conscientious objector does not really have a choice about whether to act upon his conscience, since the result of not acting upon it will bring devastating harm to his moral personhood. If one has only two options to choose from and both are extremely bad (acting against one's conscience or acting upon one's conscience and consequently suffering a meaningful sanction) one cannot be perceived as autonomous in any meaningful sense.

All of the above is true regarding the religious and non-religious conscience alike. This is also a good way to respond to Garvey's argument concerning the comparison between religion and insanity in relation to lack of choice. If the religious believer does not choose his belief and does not have the free will to act against it, then the same thing can be said about many non-religious conscientious objectors. Thus, even if the insanity analogy is accurate, it fails to establish that religion is special in that respect.

If the 'lack of choice' argument is true, it affects the nature of the justification for granting conscientious exemptions. One way to justify granting conscientious exemptions is to turn to the principle of autonomy that states that people should be able to make their own choices and have an adequate range of good options from which to choose. By granting conscientious exemptions we are tolerating the other's wrong yet autonomous choices. A different, presumably better way to justify granting conscientious exemptions is to acknowledge that, in matters of conscience, people do not have a real choice. This lack of choice results from the fact that one cannot choose one's conscience and also from the fact that acting contrary to one's conscience results in severe harm to one's personhood. So, when we grant conscientious exemptions we are tolerating the other's wrong and unchosen conscience—precisely because it is unchosen.

This way of understanding the justification for granting conscientious exemptions is important when we are trying to answer the question of why conscientious convictions are different from mere preferences. Three criteria can be taken into account in order to differentiate between claims of conscience and claims of preference: vulnerability, ability to choose and moral personhood. Views according to which no conscientious exemptions should ever be granted from legal rules eliminate the distinction between conscientious beliefs and preferences, as all are equally not being tolerated.[149] The distinction does exist, however. It does not result from differences in terms of vulnerability, as 'general' or 'neutral' laws may adversely affect preferences and

---

[149] Barry (n 2 above) 46, 50. For an evaluation of the 'no-exemption' approach see Leiter (n 26 above) 94–108.

conscientious convictions alike. Neither does it result from a difference in the ability to choose, as we do not choose either our conscience or our preferences: we simply have them. The distinction between conscience and preference results from the fact that severe harm to one's moral personhood is only inflicted when one decides or is being compelled to act contrary to one's conscience (rather than to one's preferences) in order to avoid a meaningful sanction. Yet, the fact that severe harm to one's moral personhood is inflicted when one acts against one's conscience is only important if we assume that one does not choose one's conscience and cannot simply will it to change. Maclure and Taylor, for example, argue that imposing a 'restriction of conscience' rather than a 'restriction of preference' inflicts 'moral harm' and violates one's moral integrity and self-respect. This is no doubt true. But, if conscience and religious faith can be chosen, as Maclure and Taylor argue,[150] then believers have the ability to adapt their beliefs and life plan to the conditions with which they must come to terms. They can simply choose to modify their conscience—and if they choose otherwise they should be responsible for their choice. Thus, convictions of conscience may be a 'particular type of subjective preference' as noted by Maclure and Taylor,[151] but not just because of the 'harm to the moral personhood' criterion. Conscientious convictions are special because of the special harm that is caused to a person who acts against his *non-chosen* moral convictions, which also cannot be changed at will.

While Maclure and Taylor wrongly argue that conscientious convictions are chosen, Bedi wrongly argues that only conscientious convictions are not chosen whereas mere preferences are in fact chosen—and that that fact differentiates between the two. Bedi addresses this point within the context of religious conscientious exemptions, yet his arguments should be applied to non-religious conscientious exemptions as well. Bedi argues that in order to prefer religious beliefs to mere preferences,

> we must see the religious practice as effectively unchosen, rigid and inhospitable to contestation … the more the religious group is seen as just like any other voluntary association or preference, the more difficult it becomes to justify an exemption.[152]

---

[150] J Maclure and C Taylor, *Secularism and Freedom of Conscience* (Cambridge MA, Harvard University Press, 2011) 82, 100: 'freedom of religion allows people to adopt the religious beliefs of their choice'.

[151] Maclure and Taylor (n 150 above) 73.

[152] S Bedi, 'Debate: What is so Special About Religion? The Dilemma of the Religious Exemption' (2007) 15 *The Journal of Political Philosophy* 235. See also p 237: 'as we move in the direction of anti-primordialism—as the literature seems to be doing—we undercut the ability to grant an exemption, to treat religion as special or different from a mere preference or voluntary association'. Bedi also discusses other arguments that, in his view, cannot adequately answer why religion is special when compared to mere preferences: the value of diversity, equal respect, tradition, non-instrumentality, cost and normativity (see pp 241–47). For a more simplistic view, according to which religious belief is no different from any other preference, see Barry (n 2 above) 35.

This view has more general implications. Bedi explains that

> on the one hand, contemporary theory has come to see religious affiliations and practices as contingent, open-ended and freely constructed. On the other hand, in order to justify different or special treatment for such groups we must view these affiliations as unchosen, static and not freely constructed.[153]

Bedi demonstrates that 'free choice' could not be the right justification for granting religious exemptions and not merely preference-based exemptions. Bedi's argument is mostly descriptive. He does say that he strongly doubts that religion occupies one extreme or the other (ie, religion as complete choice and religion as complete lack of choice), but his main argument is simply that, in order to create a distinction between religion and mere preferences with respect to the issue of legal exemptions, religion should be perceived as largely non-chosen, static and not freely constructed. The fact is, however, that our preferences are also unchosen. They are dictated by our genes, brain activity, childhood experiences or traumas, socialisation, environment, and unconscious cognitive and emotional factors—all of which are beyond our control. We do not choose our preferences. We simply have them and cannot change them at will. Therefore, the 'lack of choice' argument, when it stands alone, cannot explain the difference between conscientious convictions and mere preferences.

Within the specific context of conscientious exemptions, whether religious or not, the importance of the 'lack of choice' argument should not be overstated. Roberts and Lester claim that 'one reason to choose greater tolerance instead of lesser sensitivity in the case of religion is that many religious believers feel their beliefs are immutable or non-negotiable ... people should not be blamed for matters outside of their control'.[154] The first part of the argument is true. The fact that religion and conscientious convictions are not chosen provides one reason for tolerating religion—and conscientious objectors. The second part of the argument ('people should not be blamed for matters outside of their control') should be treated with caution. Even if the argument that religion is indeed not chosen is established it does not follow that religious exemptions should be granted in certain cases or at all—or that religion should be tolerated in certain cases or at all. More reasons are required here. Accordingly, there may be good reasons for not tolerating religion and conscientious objectors—even if religion and conscientious convictions are not chosen. People may not be morally responsible for 'matters outside of their control'—but they may be legally responsible for them.

---

[153] Bedi (n 152 above) 235.
[154] P Roberts and E Lester, 'The Distinctive Paradox of Religious Tolerance: Active Tolerance as a Mean Between Passive Tolerance and Recognition' (2006) 20 *Public Affairs Quarterly* 347, 351.

Thus, the 'lack of choice' argument has conceptual and moral implications within the issue of conscientious exemptions. Whatever these exact implications may be, the 'lack of choice' argument does not support the pro-religion approach, as the argument applies equally to both religious and non-religious conscientious objections.

(iv) The Difficulty of Defining Religion

An argument against giving priority to religious conscientious objections over non-religious ones is that such a preference would require the legislature and judiciary: (a) to define what 'religion' is (this difficulty alone also applies to anti-religion approaches); (b) to decide the sincerity of the claim that the objector holds religious beliefs; (c) to decide the centrality of relevant beliefs to the objector's life; (d) to decide whether the free exercise of religion was burdened by the state enactment in question; and (e) to determine the effect that violating the religious norm will have on the believer. In short, the state would have the power to decide issues of definition, sincerity, centrality, burden and effect. Giving this power to the state's organs, the argument goes, might jeopardise religious liberty, and especially that of religious minorities and unpopular religions, since giving this power to the state's organs might lead to the approval of certain religious beliefs and the disapproval of others, by applying (hidden) irrelevant reasons. It might also lead to legal instability.[155]

This argument against the pro-religion approach is not very convincing. The result of accepting this argument would be granting equal treatment to both religious and non-religious conscientious objectors.[156] This solution, however, merely shifts the problems of definition, sincerity, centrality, burden and effect from the ground of religion to the ground of conscience. In other words, all of the problems would remain. We would still have to face the risk of governmental disapproval of minorities or unpopular conscientious objectors by classifying their objection as non-conscientious or insincere. Therefore, the risk of uncertainty also remains. These are probably the inevitable results of any approach that is willing to grant conscientious exemptions in more than just rare cases.

(v) The 'Religion is Special' Argument

Many of those who argue for privileging religion within the context of granting conscientious exemptions—and within other contexts as well—base their

---

[155] Marshall (n 43 above) 386–87. See also W Marshall, 'What is the Matter with Equality?: An assessment of the Equal Treatment of Religion and Nonreligion in the First Amendment Jurisprudence' (2000) 75 *Indiana Law Journal* 193, 208–11.

[156] Marshall (n 155 above) 216.

argument on the fact that 'religion is special'. It is argued that religion has unique virtues that should be protected in a special way by the state. An important question at this stage would be whether these virtues are content-based or content-neutral.

Roberts and Lester, for example, argue that

> not only is religion something about which people feel strongly, it is also the paradig-matic example of a comprehensive belief. This comprehensiveness, religion's ability to organize a life, is the primary reason for religion's distinctiveness and for the need for active tolerance.[157]

Here we have two content-neutral reasons for tolerating religion: people feel strongly about it—and it is a comprehensive belief. Even if religion is in fact distinctive in that respect this cannot be a sufficient, conclusive or even weighty reason for granting religious claims special positive treatment, or positive treatment at all. The fact that people feel strongly about a compre-hensive view, ideology or belief may provide a reason to tolerate that view. This reason, however, ignores the content of the comprehensive view and is therefore a weak reason for tolerating that view. The content of the view held and the effect that it has on its holders, third parties and the public and politi-cal sphere should also be taken into account. These content-based considera-tions can provide compelling reasons for not tolerating or respecting views about which people feel strongly. Views, ideologies or beliefs are normally not worthy of respect—and are not entitled to be tolerated—merely because they are comprehensive and valuable to their holders. This approach is plainly impossible in a world where people have competing and contradictory views, ideologies or beliefs. Contradictory views and ways of life cannot be simulta-neously tolerated in full. This is plain logic. When the state reconciles (and it has to reconcile) contradictory views—it is often a zero sum game. When the state tolerates intolerant views, behaviour or way of life—someone is being harmed or offended. When the state tolerates behaviour or ways of life which are incompatible with interests of others—those others are being harmed or offended. The only question is whether reconciling contradictory views should be based on content-neutral reasons or on content-based reasons. Reconciling such contradictions can be done by applying only content-neutral criteria (eg more comprehensive views that are uniquely important to their holders are entitled to more protection or accommodation). This, however, might result in prioritising immoral and intolerant views simply because they are com-prehensive and uniquely important to their holders. Applying content-based criteria to the 'is religion special?' question means that more content-based features of religion should be found, and they may or may not be distinctive,

---

[157] Roberts and Lester (n 154 above) 350.

in order to justify tolerance or respect towards religious claims for protection or accommodation.

A common way of refuting the argument that religion is special in a sense that justifies special protection from otherwise valid laws is trying to prove that many, if not all, virtues that people attribute to religion can be found in non-religious values and practices.[158] Marshall, for example, acknowledges the following features of religion, which are suggested by supporters of the value-based, pro-religion approach: religious groups act as mediating institutions between the individual and the government; religious pluralism and flourishing provide moral principles that help in promoting self-government; and the multiplicity of religion is both a buffer against state power and a factor in cultural diversity.[159] However, the values inherent in pluralism are also advanced, Marshall states, by the protection of non-religious groups.

Leiter approaches this when he asks if there is a credible *principled* argument for tolerating religion *qua* religion: that is, an argument that would explain why, as a matter of moral or other principle, we ought to accord special legal and moral treatment to religious practices.[160] Leiter submits that

> if there is a special reason to tolerate religion it has to be because there are features of religion which warrant toleration and these features are either: 1. Features that all and only religious beliefs have, either as a matter of (conceptual or other) necessity or as a contingent matter of fact; or 2. Features which other beliefs have, or might have, but which in these other cases possession of the features would not warrant principled toleration.[161]

Leiter's conclusion, following detailed argumentation that will not be elaborated here, is that there are no such features; that is, that if we have reasons to tolerate religion, this is not because of anything that has to do with it being religion as such.[162] Leiter is right when he argues that there is nothing special about religion that justifies singling out religion for positive treatment. Leiter, however, fails to identify that there is something special about religion after all that justifies singling out religion for a negative or simply cautious treatment. This is so because Leiter applies his arguments to a very broad definition of religion—too broad to be helpful. He refers to the categorical nature

---

[158] For a recent and convincing argument along this line see M Schwartzman, 'What if Religion is not Special?' (2012) 79 *University of Chicago Law Review* 1351. For an interesting response see T Berg 'Secular Purpose, Accommodations, and Why Religion is Special (Enough)' (2013) 80 *University of Chicago Law Review Dialogue* 24.

[159] Marshall (n 43 above) 381.

[160] Leiter (n 26 above) ch 3.

[161] Leiter (n 26 above) 15.

[162] Leiter (n 26 above) ch 3. See also Anthony Ellis 'What is Special about Religion?' (2006) 25 *Law and Philosophy* 219. Ellis, like Leiter, argues that there is nothing special about religion that can justify granting it special treatment or objecting to having an established religion.

of religious commands and the insulation of religious beliefs from evidence (or the fact that religious beliefs involve, explicitly or implicitly, the metaphysics of ultimate reality) as the main characteristics of religion (while claiming that these are not features that can be found only within religion). These features alone do not provide special reasons for not tolerating religion.[163] Defining religion broadly in an attempt to reach wide common ground that would allow a general argument about 'religion' as such may result in conclusions that are not sufficiently definitive. Narrowing the scope of the argument or applying it within the context of the most well-known, influential and popular religions (rather than 'religion' as such) leads to the conclusions that were presented in Chapter five about the links between religion and intolerance. Thus, religion is in fact special, unique or distinct, yet its distinctiveness provides reasons for not tolerating it. There are, of course, reasons for tolerating religion, yet these reasons do not result from characteristics that can only be found in religion.

(vi) The Anti-Establishment Argument

Some aspects of the links between the establishment of religion and the estab-lishment of intolerance were described in Chapter five, where I discussed the second reason for the intolerant nature of religion (the fact that religion aspires to gain formal control over its believers, other religious believers and heretics alike). I argued there that the attempt to describe society in religious terms or the claim to shape the public sphere in the light of religious beliefs is actually a claim for the dominance of a certain religious belief. Accordingly, the arguments for having an established *religion* are never arguments for having established *religions* (in the same state). Having established religions in the same state is practically impossible due to the intolerant nature of religion. In other words, arguments for establishment are always arguments for preferring one religion to others. This alone should strip the argument for establishment from any moral weight. In the following I will elaborate on some of the implications of the anti-establishment argument, which is obviously an argument against the pro-religion approach.

The anti-establishment argument is considered to be one of the most pow-erful arguments against favouring religion and religious conscientious objec-tions. However, all too often the anti-establishment argument is also used in order to defend state neutrality and to object to the 'establishment of secular-ism'. I will not discuss here the whole anti-establishment argument with regard to the place that religion should have in the public and political spheres, as it exceeds the scope of this book. I will limit the discussion to a few narrow argu-ments within this context, which tend to wrongly equate the establishment of

---

[163] Leiter (n 26 above) 59–60.

religion with the establishment of secularism—and to misconceive the links between the establishment of religion and the principle of tolerance.

Martha Nussbaum, when presenting her complex view, which has both egalitarian and liberal value-based characteristics, responds to a possible pro-religion attack on this view. She calls the person who supports the pro-religion approach 'establishmentarian'.[164] This person may think that it is permissible for a state to regard itself as a monotheistic nation, for example, and to grant symbolic and legal priority to monotheistic religions over polytheism, nontheism, atheism and agnosticism. A different kind of establishmentarian may think that it is only permissible to favour religion as a category over non-religion. Nussbaum's response to the establishmentarian is that his view does not treat people as equals, as it asks some to subordinate their conscientious commitments to those of others. She adds that even a benign establishmentarianism can have quite far-reaching effects that are disadvantageous to minorities.[165] Jocelyn Maclure and Charles Taylor argue along these lines when they claim that the problem with the establishment of religion is that it makes members of other religions and secular citizens into second-class citizens. Accordingly, the establishment of secularism makes all religious citizens into second-class citizens. Therefore, both forms of establishment should be rejected.[166]

These views miss one important point. The problem with the establishmentarian is not that he asks some to subordinate their conscientious commitments to those of others, but that he asks non-religious people to subordinate their conscientious commitments to religion. Accordingly, the problem is not that establishmentarianism can have far-reaching effects that are disadvantageous to minorities, but the fact that the reasons for disadvantaging minorities are religious ones. There is nothing necessarily wrong with subordinating the conscientious commitments of utterly illiberal, intolerant people to some basic liberal values; nor is there anything necessarily wrong with disadvantaging illiberal, intolerant minorities in order to protect the rights of others, or the rights of sub-groups within the minority group, when these rights are perceived from the liberal standpoint.

In other words, when Nussbaum explains why the establishmentarian's view does not treat people as equals, it seems that all she is claiming is that the establishmentarian does not treat everyone the same (as no one should be asked to subordinate his conscientious commitments to those of others). But are we really required to treat everyone the same (including racists, homophobes and the fanatically religious)? How does a regime in which no one is

---

[164] Nussbaum (2007) (n 101 above) 352.
[165] Nussbaum (2007) (n 101 above) 353.
[166] Maclure and Taylor (n 150 above) 9, 13; Nussbaum (2012) (n 101 above) 133–36.

asked to subordinate his conscientious commitments to those of others work in practice? The quandary increases when Nussbaum states that, since the human internal capability of conscience is a delicate and vulnerable thing and since it is worthy of equal respect, 'it is worthy of equal support' (from law and institutions).[167] Even if her purpose were to promote equal respect rather than equal treatment, the criticism remains. Equal respect does not mean that there is something inherently wrong with treating people differently, even when the reason for treating them differently is their (intolerant) values or way of life. Alternatively, if equal respect means exactly that, then the argument would be that not everyone is entitled to equal respect.[168] More accurately, people are worthy of equal respect in a narrow sense, which 'secures the essential distributive conditions of the self-respecting integrity of each and every person against utilitarian impersonality'.[169] Here 'equal respect' means that all humans qua humans have rights that trump over utilitarian calculations. However, equal respect does not mean that all views, beliefs, expressions and conscience are worthy of equal respect regardless of their content (ie their morality, rationality, validity etc)—and simply because someone holds them.

An interesting yet misguided argument about the links between the establishment of religion and the principle of tolerance was suggested by Leiter, who argued that 'nothing in the principle of toleration is incompatible with state establishment of religion'.[170] In order to prove this point, Leiter refers to the UK and Germany, which do have established religions alongside a 'robust regime of liberty of conscience' and a public culture of tolerance or pluralism. He then refers to the United States, which does not have an established religion yet falls behind the UK and Germany in the toleration or pluralism contest. The UK and Germany, with their established religions, may be more tolerant or pluralistic than the United States, but this does not prove Leiter's argument. The public sphere in the UK and Germany could have been even more tolerant or pluralistic if the UK and Germany did not have established religions.[171] One example from England can prove this point. A combination of historical, cultural and legal circumstances (including the fact that the 'Church of England' is the established church of England) led to the current and unfortunate situation in which 22 per cent of primary schools in England are Church of England schools. A further 10 per cent are Roman Catholic

---

[167] Nussbaum (2007) (n 101 above) 355.
[168] I have discussed this point in Chapter three with reference to the limits of tolerance.
[169] Richards (n 95 above) 84.
[170] Leiter (n 26 above) 118.
[171] A quick look at the British Humanist Association website can provide a few notable examples (humanism.org.uk).

Schools.[172] This means that one in three primary schools in England is a state-funded religious school. This also means that in some areas in England, secular and non-Christian families struggle to find a non-faith primary school nearby. This is probably not the best example of a pluralistic and tolerant public sphere. I imagine that most Church of England schools pride themselves in applying a tolerant, respectful and inclusive environment and this may be true, but only to a limited extent—precisely because they are faith schools and because religious people, teachers and schools tend to take religion seriously. A certain Church of England school in a certain village in England, gives its pupils 'excellence certificates' on which it is written 'to be the best we can be in our Christian family', even though the school knows very well that many of its pupils come from non-religious or non-Christian families (because there are no non-faith schools nearby). This is not what a tolerant and pluralistic public sphere feels like—and this is partly the result of England having an established Church.

Thus, states like Germany and the UK that do have an established religion may still be tolerant or pluralistic but not so much as they could have been had they been secular states. Accordingly, the public sphere in the United States would have probably been even more intolerant if there were an established religion. The fact that some states that do have established religions are more tolerant than some states that don't does not negate the link between the establishment of religion and intolerance. It simply means that there are numerous cultural, social, political and legal variants that determine the kind and the amount of tolerance in democratic states. Establishing religion is merely one of those variants.

Leiter does argue that state establishment of religion is not incompatible with the principle of tolerance as long as non-religious claims of conscience are not burdened as a result. This condition, however, is too narrow. Even a 'benign' established religion, such that does not burden non-religious claims of conscience, can and normally does adversely affect the well-being, interests and rights of atheists, agnostics and those who believe in 'wrong' religions. It can do so in numerous ways, both legal and non-legal, which will not burden non-religious claims of conscience yet will still be intolerant by their nature.

Establishing religion will almost always decrease the amount of liberal and justified tolerance in society and will significantly increase the potential of that society to be more intolerant. This is so because of the unique theoretical and empirical links between religion and intolerance. As such links do not exist with regard to secularism, it cannot be argued that establishing secularism will almost always decrease the amount of liberal and justified tolerance in society.

---

[172] www.gov.uk/government/publications/maintained-faith-schools.

VIII. ANTI-RELIGION APPROACHES

There are many possible explanations for what some scholars perceive to be the hostility of liberal constitutional theory towards religion.[173] It is argued that this hostility disfavours religious claims to be granted conscientious exemptions. I will not discuss these reasons here. The meaningful links between religion and intolerance were described in Chapter five. If indeed there are meaningful and unique links between certain types of religion and intolerance, and if illiberal intolerance should not be tolerated by the liberal state, then this is one good reason for treating some religious claims to conscientious exemptions with caution.

I described earlier how Martha Nussbaum defends her semi-egalitarian, semi-value-based approach by responding to a possible establishmentarian attack.[174] To make her point, Nussbaum also responds to a possible attack from what she calls the anti-religionist:

> The anti-religionist thinks that all religion should be disfavored in the public square—not for reasons of equality, or liberty, but because he or she thinks religion somewhat embarrassing, a relic of a pre-scientific era, and a source of nothing but trouble. We can best build lasting democracies, thinks the anti-religionist, if we discourage religion and build on secular scientific rationality. Of course we should not repress religion or legally penalize religious people or religious observance. But we should certainly discourage it, and there is absolutely no reason to bend over backwards to give it space to unfold itself.[175]

What is wrong with anti-religionism? The first problem, according to Nussbaum, is that it is likely to be especially harsh towards minority religions. Since the religion of the majority is so much a part of the dominant laws and customs, it does not stand out and, therefore, does not look particularly religious.[176] If what Nussbaum describes is indeed the case and the religion of the majority is part of the dominant laws and customs, then we in fact face a sophisticated form of establishmentarianism. Establishmentarianism generates various problems and should be rejected, even according to Nussbaum's approach. Genuine anti-religionists will oppose all religions and presumably especially the majority religion and its influence on the public sphere and the public or political discourse. We should not rush to assume that anti-religionism is likely to be especially harsh towards minority religions. This is certainly not the most reasonable outcome of anti-religionism. It is equally reasonable to assume that the main concern of anti-religionists would be to eradicate the

[173] Marshall mentions the irrational nature of religion, its communal nature and the fact that it is based upon notions of absolutism and obligations to a transcendent authority: (n 43 above) 404–12.

[174] See text to n 164 above.

[175] Nussbaum (2007) (n 101 above) 353.

[176] Nussbaum (2007) (n 101 above) 354.

influence that the religion of the majority has on the public, political and legal spheres, while allowing minority, 'non-public' or 'non-political' religions more freedom, precisely because, and if, they pose little danger to the public and political nature of the state. Put differently, it appears that Nussbaum finds it hard to comprehend how a genuine yet not utopian anti-religionism may look like.

Nussbaum's second problem with anti-religionists is that they 'simply do not have very much respect for the capability of conscience, not in so far as it exercises itself in a religious way'.[177] This description is doubtless true, but it is merely a description of the natural consequences of anti-religionism. It fails to explain why these consequences are undesirable. It fails to explain why equal respect should be given to a religious conscience, or more specifically, to every religious conscience. In Chapter five I explored the meaningful and unique links between some religions and intolerance, and argued that they constitute a good reason why not to give equal respect to some religious consciences.

Nussbaum's third and most basic objection to anti-religionism is that 'even a fair anti-religionism is not compatible with a thoroughgoing commitment to equal respect'.[178] In more detail, Nussbaum argues that 'this is not a very good stance to take toward one's fellow citizens, in a world full of mystery and complexity, where it is a very good bet that nobody, not the anti-religionist either, has the ultimate solution to questions about the meaning of life and death that have plagued humanity ever since humanity began to exist'.[179] This may be true but is beside the point. The arguments about religious exemptions, and more generally about the free exercise and establishment of religion, rarely focus on 'the meaning of life and death'. They are arguments about political morality, well-being and rights—and therefore duties—that people have. We do not need to believe that we have found the meaning of life and death, the point where life on earth began—and the reason for that—and so on, in order to believe that we know better how people should, and, more importantly, should not live their lives, at a certain time and in a certain place. When a perfectionist-liberal submits that autonomy, freedom and equality (as he perceives them) should be protected and promoted by various means, and by the state, and when he argues that illiberal or intolerant practices that diminish autonomy, freedom and equality, should not be tolerated, he does not claim that he has the ultimate solution to questions about the meaning of life and death. He may plead ignorance on these matters. Moreover, if Nussbaum is right in her claim that we should assume that nobody has the ultimate solution to these questions, then we should avoid basing decisions about the rights and duties that

---

[177] Nussbaum (2007) (n 101 above) 354, and see also, on the same page: 'Because it thinks that religion is fundamentally not very important, it is not likely to go out of its way to give people dispensations from laws of general applicability on grounds of conscience'.

[178] Nussbaum (2007) (n 101 above) 355.

[179] Nussbaum (2007) (n 101 above) 355.

(religious) people have on the fact that they think they do know the answers to these questions. The political and legal discourse should ignore these metaphysical questions and concentrate on two main familiar questions: how people should behave, and how they should behave towards each other. There are huge disagreements about the answers to these questions, but the argument is conducted within the scope of political morality and reason rather than metaphysics. In Chapter three I referred to one specific argument within this subject, when I made a detailed argument, taken from the area of political morality, according to which there are good reasons not to tolerate, and at times not to respect, those who behave in a way that contradicts and threatens basic liberal values.

IX. CONCLUSION: IS RELIGION SPECIAL?

In this chapter, I evaluated and ultimately rejected four possible approaches to conscientious exemptions: the neutral approach; the equal regard approach; the liberal value-based approach; and the pro-religion approach.

With regard to the neutral and the equal regard approaches, the argument that illiberal intolerance should normally not be tolerated provides one reason, among others, why the content of someone's conscience is significant when deciding when to grant conscientious exemptions. With regard to the liberal, value-based approach, and the pro-religion approach, the argument about the links between religion and intolerance, combined with the argument about intolerance as a limit on tolerance, provides one reason why the religious content of one's conscience is a relevant consideration when deciding whether or not to grant an exemption, and why it is normally a reason for not granting an exemption.

The religiosity of someone's conscience should not be a decisive reason for granting or refusing conscientious exemptions. The issue is far too complicated to be decided on the basis of one specific reason.[180] More specifically, there are three main questions that should be answered here: firstly, should the religiosity of the conscience be a relevant reason within the balance of reasons? Secondly, should it be a reason for granting or refusing conscientious exemptions? And, thirdly, what should be the weight of that reason? The answers to the first two questions rely on much of what has been said thus far. The third question will be briefly addressed within the concluding remarks to the book.

---

[180] See, for example, McConnell and Posner's helpful classification of the reasons for not granting exemptions into four categories: the prevention of negative externalities (ie costs or burdens imposed on third parties); the provision of public goods; paternalism; and the enforcement of morality: (n 78 above) 46–51.

For a slightly different classification, see Greenawalt (n 1 above) 318–21, who distinguishes between rules directly protecting others from harm; rules imposing shared burdens; paternalistic laws; and rules establishing the conditions for benefits and privileges.

7
Conclusion

I. A SHORT INTRODUCTION TO THE CONCLUSION

IN THIS BOOK I have presented the following main arguments: first, the limit of liberal tolerance is illiberal intolerance, ie illiberal intolerance should almost never be tolerated by the tolerant-liberal state; secondly, there are meaningful and special links between certain religions—and certainly the most common and influential ones—and intolerance. Because of these links most adherents of most religions are more likely to be intolerant and act intolerantly than non-religious people. If these arguments are true they may provide a reason for the tolerant-liberal state not to tolerate religion as such. They certainly provide a reason for the tolerant-liberal state not to tolerate religious claims for accommodation or religious claims for exemptions from legal rules. At this point it can be asked what 'religion' adds to the argument about the limits of liberal tolerance. If illiberal intolerance should not be tolerated by the liberal state, is there something special to be said about religious-illiberal intolerance? Can't we simply argue that illiberal intolerance—whether religious or not—should not be tolerated? Within the context of conscientious exemption, can't we argue that conscientious objections—whether religious or not—should not be tolerated if they rely on intolerant values? What does the religiosity of the 'intolerant conscience' or the religiosity of a demand for accommodation add to the equation?

II. WHY AND WHEN THE RELIGIOSITY OF A CLAIM FOR ACCOMMODATION OR EXEMPTION MATTERS

If the arguments about the limits of liberal tolerance and about the links between religion and intolerance are valid, it is quite clear that the religiosity of claims for accommodation or exemption should be a relevant reason within the balance of reasons, and that it should normally be a reason for refusing to accommodate religion or to grant an exemption. For the sake of simplicity I will mainly refer to religious claims for conscientious exemptions but the rationale of the proposed approach applies to all claims for accommodation and to the general relationship between religion and the tolerant-liberal state. We can think of two main possible cases:

> Case 1: the religious claim for exemption is directly based on intolerant and anti-liberal values or practices. Such are, for example, homophobic or racist views and unjustly discriminatory practices (eg a refusal to provide services to homosexuals; excluding women from the public sphere; 'separate but equal' practices and so on).
>
> Case 2: the religious claim is based on religious values or practices that may be irrational or morally misguided but are not necessarily intolerant and anti-liberal (eg a refusal to perform abortion or to provide contraception; displaying religious symbols in the public sphere; a refusal to wear safety helmets; a refusal to work on the religious day of rest; a refusal to receive or allow medical treatment and so on).

These two possible cases do not reflect all relevant considerations that should be taken into account when deciding the state's response to claims for religious exemption or accommodation. Further considerations include the harm that may be caused to the rights and interests of all involved and the importance of relevant public or state interests. These cases, however, aim to focus on the content of the values that ground the claim for exemption, as this is normally a neglected aspect in contemporary theory and practice.

As to the first case, any conscientious objection that is based on intolerant values, whether religious or not, should not be tolerated, either by refusing to grant conscientious exemptions or by other means. But religion makes things worse in the sense that religious intolerance generally poses a greater threat to liberal democracies than non-religious intolerance (all other things being equal)—precisely because of the unique links between religion and intolerance. Moreover, and because of these unique links, religion makes things worse when religious intolerance accompanies or reinforces intolerant attitudes and behaviours that are not necessarily religious (eg when religion accompanies or reinforces racism, homophobia, patriarchy, nationalism or totalitarianism). The links between religion and intolerance should lead the authorities to apply a more cautious, perhaps suspicious attitude towards religious claims to be granted conscientious exemptions, even though the decision would have to be made mainly on a case-by-case basis, ie according to the content of the values that ground each and every conscientious objection, whether it be religious or not. There are various ways of not tolerating intolerant conscientious objectors. The authorities may grant them an exemption but condemn their values or behaviour. The authorities may also grant them an exemption and, at the same time, deny them any governmental support or subsidy.[1] In appropriate cases, the authorities can also refuse to grant an exemption.

---

[1] For a persuasive argument that the state should not grant tax benefits to institutions that discriminate on the basis of sex (rather than just on the basis of race) even if the discriminatory practice is based on religious grounds, see: C Corbin, 'Expanding the Bob Jones Compromise'

The state should always express an attitude of intolerance towards intolerant conscientious objectors. The exact nature of that attitude may vary. This is where religion matters.

As to the second case: religious claims or claims from religious institutions for exemptions, accommodation, state funding, tax benefits, special treatment and so on may not be tolerated or accepted even when they do not directly rely on intolerant values. Accordingly, religious symbols may not be displayed in certain places (the public sphere, state institutions, 'public' institutions etc) even when the symbol itself does not convey intolerant values. This is so because religion is inherently intolerant and because the liberal state should not support or endorse, directly or indirectly, intolerant ideologies or sets of beliefs. We should also consider the need to avoid shaping the public sphere according to religious values—even when they are not necessarily intolerant. Inserting religious symbols, values and reasoning into the public sphere creates an accommodating atmosphere that in turn may strengthen cultural, social and political religious tendencies—and religion itself. A tolerant-liberal state should not create an accommodating atmosphere for ideologies—including religious ones—that are intolerant and illiberal by their nature. This is especially the case with regard to 'regulatory religions' (religions that regulate many aspects of their adherents' lives), as accommodating such religions requires numerous legal and social adjustments, which, when examined separately may not cause great concern, but when put together run against the secular and rational nature of a tolerant-liberal democracy.[2] A tolerant-secular-liberal state should not limit non-religious people's freedoms and opportunities and should not distribute rights, benefits and duties by subscribing to religious values and reasoning or by avoiding evaluating the content of such values.

Within the context of conscientious exemption, the state has good reason, although not necessarily a conclusive reason, not to grant religious conscientious exemptions, even in cases where the claims to be granted exemptions are not based directly on intolerant values, beliefs or conscience. The state may have such a reason because of the special links between certain religions and intolerance. The stronger the link regarding a certain religion, the stronger is the reason for not granting religious conscientious exemptions to its adherents

---

in A Sarat (ed), *Legal Responses to Religious Practices in the United States: Accommodation and its Limits* (Cambridge, Cambridge University Press, 2012) 123. For a similar view regarding the denial of state funds to institutions that discriminate, see another article from the above collection: C Brettschneider, 'How Should Liberal Democracies Respond to Faith Based Groups that Advocate Discrimination? State Funding and Non-Profit Status', ibid, 72.

[2] For good examples within the UK context see: D McGoldrick, 'Accommodating Muslims in Europe: From Adopting Sharia Law to Religiously Based Opt Outs from Generally Applicable Laws' (2009) 9 *Human Rights Law Review* 627–35 (although McGoldrick does not use these examples to make an argument for a secular, tolerant-liberal democracy in the way it is made here).

or for not tolerating them in alternative ways. The tolerant-liberal state should aspire to protect and strengthen its liberal, secular nature. Tolerating religious conscientious objectors who act upon a conscience that is not intolerant may still support, even if indirectly, institutions or practices of that religion that are intolerant.

III. AND A FINAL CONCLUSION

If illiberal intolerance should not be tolerated and if there are links between religion and intolerance, then the religiosity of a legal, political or social claim is always a reason for not tolerating that claim. The only question that can be asked at this stage concerns the weight that ought to be accorded to the religiosity of such a claim. Should it merely be a relevant reason to be considered or should it be a weighty reason for not tolerating the claim? For all of the reasons mentioned throughout the book, the religiosity of a claim for accommodation should definitely be a relevant reason for not tolerating that claim. For the same reasons there is a strong case for seeing the religiosity of such claims as a strong or weighty reason for not tolerating them. It should not, however, be an overriding or conclusive reason for not tolerating such claims as there are always reasons for tolerating religious claims for accommodation or exemption. In some cases those reasons may override the reasons against tolerating such claims and may therefore justify accommodation or granting exemptions. The purpose of this book was not to provide a detailed recipe for deciding these cases but rather to highlight some relevant considerations and the weight that ought to be accorded to them.

IV. POST-CONCLUSION: A NOTE ABOUT RELIGION, THE ACADEMIC WORLD AND THE REAL WORLD

In the following I will refer to debates about religion amongst academics as this is the world where I live and work—but the rationale of this brief note can be applied more broadly and within other contexts as well.

Anti-religion academic arguments often encounter a harsh response from some academics—and I have had my fair share of such a response. By 'harsh response' I do not mean torture, imprisonment or execution (which are still carried out against atheists and members of 'wrong' religions in some parts of the world) but rather a verbal response. Anti-religion academic arguments also often cause great inconvenience amongst some well-educated and well-informed academics, whether they are religious, multiculturalists, pluralists or neutral liberals. Using the term 'anti-religion' may itself cause inconvenience and may be perceived as radical, provocative or simply impolite (while the term 'pro-religion' does not seem to raise any similar difficulties, even though 'pro-religion' often means 'anti-atheism' or 'anti-atheists'). The harsh academic response to anti-religion arguments cannot be explained only by the fact that 'religious matters' or religion may be seen as a mixture of faith and identity that results in an unflattering critique of religion being perceived as an attack on one's identity or community. This reason, together with others, can explain why any harsh response towards anti-religion arguments and anti-theist people is carried out, including by fanatical, narrow-minded and generally intolerant religious people. The interesting question is why well-educated and well-informed academics, who are normally tolerant people, respond so harshly.

Quite paradoxically, one of the main reasons for this harsh response is precisely that these academics are generally tolerant. Many of them and their close ones may have a perception of 'religion as quest', which may prescribe tolerance and even acceptance. With regard to many religious academics— some of them are dear colleagues—their religion and religious belief are not sources of intolerance. Some of them are probably more tolerant and virtuous than some of their non-religious colleagues. Others do not think that religion is special or that religious claims should be accorded special weight even though they themselves are deeply religious. In most parts of the academic world, at this stage of history, people of different religions, atheists and anti-theists normally get along and religious persecution or intolerance is relatively rare. So, for many religious academics the academic attack on religion seems detached from their own experience and from their internal point of view of their religion. Academic and personal integrity, however, should lead religious, multiculturalist and neutral-liberal academics to acknowledge the clear, unique and troubling links between religion and intolerance. These theoretical and empirical links are historically proven and unfortunately are being proven time and time again worldwide. Religion is not the source of all evil and it does not poison everything—but it has great potential and proven ability to cause great evil and to poison almost everything. Academic and personal integrity should lead religious academics to acknowledge that throughout history and still today, too many religious people and religious leaders have not perceived religion as a quest and that for too many religious people religion does not prescribe tolerance. Religious academics should admit that when we debate about religion we do sit in an ivory tower, amusing ourselves with inclusive constitutional and moral principles, whereas in the real world, religion, religious institutions, religious leaders, religious states and religious believers (who may be 'extremists' but are genuinely religious rather than 'distorting' existing religions) probably cause more harm than good. This does not mean that religion does not have positive virtues or that it cannot be used for good purposes but honest people should not ask themselves what their personal experience of having a religious belief is, but rather what the common effects of religion are on our world. The inevitable answer is that the troubling theoretical and empirical links between religion and intolerance are of great concern, and that these links should not be ignored when we decide political and legal disputes about religion in a tolerant-liberal democracy.

Bibliography

ABBOTT, EP, 'Atheism and the Religious Liberty Protection Act: A Place for Everyone or Everyone in their Place' (2000/2001) 2 *Rutgers Journal of Law and Religion* 4

ABEL, R, *Speech and Respect: Hamlyn Lectures Series* (London, Sweet & Maxwell, 1994)

ABU-NIMMER, M, *Nonviolence and Peace Building in Islam: Theory and Practice* (Gainesville FL, University Press of Florida, 2003)

ACKERMAN, B, *Social Justice and the Liberal State* (New Haven CT, Yale University Press, 1980)

ADAMS, NA, 'A Human Rights Imperative: Extending Religious Liberty Beyond the Border' (2000) 33 *Cornell International Law Journal* 1

ALEXANDER, L, 'Harm, Offense, and Morality' (1994) 7 *Canadian Journal of Law & Jurisprudence* 199

ALLPORT, G, *The Nature of Prejudice* (New York, Basic Books Publishers, 1954)

—— 'Religious Context of Prejudice' (1966) 5 *Journal for the Scientific Study of Religion* 447

ALLPORT, G, and ROSS, J, 'Personal Religious Orientation and Prejudice' (1967) 5 *Journal of Personality and Social Psychology* 432

ALTEMEYER, B, and HUNSBERGER, B, 'Authoritarianism, Religious Fundamentalism, Quest, and Prejudice' (1992) 2 *International Journal for the Psychology of Religion* 113

ANDERSON, J, *Studies in Empirical Philosophy* (Sydney, Sydney University Press, 1962), electronic edition (2000) available at: setis.library.usyd.edu.au/anderson

ARIAN, A, ET AL, *Auditing Israeli Democracy—2010: Democratic Values in Practice* (The Israel Democracy Institute, 2010) (in Hebrew)

AUDI, R, 'Religion and the Ethics of Political Participation' (1990) 100 *Ethics* 386

—— 'The Place of Religious Argument in a Free and Democratic Society' (1993) 30 *San Diego Law Review* 677

—— *Democratic Authority and the Separation of Church and State* (Oxford, Oxford University Press, 2011)

—— *Rationality and Religious Commitment* (Oxford, Oxford University Press, 2011)

AUGENSTEIN, D, 'Tolerance and Liberal Justice' (2010) 23 *Ratio Juris* 437

AUGUSTINE, St, 'Epistle to Vicentius' in P Schaff (ed), *St Augustine: The Confessions and Letters of St Augustine I* (1886, 1st edn 408)

BAMFORTH, N, and RICHARDS, D, *Patriarchal Religion, Sexuality, and Gender: A Critique of New Natural Law* (Cambridge, Cambridge University Press, 2008)

BARAK, A, *Proportionality: Constitutional Rights and their Limitations* (Cambridge, Cambridge University Press, 2012)

BARRY, B, *Justice as Impartiality* (Oxford, Oxford University Press, 1995)

—— *Culture and Equality* (Cambridge, Polity Press, 2001)

BATSON, CD, 'Religion as Prosocial: Agent or Double Agent?' (1976) 15 *Journal for the Scientific Study of Religion* 29

—— 'Religious Orientation and Overt Versus Covert Racial Prejudice' (1986) 50 *Journal for the Scientific Study of Religion* 175

BATSON, CD, and BURRIS, C, 'Personal Religion: Depressant or Stimulant of Prejudice and Discrimination?' in MP Zanna and JM Olson (eds), *The Psychology of Prejudice* (Hillsdale NJ, Lawrence Erlbaum Associates, 1993)

BATSON, CD NAIFEH, SJ and PATE, S, 'Social Desirability, Religious Orientation, and Racial Prejudice' (1978) 17 *Journal for the Scientific Study of Religion* 31

BATSON, CD, and SCHOENRADE, PA, 'Measuring Religion as Quest: 1. Validity Concerns' (1991) 30 *Journal for the Scientific Study of Religion* 416

—— 'Measuring Religion as Quest: 2. Reliability Concerns' (1991) 30 *Journal for the Scientific Study of Religion* 430

BATSON, CD, SCHOENRADE, P, and VENTIS, WL, *Religion and the Individual: A Social-Psychological Perspective* (Oxford, Oxford University Press, 1993)

BEDI, S, 'Debate: What is so Special About Religion? The Dilemma of the Religious Exemption' (2007) 15 *The Journal of Political Philosophy* 235

BEERS, D, 'Extension Versus Invalidation of Underinclusive Statutes: A Remedial Alternative' (1975) 12 *Columbia Journal of Law & Social Problems* 115

BEIT-HALLAHMI, A, and ARGYLE, M, *The Psychology of Religious Behavior, Belief and Experience* (London, Routledge, 1997)

BEIT-HALLAHMI, B, *Psychological Perspectives on Religion and Religiosity* (London, Routledge, 2015)

BERG, TC, 'What Hath Congress Wrought? An Interpretive Guide to the Religious Freedom Restoration Act' (1994) 39 *Villanova Law Review* 1

—— 'Can Religious Liberty Be Protected as Equality?' (2007) 85 *Texas Law Review* 1185

BIZAR, DM, 'Remedying Underinclusive Entitlement Statutes: Lessons From a Contrast of the Canadian and U.S. Doctrines' (1992) 24 *University of Miami Inter-American Law Review* 121

BLOOM, A, *Closing of the American Mind* (New York, Simon & Schuster, 1987)

BOLLINGER, L, *The Tolerant Society* (Oxford, Oxford University Press, 1986)

BOYLE, K, and SHEEN, J, *Freedom of Religion and Belief—A World Report* (London, Routledge, 1997)

BRADNEY, A, *Religions, Rights and Laws* (Leicester, Leicester University Press, 1993)

BRAITHWAITE, C, *Conscientious Objection to Various Compulsions Under British Law* (The University of Michigan, William Sessions Limited, 1995)

BRETTSCHNEIDER, C, *When the State Speaks, What Should It Say?: How Democracies Can Protect Expression and Promote Equality* (Princeton NJ, Princeton University Press, 2012)

—— 'How Should Liberal Democracies Respond to Faith Based Groups that Advocate Discrimination? State Funding and Non-Profit Status' in A Sarat (ed), *Legal Responses to Religious Practices in the United States: Accommodation and its Limits* (Cambridge, Cambridge University Press, 2012) 72

BROWN, W, *Regulating Aversion: Tolerance in the Age of Identity and Empire* (Princeton NJ, Princeton University Press, 2006)

BURNS, RP, 'The Tasks of the Philosophy of Law' (2007) 3, available at: ssrn.com/abstract=1016124

CANETTI-NISIM, D, 'Two Religious Meaning Systems, One Political Belief System: Religiosity, Alternative Religiosity and Political Extremism' in L Weinberg and A Pedhazur (eds), *Religious Fundamentalism and Political Extremism* (London, Routledge, 2004)

CAPOTORTI, F, *Study on the Rights of Persons Belonging to Ethnic, Religious and Linguistic Minorities* (United Nations, 1979)

CARTER, S, 'Evolution, Creationism, and Treating Religion as a Hobby' (1987) *Duke Law Journal* 977
—— *The Culture of Disbelief: How American Law and Politics Trivialize Religious Devotion* (New York, Anchor Books, 1994)
CASTELLIO, S, *Concerning Heretics, whether they are to be persecuted and how they are to be treated* (RH Bainton trans and ed) (New York, Octagon Books, 1965)
CHAPLIN, J, 'How Much Cultural and Religious Pluralism can Liberalism Tolerate?' in J Horton (ed), *Liberalism, Multiculturalism and Toleration* (Basingstoke, Palgrave MacMillan, 1993)
CHIU, DC, 'The Cultural Defense: Beyond Exclusion, Assimilation, and Guilty Liberalism' (1994) 82 *California Law Review* 1053
CHRISTIANS, LL, 'Religious Law and Secular Law in Democracy: The Evolutions of the Roman Catholic Doctrine After the Second Vatican Council' [2006] *Brigham Young University Law Review* 661
COHEN-ALMAGOR, R, *The Scope of Tolerance: Studies of the Cost of Free Expression and Freedom of the Press* (London, Routledge, 2006)
COHEN-ELIYA, M, and PORAT, I, *Proportionality and Constitutional Culture* (Cambridge, Cambridge University Press, 2013)
COHN, HH, 'The Law of Religious Dissidents: A Comparative Historical Survey' (2000) 34 *Israel Law Review* 39
—— 'Religious Intoleration and the Law' (1966) 12 *New York Forum* 257
COLBURN, B, 'Forbidden Ways of Life' (2008) 58 *The Philosophical Quarterly* 618
CORBIN, C, 'Expanding the Bob Jones Compromise' in A Sarat (ed), *Legal Responses to Religious Practices in the United States: Accommodation and its Limits* (Cambridge, Cambridge University Press, 2012) 123
COSTIGANE, H, 'A History of the Western Idea of Conscience' in J Hoose (ed), *Conscience in World Religions* (Notre Dame, The University of Notre dame Press, 1999)
COTTINGHAM, J (ed), *Western Philosophy: An Anthology* (New York, Wiley, 2008)
D'ARCY, E, *Conscience and Its Right to Freedom* (London, Sheed & Ward Ltd, 1961)
DAWKINS, R, *The God Delusion* (New York, Bantam Books, 2006)
DE-BLOIS, M, 'The Foundation of Human Rights: A Christian Perspective' in P Beaumont (ed), *Christian Perspective on Human Rights and Legal Philosophy* (Carlisle, Paternoster Press, 1998)
DERRIDA, J, 'Autoimmunity: Real and Symbolic Suicides' in G Borradori (ed), *Philosophy in a Time of Terror* (Chicago IL, The University of Chicago Press, 2003) 127
DINSTEIN, Y, 'Freedom of Religion and the Protection of Religious Minorities' in Y Dinstein and M Tabory (eds), *The Protection of Minorities and Human Rights* (Boston MA, Martinus Nijhoff Publishers, 1992)
DOE, N, and JEREMY, A, 'Justifications for Religious Autonomy' in R O'Dair and A Lewis (eds), *Law and Religion—Current Legal Issues*, vol 4 (Oxford, Oxford University Press, 2001)
DRINAN, RF, 'Reflections of the Demise of the Religious Freedom Restoration Act' (1997) 86 *Georgetown Law Journal* 101
DUCK, RJ, and HUNSBERGER, B, 'Religious Orientation and Prejudice: The role of Religious Proscription, Right-Wing Authoritarianism and Social Desirability' (1999) 9 *International Journal for the Psychology of Religion* 157

DURIEZ B, LUYTEN, P, SNAUWAERT, B, and HUTSEBAUT, D, 'The Importance of Religiosity and Values in Predicting Political Attitudes: Evidence for the Continuing Importance of Religiosity in Flanders (Belgium)' (2007) 5 *Mental Health, Religious and Culture* 35

DWORKIN, R, 'Liberalism' in S Hampshire (ed), *Public and Private Morality* (Cambridge, Cambridge, 1978) 113

—— *Taking Rights Seriously* (Cambridge MA, Harvard University Press, 1977)

—— *A Matter of Principle* (Oxford, Oxford University Press, 1985)

—— *Law's Empire* (Cambridge MA, Harvard University Press, 1986)

—— *Sovereign Virtue: The Theory and Practice of Equality* (Cambridge MA, Harvard University Press, 2000)

—— *Is Democracy Possible Here?* (Princeton NJ, Princeton, 2006)

D'COSTA, G, 'Christian Orthodoxy and Religious Pluralism: A Response to Terrence W. Tilley' (2007) 23 *Modern Theology* 435

EISENSTEIN, MA, 'Rethinking the Relationship Between Religion and Political Intolerance in the US' (2006) 28 *Political Behaviour* 327

EISGRUBER, CL, and SAGER, LG, 'Mediating Institutions: Beyond the Public/Private Distinction: The Vulnerability of Conscience: The Constitutional Basis for Protecting Religious Conduct' (1994) 61 *University of Chicago Law Review* 1245

—— 'Chips Off Our Block? A Reply to Berg, Greenawalt, Lupu and Tuttle' (2007) 85 *Texas Law Review* 1273

—— *Religious Freedom and the Constitution* (Cambridge MA, Harvard University Press, 2007)

ELLISON, CG, and MUSICK, MA, 'Southern Intolerance: A Fundamentalist Effect?' (1993) 72 *Social Forces* 379

ELY, J, *Democracy and Distrust: A Theory of Judicial Review* (Cambridge MA, Harvard University Press, 1980)

ENDICOTT, T, 'The Impossibility of the Rule of Law' (1999) 19 *Oxford Journal of Legal Studies* 1

ENOCH, D, 'Once You Start Using Slippery Slope Arguments, You're on a Very Slippery Slope' (2001) 21 *Oxford Journal of Legal Studies* 629

—— 'A Right to Violate One's Duty' (2002) 21 *Law and Philosophy* 355

ERASMUS, 'On Mending the Peace of the Church' in JP Dolan (ed), *The Essential Erasmus* (New York, Plume, 1964, 1st edn 1536)

EVANS, MD, *Religious Liberty and International Law in Europe* (Cambridge, Cambridge University Press, 1997)

—— 'Human Rights, Religious Liberty, and the Universality Debate' in R O'Dair and A Lewis (eds), *Law and Religion—Current Legal Issues*, vol 4 (Oxford, Oxford University Press, 2001)

FEINBERG, J, *The Moral Limits of the Criminal Law—Harm to Others* (Oxford, Oxford University Press, 1984)

FINNIS, J, *Natural Law and Natural Rights* (Oxford, Oxford University Press, 1980)

FISH, S, *There's No Such Thing as Free Speech—and it's a Good Thing Too* (Oxford, Oxford University Press, 1994)

—— 'Mission Impossible: Settling the Just Bounds Between Church and State' (1997) 97 *Columbia Law Review* 2255

FOX, GH, and NOLTE, G, 'Intolerant Democracies' (1995) 36 *Harvard International Law Journal* 1

FREEMAN, GC, 'The Misguided Search for the Constitutional Definition of Religion' (1983) 71 *Georgetown Law Journal* 1519, 1548

FRANKFURT, H, 'Equality as a Moral Idea' (1987) 98 *Ethics* 21

—— 'Equality and Respect' (1997) 64 *Social Research* 3

FULTON, AS, GORSUCH RL, and MAYNARD, EA, 'Religious Orientation, Antihomosexual Sentiment, and fundamentalism Among Christians' (1999) 38 *Journal for the Scientific Study of Religion* 14

GAERTNER, S, and DOVIDIO, J, 'The Aversive Form of Racism' in S Gaertner and J Dovidio (eds), *Prejudice, Discrimination, and Racism* (Orlando FL, Academic Press, 1986)

GALANTER, M, 'Religious Freedoms at the United States: A Turning Point?' (1966) *Wisconsin Law Review* 217

GALEOTTI, A, *Toleration as Recognition* (Cambridge, Cambridge University Press, 2002)

GANS, C, *Philosophical Anarchism and Political Disobedience* (Cambridge, Cambridge University Press, 1992)

—— 'Right and Left: Ideological Disobedience in Israel' (2002) 36 *Israel Law Review* 19

GARVEY, JH, 'Free Exercise and the Values of Religious Liberty' (1986) 18 *Connecticut Law Review* 779

—— 'All Things Being Equal…' [1996] *Brigham Young University Law Review* 587

GAY DA, and Ellison, CG, 'Religious Subcultures and Political Tolerance: Do Denominations Still Matter?' (1993) 34 *Review of Religious Research* 311

GEDICKS, FM, *The Rhetoric of Church and State* (Durham NC, Duke University Press, 1995)

—— 'An Unfirm Foundation: The Regrettable Indefensibility of Religious Exemptions' (1998) 20 *University of Arkansas at Little Rock Law Journal* 555

—— 'The Improbability of Religion Clause Theory' (1997) 27 *Seton Hall Law Review* 1233

GEORGE, RP, *Making Men Moral: Civil Liberties and Public Morality* (Oxford, Oxford University Press, 1993)

GEY, S, 'Why is Religion Special? Reconsidering the Accommodation of Religion Under the Religion clauses of the First Amendment' (1990) 52 *University of Pittsburgh Law Review* 75

—— 'When is Religious Speech not "Free Speech"?' [2000] *University of Illinois Law Review* 379

GORSKY, J, 'Conscience in Jewish Tradition' in J Hoose (ed), *Conscience in World Religion* (Leominster, Gracewing Publishing, 1999)

GREEN, L, 'On Being Tolerated' in M Kramer, C Grant, B Colborn, and A Hatzistavrou (eds), *The Legacy of HLA Hart: Legal, Political, and Moral Philosophy* (Oxford, Oxford University Press, 2008) 277

GREENAWALT, K, 'Religion as a Concept in Constitutional Law' (1984) 72 *California Law Review* 753, 766–67

—— *Religious Convictions and Political Choice* (New York, Oxford University Press, 1988)

—— *Conflicts of Law and Morality* (Oxford, Oxford University Press, 1989)

—— 'Religious Convictions and Political Choice: Some Further Thoughts' (1990) 39 *DePaul Law Review* 1019

—— 'How Does "Equal Liberty" Fare in Relation to Other Approaches to the Religious Clauses?' (2007) 85 *Texas Law Review* 1217

GRISEZ, G, *The Way of the Lord Jesus: I: Christian Moral Principles* (Chicago IL, Franciscan Press, 1983)

GUIORA, A, *Freedom from Religion: Rights and National Security* (Oxford, Oxford University Press, 2013)

GUISO, L, SAPIENZA, P, and ZINGALES, L, 'People's Opium? Religion and Economic Attitudes'(2003) 50 *Journal of Monetary Economics* 225

HALL, J, *Law, Social Science and Criminal Theory* (Publication of the Comparative Criminal Law Project, vol 14, 1982)

HALL, TL, 'Religion and Civic Virtue: A Justification of Free Exercise' (1992) 67 *Tulane Law Review* 87

HAMMER, LM, *The International Human Right to Freedom of Conscience* (Farnham, Ashgate, 2001)

HAREL A, and SHENRACH, A, 'Segregation of Men and Women in Public Transportation' (2003) 3 *Allay Mishpat* 71 (in Hebrew)

HARRIS, S, *The End of Faith: Religion, Terror, and the Future of Reason* (New York, WW Norton & Company, 2004)

HART, HLA, *The Concept of Law* (Clarendon Law Series), 2nd edn (Oxford, Oxford University Press, 1994)

—— 'Are There Any Natural Rights' in A Quinton (ed), *Political Philosophy* (Oxford, Oxford University Press, 1967)

HEYD, D, 'Introduction' in D Heyd (ed), *Toleration: An Elusive Virtue* (Princeton NJ, Princeton University Press, 1996)

HIGGINS, R, *Problem and Process: International Law and How We Use It* (Oxford, Oxford University Press, 1994)

HITCHENS, C, *God is not Great: How Religion Poisons Everything* (London, Atlantic Books, 2007)

HOGG, MA, 'Social Identity' in MR Leary and JP Tangney (eds), *Handbook on Self and Identity* (New York, The Guilford Press, 2003)

HOOD, RW, HILL, PC, and SPILKA, B, *The Psychology of Religion: An Empirical Approach*, 4th edn (New York, The Guilford Press, 2009)

HORTON, J, 'Three (Apparent) Paradoxes of Toleration' (1994) 17 *Synthesis Philosophica* 7

—— 'Toleration as a Virtue' in D Heyd (ed), *Toleration: An Elusive Virtue* (Princeton NJ, Princeton University Press, 1996) 29

HORWITZ, P, 'The Sources and Limits of Freedom of Religion in a Liberal Democracy: Section 2(a) and Beyond' (1996) 54 *University of Toronto Faculty of Law Review* 1

HUME, D, *Dialogues Concerning Natural Religion* (The Hafner Library of Classics, Edited and Introduction by Henry D Aiken 1963, 1st edn 1779)

HUNSBERGER, B, and JACKSON, LM, 'Religious, Meaning and Prejudice' (2005) 61 *Journal of Social Issues* 807

IANNACCONE, LR, and BERMAN, E, 'Religious Extremism: The Good, the Bad, and the Deadly' (2006) 128 *Public Choice* 109

JAYAWICKRAMA, N, *The Judicial Application of Human Rights Law—National, Regional and International Jurisprudence* (Cambridge, Cambridge University Press, 2002)

JELEN, TG, and WILCOX, C, 'Denominational Preferences and the Dimensions of Political Tolerance' (1990) 51 *Sociological Analysis* 69

—— 'Evangelicals and Political Tolerance' (1990) 18 *American Politics Quarterly* 25

JONES, JW, 'Why Does Religion Turn Violent? A Psychoanalytic Exploration of Religious Terrorism' (2006) 93 *Psychoanalytic Review* 167

KELSAY, J, *Arguing the Just War in Islam* (Cambridge MA, Harvard University Press, 2007)

KIRKPATRICK, LA, 'A Psychometric Analysis of the Allport-Ross & Feagin Measures of Intrinsic-Extrinsic Religious Orientation' in M Lynn and D Moberg (eds), *Research in the Social Scientific Study of Religion* (Greenwich, JAI Press Inc, 1989)

KRAMNICK, I, and MOORE, L, *The Godless Constitution: The Case Against Religious Correctness* (New York, WW Norton, 1996)

KUGLER, Y, 'On the Possibility of a Criminal Law Defence for Conscientious Objection' (1997) 10 *Canadian Journal of Law and Jurisprudence* 387

KUNG, H, *Freud and the Problem of God* (New Haven CT, Yale University Press, 1979)

KURLAND, PB, 'The Supreme Court, Compulsory Education, and the First Amendments' Religion Clauses' (1973) 75 *West Virginia Law Review* 213

KYMLICKA, W, *Multicultural Citizenship: A Liberal Theory of Minority Rights* (Oxford, Clarendon, 1995)

LAYCOCK, D, 'The Religious Freedom Restoration Act' [1993] *Brigham Young University Law Review* 221

—— 'Religious Liberty as Liberty' (1996) 7 *Journal of Contemporary Legal Studies* 313

LEAL, D, 'Against Conscience: A Protestant View' in J Hoose (ed) *Conscience in World Religions* (Notre Dame, The University of Notre dame Press, 1999)

LEITER, B, *Why Tolerate Religion* (Princeton NJ, Princeton University Press, 2012)

—— 'Why Tolerate Religion?' *Constitutional Commentary* (2008) 32 (Available at SSRN: ssrn.com/abstract=904640

LEVY, JT, 'Classifying Cultural Rights' in I Shapiro and W Kymlicka (eds), *Ethnicity and Group Rights* (New York and London, New York University Press, 1997)

LIPSON, JC, 'On Balance: Religious Liberty and Third Party Harms' (2000) 84 *Minnesota Law Review* 589

LOCKE, J, *A Letter Concerning Toleration* (Indianapolis IN, Hackett Publishing Company, 1983; first published in 1689)

LUPO, I, 'Where rights Begin: The Problem of Burdens on the Free Exercise of Religion' (1989) 102 *Harvard Law Review* 933

—— 'The Trouble with Accommodation' (1992) 60 *George Washington Law Review* 743

—— 'To Control Faction and Protect Liberty: A General Theory of the Religion Clauses' (1996) 7 *Journal of Contemporary Legal Studies* 357

—— 'The Case Against Legislative Codification of Religious Liberty' (1999) 21 *Cardozo Law Review* 565

MACEDO, S, 'Transformative Constitutionalism and the Case of Religion: Defending the Moderate Hegemony of Liberalism' (1998) 26 *Political Theory* 56

MACKLEM, P, 'Guarding the Perimeter: Militant Democracy and Religious Freedom in Europe' (2012) 19 *Constellations* 575

MACLURE, J, and TAYLOR, C, *Secularism and Freedom of Conscience* (Cambridge MA, Harvard University Press, 2011)

MARCUS, EN, 'Conscientious Objection as an Emerging Human Right' (1998) 38 *Virginia Journal of International Law* 507

MARCUSE, H, 'Repressive Tolerance' in RP Wolff (ed), *A Critique of Pure Tolerance* (London, Jonathan Cape Publishers, 1969) 65

MARSHALL, WP, 'The Case Against the Constitutionally Compelled Free Exercise Exemption' (1990) 40 *Case Western Reserve Law Review* 357

—— 'What is the Matter with Equality?: An assessment of the Equal Treatment of Religion and Nonreligion in the First Amendment Jurisprudence' (2000) 75 *Indiana Law Journal* 193

MARTINEZ-TORRON, J, 'The European Court of Human Rights and Religion' in R O'Dair and A Lewis (eds), *Law and Religion—Current Legal Issues*, vol 4 (Oxford, Oxford University Press, 2001)

MATSUDA, MJ, 'Public Response to Racial Speech: Considering the Victim's Story' (1989) 87 *Michigan Law Review* 2320

McCLOSKY, H, and BRILL, A, *Dimensions of Tolerance* (New York, Russell Sage Foundation, 1983)

McCONNELL, M, 'Accommodation of Religion' [1985] *Supreme Court Review* 1

—— 'Neutrality Under the Religious Clauses' (1986) 81 *Northwestern University Law Review* 146

—— 'The Origins and Historical Understanding of Free Exercise of Religion' (1990) 103 *Harvard Law Review* 1409

—— 'Religious Freedom at a Crossroads' (1992) 59 *University of Chicago Law Review* 115

—— 'The Problem of Singling Out Religion' (2000) 50 *DePaul Law Review* 1

McCONNELL, M, and POSNER, RA, 'An Economic Approach to Issues of Religious Freedom' (1989) 56 *University of Chicago Law Review* 1

McFARLAND, SG, 'Religious Orientations and the Targets of Discrimination' (1989) 28 *Journal for the Scientific Study of Religion* 324

McGOLDRICK, D, 'Accommodating Muslims in Europe: From Adopting Sharia Law to Religiously Based Opt Outs from Generally Applicable Laws' (2009) 9 *Human Rights Law Review* 627

MENDUS, S, 'Introduction' in S Mendus (ed), *Justifying Toleration: Conceptual and Historical Perspectives* (Cambridge, Cambridge University, 1988)

—— 'My Brother's Keeper: The Politics of Intolerance' in S Mendus (ed) *The Politics of Toleration* (Edinburgh, Edinburgh University Press, 1999)

MENSCHING, G, *Tolerance and Truth in Religion* (trans HJ Klimkeit) (Tucaloosa AL, University of Alabama Press, 1971)

MILL, JS, *On Liberty* (London, JW Parker & Son, 1859)

—— *On Liberty* and *The Subjection of Women* (Ware, Wordsworth Classics of World Literature, 1996, first published in 1859 and 1869 respectively)

MOMEN, M, *An Introduction to Shi'i Islam: The History and Doctrines of Twelver Shi'ism* (New Haven CT, Yale University Press, 1987)

MORTENSEN, R, 'Rendering to God and Caesar: Religion in Australian Discrimination Law' (1995) 18 *University of Queensland Law Journal* 208

MOSKOS, CC, and CHAMBERS, JW (eds), *The New Conscientious Objection—From Sacred to Secular Resistance* (Oxford, Oxford University Press, 1993)

MURPHY, J, 'Marxism and Retribution' in J Waldron (ed), *Philosophy of Law* (Oxford, Oxford University Press, 1994)

MUTTART, D, *The Empirical Gap in Jurisprudence: A Comprehensive Study of the Supreme Court of Canada* (Toronto, University of Toronto Press, 2007)

NAGEL, T, 'Moral Conflict and Political Legitimacy' (1987) 16 *Philosophy and Public Affairs* 215

—— *Equality and Partiality* (Oxford, Oxford University Press, 1991)

NEPSTAD, SE, 'Religion, Violence, and Peacemaking' (2004) 43 *Journal for the Scientific Study of Religion* 297

NEUBERG, S, WARNER, C, MISTLER, S, HILL, E, and BERLINS, A, 'Religious Infusion and Intergroup Conflict: Results from the Global Group Relations Project', APSA 2011 Annual Meeting Paper, available at: ssrn.com/abstract=1901492

—— 'Religious Infusion and Intergroup Conflict: Results from the Global Group Relations Project' (2014) 25 *Psychological Science* 198

NEWEY, G, 'Is Democratic Toleration a Rubber Duck?' (2001) 7 *Res Publica* 315

NICHOLSON, PP, 'Toleration as a Moral Idea' in J Horton and S Mendus (eds), *Aspects of Toleration* (London, Routledge, 1985)

NIEBUHR, R, *The Return toPrimitive Religion* (Winter 1938) 3 *Christendom* 5
—— *The Children of Light and the Children of Darkness* (1972, 1st edn 1944)
NOTE, 'The Supreme Court—Leading Cases: Religious Freedom Restoration Act' (2006) 120 *Harvard Law Review* 341
NUSSBAUM, M, *Sex and Social Change* (New York, Oxford University Press, 1999)
—— 'Radical Evil in the Lockean State: The Neglect of the Political Emotions' (2006) 3(2) *Journal of Moral Philosophy* 159
—— 'Liberty of Conscience: The Attack on Equal Respect' (2007) 8 *Journal of Human Development* 337
—— *The New Religious Intolerance: Overcoming the Politics of Fear in an Anxious Age* (Cambridge, The Belknap Press, 2012)
O'DEA, TF, and O'DEA, J, *The Sociology of Religion* (Upper Saddle River, Prentice-Hal, 1983)
OLSON, RE, *The Mosaic of Christian Belief* (Downers Grove, InterVarsity Press, 2002)
PARFIT, D, 'Equality and Priority' (1997) 10 *Ratio* 202
PARGAMENT, KI, *The Psychology of Religion and Coping: Theory, Research, Practice* (New York, The Guilford Press, 1997)
PARKINSON, P, 'Accommodating Religious Beliefs in a Secular Age: The Issue of Conscientious Objection in the Workplace' (2011) 34 *University of New South Wales Law Journal* 281
PERES, Y, and YUCHTMAN-YA'AR, E, *Between Consent and Dissent: Democracy and Peace in the Israeli Mind (Rights & Responsibilities)* (Lanham MD, Rowman & Littlefield Publishers, 2000)
PERRY, JM, *Tillich's Response to Freud: A Christian Answer to the Freudian Critique of Religion* (Lanham MD, University Press of America, 1988)
PERRY, M, *Morality, Politics, and Law: A Bicentennial Essay* (New York, Oxford University Press, 1988)
—— *Love and Power: The Role of Religion and Morality in American Politics* (New York, Oxford University Press, 1991)
—— 'Religious Morality and Political Choice: Further Thoughts—And Second Thoughts—On Love and Power' (1993) 30 *San Diego Law Review* 703
PICKERING, WSF, *Durkheim's Sociology of Religion—Themes and Theories* (Cambridge, Lutterworth Press, 1984)
PINTO, M, 'What Are Offences to Feelings Really About?: A New Regulative Principle for the Multicultural Era' (2010) 30 *Oxford Journal of Legal Studies* 695
POPPER, K, *The Open Society and Its Enemies* (London, Routledge, 1945)
RADAY, F, 'Culture, Religion and Gender' (2003) 1 *International Journal of Constitutional Law* 663
—— Modesty Disrobed—Gendered Modesty Rules under the Monotheistic Religions' in Marie Failinger, Elizabeth Schiltz and Susan Stabile (eds), *Feminism, Law and Religion* (Farnham, Ashgate, 2013) 283
RAPHAEL, DD, 'The Intolerable' in S Mendus (ed), *Justifying Toleration: Conceptual and Historical Perspectives* (Cambridge, Cambridge University Press, 1988)
RAWATT, WC, Associations Between Religious Personality Dimensions and Implicit Homosexual Prejudice' (2006) 45 *Journal for the Scientific Study of Religion* 397
RAWATT, WC, FRANKLIN, LM, and COTTON, M, 'Patterns and Personality Correlates of Implicit and Explicit Attitudes Toward Christians and Muslims' (2005) 44 *Journal for the Scientific Study of Religion* 29

RAWLS, J, *A Theory of Justice* (Cambridge MA, Harvard University Press, 1971)
—— 'Justice as Fairness: Political not Metaphysical' (1985) 14 *Philosophy & Public Affairs* 223
—— *Political Liberalism* (New York, Columbia University Press, 1993)
—— *A Theory of Justice*, Revised edn (Cambridge MA, Harvard University Press, 1999)
RAZ, J, *The Authority of Law* (Oxford, Oxford University Press, 1979)
—— *The Morality of Freedom* (Oxford, Clarendon Press, 1986)
—— 'Autonomy, Toleration and the Harm Principle' in R Gavison (ed), *Issues in Contemporary Legal Philosophy* (Oxford, Clarendon Press, 1987)
—— 'Facing Diversity: The Case of Epistemic Abstinence' (1990) 19 *Philosophy and Public Affairs* 3
—— 'Free Expression and Personal Identification' (1991) 11 *Oxford Journal of Legal Studies* 303
—— *Ethics in the Public Domain* (Oxford, Clarendon Press, 1994)
—— *Practical Reasons and Norms*, 2nd edn (Oxford, Oxford University Press, 1999)
—— 'Comments and Responses' in LH Meyer, SL Paulson and TW Pogge (eds), *Rights, Culture, and the Law: Themes from the Legal and Political Philosophy of Joseph Raz* (Oxford, Oxford University Press, 2003)
REISS, S, 'Why People Turn to Religion: A Motivational Analysis' (2000) 39 *Journal for the Scientific Study of Religion* 47
RICHARDS, D, *Toleration and the Constitution* (New York, Oxford University Press, 1986)
—— *Fundamentalism in American Religion and Law* (Cambridge, Cambridge University Press, 2010)
RIVERS, J, 'Religious Liberty as a Collective Right' in R O'Dair and A Lewis (eds), *Law and Religion—Current Legal Issues*, vol 4 (Oxford, Oxford University Press, 2001)
ROBERTS, P, and LESTER, E, 'The Distinctive Paradox of Religious Tolerance: Active Tolerance as a Mean Between Passive Tolerance and Recognition' (2006) 20 *Public Affairs Quarterly* 347
ROBINSON, Z, 'Rationalizing Religious Exemptions: A Legislative Process Theory of Statutory Exemptions for Religion' (2011) 20 *William & Mary Bill of Rights Journal* 133
ROGERS, MB, and OTHERS, 'The Role of Religious Fundamentalism in Terrorist Violence: A Social Psychological Analysis' (2007) 19 *International Review of Psychiatry* 253
RUNCIMAN, S, *The Medieval Manichee: A Study of the Christian Dualist Heresy* (Cambridge, Cambridge University Press, 1947)
RYAN, JE, 'Smith and the Religious Freedom Restoration Act: An Iconoclastic Assessment' (1992) 78 *Virginia Law Review* 1407
SANDBERG, R, *Religion, Law and Society* (Cambridge, Cambridge University Press, 2014)
SANDBERG, R, and DOE, N, 'Religious Exemptions in Discrimination Law' (2007) 66 *Cambridge Law Journal* 302
SANDEL, M, 'Religious Liberty—Freedom of Conscience or Freedom of Choice?' [1989] *Utah Law Review* 597
—— 'Judgmental Toleration' in RP George (ed), *Natural Law, Liberalism, and Morality* (Oxford, Oxford University Press, 1996)
SARKISSIAN, A, 'The Determinants of Tolerance in Arab Societies', APSA 2011 Annual Meeting Paper, available at: ssrn.com/abstract=1901491
SCANLON, T, 'The Difficulty of Tolerance' in T Scanlon, *The Difficulty of Tolerance: Essays in Political Philosophies* (Cambridge, Cambridge University Press, 2003)

SCHEEPERS, P, TE GROTENHUIS, M, and VAN DER SLIK, V, 'Education, Religiosity and Moral Attitudes: Explaining Cross-National Effect Differences' (2002) 63 *Sociology of Religion* 157

SCHWARTZMAN, M, 'What if Religion is not Special?' (2012) 79 *University of Chicago Law Review* 1351

SEGAL, RA, 'The Frazerian Roots of Contemporary Theories of Religion and Violence' (2007) 37 *Religion* 4

SHER, G, *Beyond Neutrality: Perfectionism and Politics* (Cambridge, Cambridge University Press, 1997)

SILVERMAN, B, 'Consequences, Racial Discrimination, And the Principle of Belief Congruence' (1974) 29 *Journal of Personality and Social Psychology* 497

SISK, GC, 'How Traditional and Minority Religions Fare in the Courts: Empirical Evidence from Religious Liberty Cases' (2005) 76 *University of Colorado Law Review* 1021

SMITH, RK, 'Converting the Religious Equality Amendment into a Statute with a Little Conscience' [1996] *Brigham Young University Law Review* 645

SMITH, S, 'The Restoration of Tolerance' (1990) 78 *California Law Review* 305

—— *Foreordained Failure: The Quest for a Constitutional Principle of Religion Freedom* (New York, Oxford University Press, 1995)

SPILKA, B, HOOD JNR, RW, HUNSBERGER, B, and GORSUCH, R, *The Psychology of Religion: An Empirical Approach*, 3rd edn (New York, The Guilford Press, 2003)

STEINBERG, DE, 'Religious Exemption as Affirmative Action' (1991) 40 *Emory Law Journal* 77

SUNSTEIN, CR, *Designing Democracy: What Constitutions Do* (New York, Oxford University Press, 2001)

TAJFEL, H, 'Social Psychology of Intergroup Relations' (1982) 33 *Annual Review of Psychology* 1

TEN, CL, 'Comment' in R Gavison (ed), *Issues in Contemporary Legal Philosophy* (Oxford, Clarendon Press, 1987)

TILLEY, TW, 'Christian Orthodoxy and Religious Pluralism: A Rejoinder to Gavin D'costa' (2007) 23 *Modern Theology* 447

TILLICH, P, *The Shaking of the Foundation* (London, SCM Press, 1948)

TRIBE, L, 'The Puzzling Persistence of Process Based Theories' (1980) 89 *Yale Law Journal* 1063

TSANG, J, and RAWATT, WC, 'The Relationship Between Religious Orientation, Right-Wing Authoritarianism, and Implicit Sexual Prejudice' (2007) 17 *The International Journal for the Psychology of Religion* 99

TUSHNET, M, 'The Constitution of Religion' (1986) 18 *Conneticut Law Review* 701

VOLOKH, E, 'A Common-Law Model for Religious Exemptions' (1999) 46 *UCLA Law Review* 1465

WALDRON, J, 'A Right to Do Wrong' (1981) 92 *Ethics* 21

—— 'A Rights Based Critique of Constitutional Rights' (1993) 13 *Oxford Journal of Law Studies* 18

—— *Law and Disagreement* (Oxford, Oxford University Press, 1999)

WALL, S, *Liberalism, Perfectionism and Restraint* (Cambridge, Cambridge University Press, 1998)

WALZER, M, *Obligations: Essays on Disobedience, War and Citizenship* (Cambridge MA, Harvard University Press, 1970)

—— *On Toleration* (New Haven CT, Yale University Press, 1997)

WATT, G, 'Giving unto Caesar: Rationality, Reciprocity and legal Recognition of Religion' in R O'Dair and A Lewis (eds), *Law and Religion—Current Legal Issues*, vol 4 (Oxford, Oxford University Press, 2001) 45

WEBER, M, *The Sociology of Religion* (trans E Fischoff) (Boston MA/London, Beacon Press/ Methuen, 1965)

WEITMAN, PJ, *Religion and the Obligations of Citizenship* (Cambridge, Cambridge University Press, 2002)

WELLMAN JNR, JK, and TOKUNO, K, 'Is Religious Violence Inevitable' (2004) 43 *Journal for the Scientific Study of Religion* 291

WHITEHEAD, AN, *Religion in the Making* (New York, Fordham University Press, 1926)

WILCOX, C, and JELEN, TG, 'Evangelicals and Political Tolerance' (1990) 18 *American Politics Quarterly* 25

WILLIAMS B, *Problems of the Self: Philosophical Papers 1956–1972* (Cambridge, Cambridge University Press, 1973)

—— 'Toleration: An Impossible Virtue?' in D Heyd (ed), *Toleration: An Elusive Virtue* (Princeton NJ, Princeton University Press, 1996)

—— 'Tolerating the Intolerable' in S Mendus (ed), *The Politics of Toleration* (Edinburgh, Edinburgh University Press, 1999)

WINTEMUTE, R, 'Accommodating Religious Beliefs: Harm, Clothing or Symbols, and Refusals to Serve Others' (2014) 77 *The Modern Law Review* 223

WULFF, DM, *Psychology of Religion: Classic and Contemporary Views*, 2nd edn (New York, John Wiley & Sons, 1997)

WYBRANIEC, J, and FINKE, R, 'Religious Regulation and the Courts: The Judiciary's Changing Role in Protecting Minority Religions from Majoritarian Rule' (2001) 40 *Journal for the Scientific Study of Religion* 427

List of Cases

Braunfeld v Brown 366 US 599 (1961)
Employment Division, Department of Human Resources v Smith 494 US 872 (1990)
Frazee v Illinois 489 US 829 (1989)
Gallaham v Holyfield 516 F Supp 1004 (ED Va 1981)
Goldman v Weinberger 475 US 503 (1986)
Gratz v Bollinger et al 123 S Ct 2325 (2003)
Hobbie v Unemployment Appeals Commission 480 US 136 (1987)
R v Edwards Books and Art [1986] 2 SCR 713
Ragen v Ministry of Transport HCJ 746/07 (2008)
Ragen v Ministry of Transport HCJ 746/07 (2011)
Refah Partisi (The Welfare Party) and Others v Turkey (Application nos 41340/98, 41342/98, 41343/98 and 41344/98), judgment of 31 July 2001 (ECtHR)
Regents of the University of California v Bakke 438 US 265 (1978)
Sherbert v Verner 374 US 398 (1963)
State v Hershberger 462 NW 2d 393 (Minn 1990)
State v Miller 538 NW 2d 573 (Wis App 1995)

Thomas v Review Board of the Indiana Employment Security Division 450 US 707 (1981)
United States v Lee 455 US 252 (1982)
United States v Seeger 380 US 163 (1965)
Welsh v Unites States 398 US 333 (1970)
Wisconsin v Yoder 406 US 205 (1972)

Index

A

Absolutism
  difficulties of applying test to conscientious exemption, 145
  key characteristic of religion, 68
  relationship with morality and law, 116
  theoretical link between religion and intolerance, 112–14

Academics
  anti-religion arguments, 201
  general tolerance, 202–3
  pro-religion arguments, 202

Alexander, L, 58
Allport, G, 74, 75, 77, 82, 122
Altemeyer, B, 83
Anderson, J, 72
Anti-establishment argument, 191–95
Anti-religionism
  academic responses, 201–2
  arguments for specialness of religion, 195–97

Augenstein, D, 23–24
Autonomy
  connection with reciprocity, 34
  importance of reasons for intolerance, 95–96
  justification for 'tolerance as a right', 32–33
  perfectionist liberalism, 56–57
  reasons to avoid harm, 16
  reciprocity, 33
  specialness of religion, 139–41

B

Barry, B, 103, 104, 110, 128
Batson, CD, 73–77, 79, 81, 82, 90, 98
Bedi, S, 186, 187
Beit-Hallahmi, B, 183
Beliefs see **Values and beliefs**
Berman, E, 105
Bollinger, L, 104
Bollinger, LC, 31
Brill, A, 81, 109, 115, 120
Burris, C, 98

C

Choice see **'Lack of choice' argument**
Christianity

conscientious exemption, 132–33
  difficulties of applying harm test, 147
  intolerant by nature, 125
  link with intolerance—empirical findings
    conclusions, 89–92
    first stage (1940–1965), 73–74
    last stage (1990s and beyond), 84–89
    second stage (1966–1975), 74–76
    third stage (1976–1990), 76–81
  origins of term 'intolerance', 65
  theoretical links with intolerance
    absolutism, 112
    community preservation, 97–98
    morality and the law, 114
    perception of 'truth', 109–12
    sacred traditions and symbols, 107
    values and beliefs, 118–19
  treatment as paradigmatic cases, 69–70, 93–94

Classification of religion
  'extrinsic religion', 74–75
  fundamentalism, 82–84
  'intrinsic religion', 74–75
  link between religion and intolerance, 90
  'religion as a means', 77
  'religion as a quest', 77
  'religion as an end', 77

Cohen-Almagor, R, 17, 47
Cohn, HH, 93, 102
Colburn, B, 33
Community preservation
  key characteristic of religion, 68
  theoretical link between religion and intolerance, 97–101

'Compelling state interest' test, 149–51
Condemnation, 46–47
Conscientious exemptions
  see also **Specialness of religion**
  as an expression of tolerance
    equality principle, 135–37
    exceptions to main argument, 133–34
    paradigm example of tolerance, 134
    perceptions of favouritism, 131–33
    possible justifications, 129–30
    sincerity of claimants, 131
    state failure to foresee harm, 130–31